THE HAND
AND
THE HOROSCOPE

Fred Gettings

Triune Books

ISBN 0 85674 013 6
Published by Triune Books, London, England
© Fred Gettings 1973
Designed and produced by
Trewin Copplestone Publishing Ltd
Printed in Great Britain by
Chapel River Press, Andover

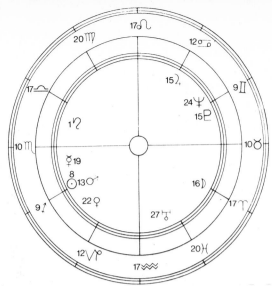

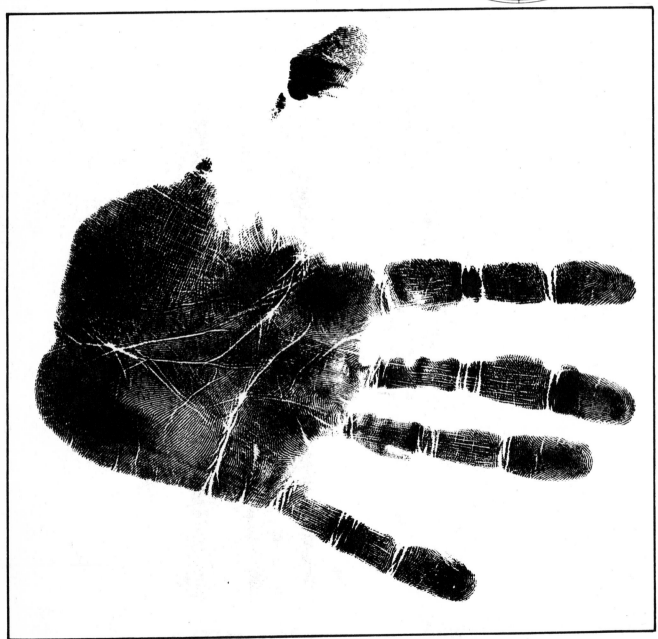

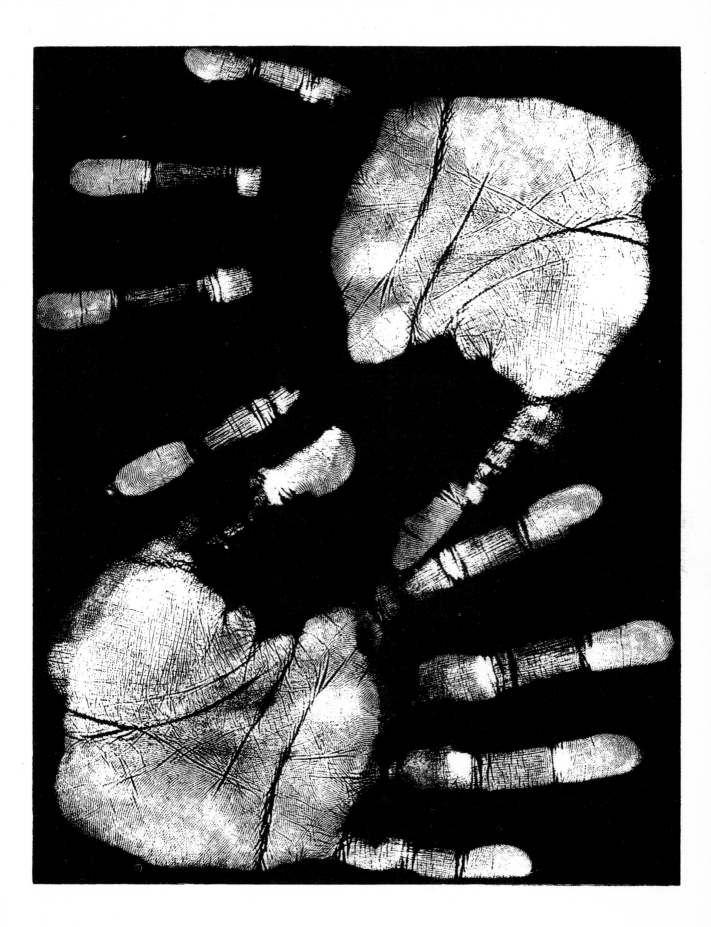

THE HAND AND THE HOROSCOPE

CONTENTS

The glossary at page 186 has been designed to facilitate cross-reference of ideas in the two areas of palmistry and astrology. Both of these studies make use of similar terms and concepts, and it is necessary in certain cases to differentiate shades of meaning in order to avoid confusion. In addition, a few occult terms, with which the layman is not often familiar, have been used in the text: such terms are explained in the glossary.

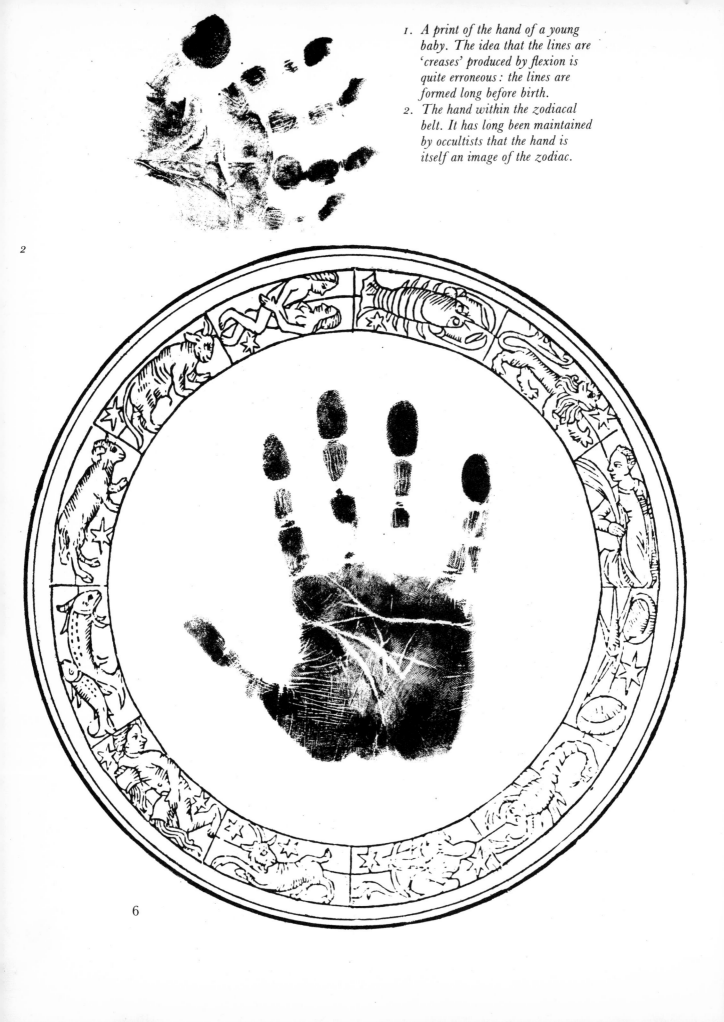

1. *A print of the hand of a young baby. The idea that the lines are 'creases' produced by flexion is quite erroneous: the lines are formed long before birth.*
2. *The hand within the zodiacal belt. It has long been maintained by occultists that the hand is itself an image of the zodiac.*

2

6

PREFACE

The greatest obstacle to seeing is the eye, runs the famous Buddhist paradox. We see the phenomena of the world, but we do not see the means by which we see these phenomena. How can we be sure that our instrument of seeing is working correctly, if we cannot investigate that instrument? How may we escape from the limitation of the senses in order to apprehend the world of reality? The ancient paradox points to the very root of the human conflict; we ourselves appear to mark the threshold between two worlds – the invisible inner world, about which we know virtually nothing, and the visible outer world, about which we tell ourselves we know a great deal. And yet we do not pay sufficient attention to the fact that the inner and the outer worlds may themselves be products of this 'threshold awareness' that we call ourself: in looking at the world so intently, we appear to have forgotten about the nature of the seeing eye. Between the two worlds invisible and visible there lurks that strange entity we call the 'self', that awareness which disappears when we sleep and yet miraculously appears each day to continue imperturbably its work of reconciling these two worlds, almost as if there might be some purpose in such an activity. It is a strange image conjured up here, but it is an image of every person who lives and experiences: we are all involved with a mystic alchemy by which the exterior becomes interiorized, and the interior becomes exteriorized.

Such an image may scarcely be understood with the mind at all, and this is mainly because of the way in which we think. One of the laws of logic demands that one should not 'make a leap' in the structure of an argument – each piece of information, each fact, must be securely linked within a structure of propositions, and must be seen as driving home to a conclusion, which itself may be used as a proposition for further elaboration. There is a beauty about this kind of logical structure, though it is a sterile one, for it can produce nothing new – the argument may be flawless, but it may lead nowhere; at best it can merely present a new way of looking at facts and materials already understood from one or more points of view. Logic is concerned with the validity of argument, not with the wisdom of argument. It therefore cannot permit leaps, which may endanger the self-imposed structure of the logical method. It is a method which does not seek for wisdom so much as for consistency, a method which is still surprisingly popular today in spite of its obvious failures in application. One of the laws which govern the acquiring of wisdom, in which one seeks to understand the world from a totality of human faculties rather than just from the single standpoint of intellect, demands precisely such a leap. The work of attaining wisdom is based on a paradox which attempts to by-pass the truth that the greatest obstacle to seeing is the eye. The acquiring of wisdom requires that we both move inwards and outwards at the same time.

When we approach the study of Man, we find that we cannot properly understand his inner world without at the same time understanding the outer world in which he lives. And yet we find that we cannot properly understand the outer world in which we live without understanding ourselves. It seems that if we wish to move inwards we must first

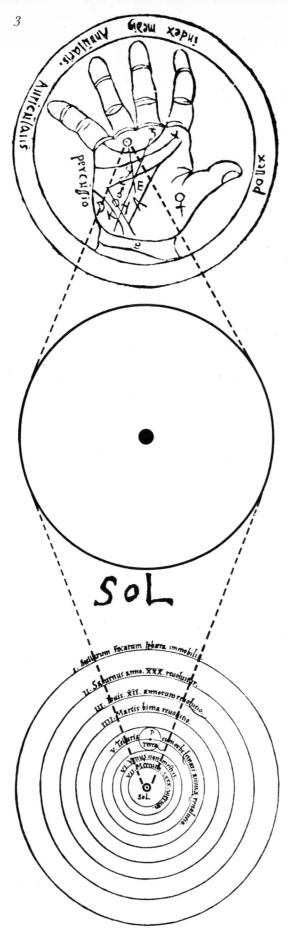

3

SoL

3. The link between the macrocosm and the microcosm. The influence of the Sun, which stands at the centre of the macrocosmic system, is manifest in the space below the ring finger, at approximately the centre of the hand. This rulership explains why the ring finger is regarded as the index of creativity and emotionality, since it is 'rooted in solar forces'.

4. The Chinese character for 'spiral'.

5. The graphic idea upon which the above character was based, indicating how the central 'seed' of

move outwards, and if we wish to move outwards, we must first move inwards: our experience teaches that the development of real understanding appears to be rather like trying to move in a spiral, centrifugal and yet centripetal at the same time. The modern Chinese character which means 'spiral' was originally a drawing of a grain seed inside a circle (figure 4), suggesting admirably the idea of growth with which a spiral is involved, and reminding us in the west of the ancient astrological glyph for the Sun (figure 3), which is a circle with a dot in the centre. This circle on one level marks the outer limits of the solar system, with the Sun at the centre; on another level it marks the outer limits of Man's perception, with Man himself at the centre; it is also, on yet another level, the human heart, with the seed of spiritual growth at the centre. It could be that this apparently simple solar glyph is the most complex symbol in the west. The analogies induced in the mind in contemplating such a glyph enable one to make the leaps requisite for the growth of knowledge. If we understand this glyph aright, we understand something of the force which links the spiral growth of cellular life with the mighty cosmic whirl of the nebulae, something of the force which links the human heart with the Sun itself, and so on. It is this order of understanding which is required to appreciate the real teachings of the occult, upon which the doctrines of astrology and palmistry are based. It requires that we look at Man, and at the world, in an entirely new way: it requires that we go in and out at the same time, for both ways are the same, and without the other neither direction is meaningful.

the solar glyph must be considered as expanding outwards in a growth towards the periphery of the macrocosm.

6. *Mediaeval drawings of the Sun often portray the spiral form to convey the vitality of the body. The Moon is frequently depicted as being lighted on the wrong side, as in this example, to indicate the idea of human guilt, in the separation of spirit (Sun) from desire and subconscious forces (Moon).*

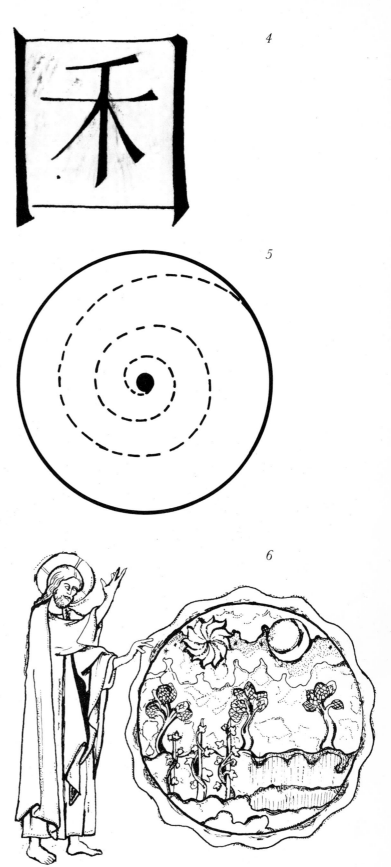

4

5

6

According to the most ancient doctrines, each part of the human frame, and indeed the human frame as a totality, is a model of the solar system. Because of this, occultists may look up into the sky in order to understand the individual man, and at the same time they may look down into some part of the body to understand the individual man. Everything is related in a divine harmony, the lowest to the highest, and one may be understood by a reference to the other because everything is part of everything, and a harmony prevails: 'The way up and the way down are the same,' said the Greeks. With such a promise, one is sadly disappointed when one attempts to relate the traditions concerning astrology with those concerning palmistry. One is disappointed because the obvious cross-reference of planetary names and designations possessed by both promise much, but on investigation appear to offer very little. Occultists are fond of saying that the hand is a model of the solar system, though appear very reluctant to expound exactly *how* and in what way it is such a model. It is the way of certain occultists to promise much, and perform little.

The reasons why these two systems of analogy no longer appear to link together, save through the husks of words, are complex, and need hardly concern us here: what will concern us here is the attempt to show how the hand, when understood correctly, may indeed be seen as a miniature individualized zodiac, a structure which parallels the zodiacal influences which operated on the personality at birth. The many attempts which have been made in the past to link

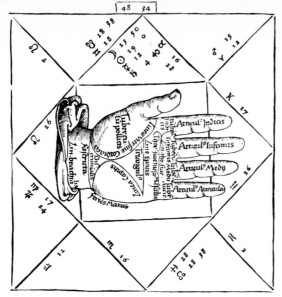

7

7. *A seventeenth-century attempt to link palmistry with astrology. Only the lines of the hand are dealt with in such systems. (From* Rothmann 'Chiromantiae'.)

8. *A plate from Belot's work on palmistry, in which an imaginative, though sterile, set of relationships between zodiacal signs and parts of the hand are presented.*

astrology with palmistry have failed mainly because the wrong system of cross-reference has been adopted: it is the purpose of this book to suggest a new system of cross-reference, a new way of relating the two, and to lay a foundation for a fresh understanding of the hand as a symbol of the microcosm which is Man. The book presupposes no previous understanding of astrology or palmistry, though a knowledge of either will obviously be useful in the correct assessment of its purpose, and indeed, the more one understands about the nature of the two systems, the more meaningful will the connection between the two become.

Astrology is a system of thought which attempts to relate Man to the universe in a meaningful and practical way. Seen in terms of metaphysical speculations, astrology is involved with the very purpose of Life, as well as with the purpose of every individual life, no matter how meaningless this may appear to be. Astrology presents Man in an interesting image which makes him 'small against the stars, so large against the sky.' He is small as a material unit, with a body composed of material elements which were quite separate before his conception, and which dissolve and separate after his death; he is large because, from this vantage point of self-awareness, he is the most real thing in the universe, and it may be said that with his perceptions he creates the universe around him, as well as his own life. Astrology is probably the only psychological system which attempts to link these two different sides of man – the objective image of a terrestrial biped with the subjective impression of a god. Because of this, real astrology is highly complex but fortunately the basis underlying the doctrine is extremely simple, and has been lucidly explained by very many astrologers. The elements of astrology may be grasped with only slight application by almost anyone and utilized in a personal way in the attempt to understand life.

Perhaps the first emotion which begins to develop with even a superficial understanding of astrology is a sense of wonderment – not only that Man should fit so perfectly into a universe which appears on first impression to be chaotic and lifeless – but that from somewhere, from a remote past, a body of teaching should have survived which enables us to place Man in a meaningful position within the structure of the universe. The sense of wonderment grows when we realize that no one knows where the doctrine behind astrology came from; no one knows who gave this incredible knowledge to the human race.

The same sense of wonderment is experienced when one looks into palmistry, for although much of the rich doctrine connected with palmistry has been lost or perverted, there still remain hints of an incredible psychological system which has somehow survived from some remarkable past. Palmistry is a body of doctrine which is sometimes confused and bewildering in its present form, but which relates in a very distinctive manner the structure of the hand, as well as the structure of the line markings on the hand, to the psychological structure of the personality. Palmistry in its practical and systematic phase is less concerned with the prediction of the future than astrology, yet it holds in common with its sister art the belief that events and so-called 'accidents' spring from

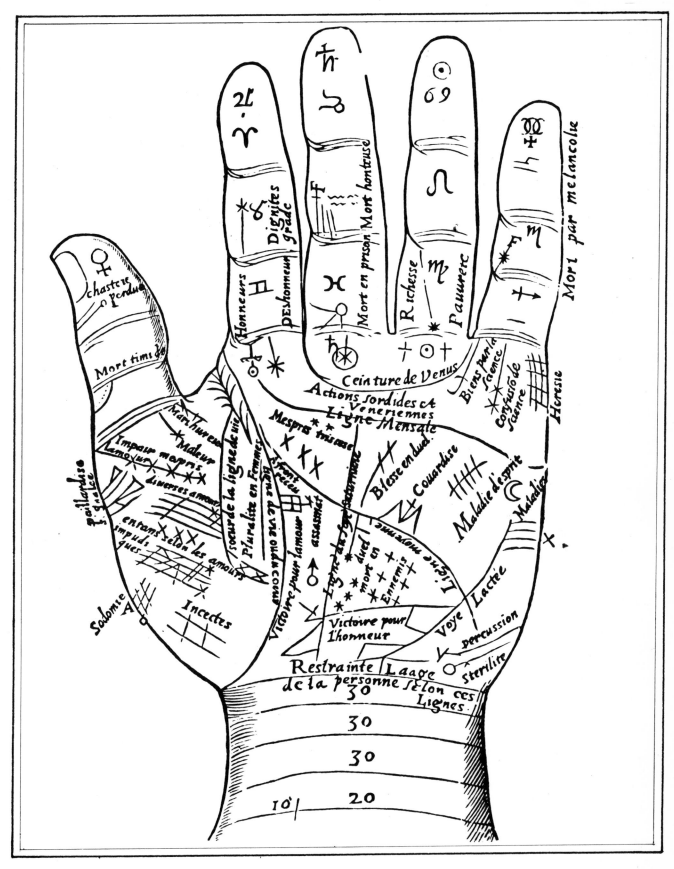

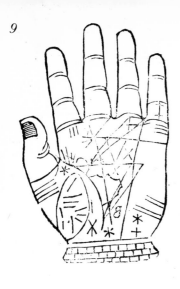

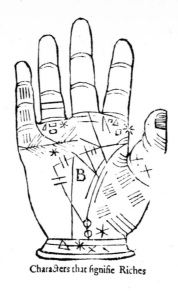

Characters that signifie Riches

9. *A sample of hand interpretation based on the 'fixed symbol' method, by which certain linear structures are taken to portend quite definite psychological traits or events. (From* Richard Saunders *'Palmistry: The Secrets thereof Disclosed').*

10. *The planetary symbols to the right find their structural equivalents in the line markings alongside them. This is fixed symbol interpretation at its most infantile. Such tables as these were common in the sixteenth and seventeenth century.*

10

Oræ hæ exhibent fe fub formis aut inufitatis aut ufitatis. Illæ, quæ & Planetarum dicuntur hæ cres, certæ funt & quali appropriatæ, cuique Planetæ, ut:

11

temperament, and these are sought out by the incarnating spirit in order that it may gain experience. The occultism which underlies astrology and palmistry teaches that just as the incarnating spirit chooses a particular body, or 'physical sheath', for a particular and distinct purpose, so does he choose a particular 'sheath of experiences' by which his life will be structured, in order to help his spiritual growth. Since these spiritual intentions may be perceived from the hand, the study of palmistry in its deepest sense may take us into metaphysical speculations just as deep as those into which astrology leads.

Astrological and palmistic doctrines both revolve around Man, and inevitably both systems have much in common. However, it is what they have most superficially in common that prevents astrology and palmistry from coming together easily. Many attempts have been made in the past to link the two systems, and these attempts, though interesting in their end product, have all been failures in their aim. This does not mean that there is no relationship between astrology and palmistry: it merely means that any attempt to link the two must be made in a new way. This book is the result of such an attempt: it shows that a correct understanding of the hand is of great value in the interpretation of the horoscope, that a correct approach to the horoscope is invaluable in understanding the hand. It shows that with a combination of astrology and palmistry a psychological system may evolve which would enable us to understand more completely the centre of the universe, which is Man, and perhaps, through this, to understand more completely the universe itself.

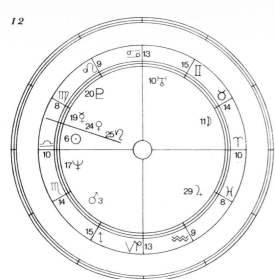

11. *Photography has enormously aided the study and recording of the morphology of the hand, which now is more generally used by palmists than strict line interpretation.*

12. *A horoscope and related hand*

13. *print. The modern approach to hand interpretation depends to a great extent on the study of the form of the hand, and takes into account factors such as papillary patterns, which few palmists before the twentieth century used in their work. The drives and forces within the horoscope are always paralleled by those in the hand.*

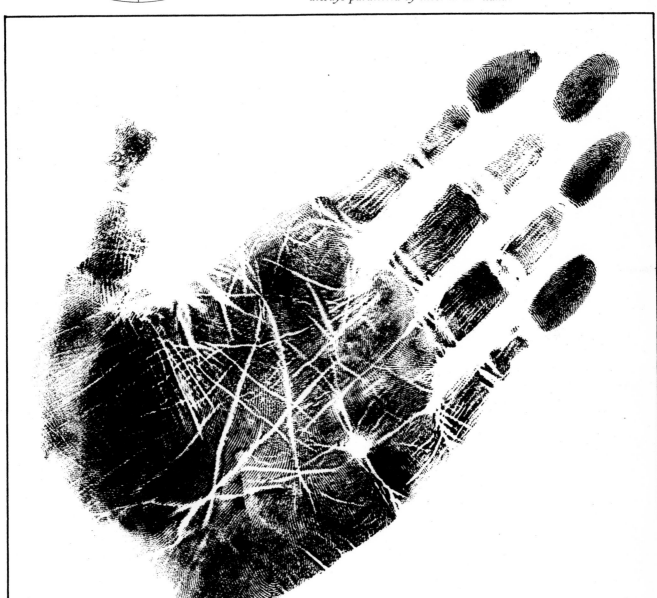

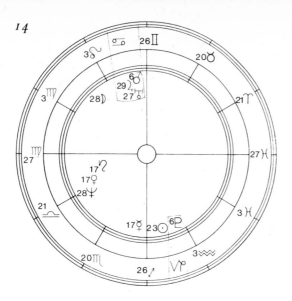

Serious astrology does not recognize the validity of 'newspaper astrology'. In this horoscope the Sun is placed in Sagittarius, which would mean that in popular terms the native would be 'born under' that sign. In fact, he would be just as strangly under the influence of Libra or Cancer, since he has three planets in each of these signs, and only two planets in Sagittarius. Real astrology is much more precise in determining 'type' than newspaper astrology would suggest.

Both astrology and palmistry are based on a system of simple doctrines which in themselves encase remarkable universal truths, and it will be necessary for anyone who wishes to pursue the theme of this book, in their own horoscope and hands, or in those of their friends, to learn the elements of astrology and palmistry, before attempting to relate the two. Because of this, the first part of the book sets out the simple elements of astrology, while the second part sets out the simple elements of palmistry, though coloured by the astrological information imparted in the first section.

The bibliography on page 184 is intended as a guide to reading for those interested in further study of both subjects which, for want of a better term, we may call astrological palmistry. The present text may in fact, be regarded as a practical commentary on the rich store of ideas housed in this bibliography. While there are many books dealing with astrology and palmistry, few are of any real value, and perhaps the most useful piece of information which the modern teacher of these subjects may give to his students is a list of what to read, and, by implication, a list of what *not* to read. It is my opinion that more rubbish has been written about astrology and palmistry than any other related occult subject, yet at the same time it is my experience that certain books on astrology contain information which will be of the greatest value and utility in regard to the problem which will be facing mankind in the next two or three decades. This is because Man has recently begun to realize that whilst perhaps he is 'going somewhere' there is no such thing as 'progress' in a material

sense: he is certainly not heading in any direction which will satisfy his personality. The ordinary sense of 'meaning' and 'progress' is based on a myth, the modern myth of materialism, for it is clear that in a world where inert matter is god, the importance of living entities may be misunderstood. This realization may ultimately help Man to rediscover within himself the meaning of his life. It offers him a chance to become more real to himself, by allowing the material world to become less real and more diffused, as the perception of Man undoubtedly requires it to be. The inner nucleus may become more intense, the present invisible more easily perceptible, as the outer impressionable material would become less clearly defined, less hypnotic, less inclined to diffuse and confuse the inner organs of perception.

Perhaps the dramatic universe is more static than we think. The mediaevalists put Man at the centre of the universe, surrounding him with circles of living entities, all of different degrees of sensibility (figure 16). It is no longer fashionable to think such an image valid, but if it is seen in its true symbolic sense we may understand that the mediaevalists were right: Man is the centre of the universe, whether he wants to be or not, for he sees the world from his own vantage point and creates the world around him. He *is* the centre – his only problem is to find out where this centre is!

The present crisis in human affairs may be traced to the fact that we have lost our centre of being. Our only hope is for a new spiritual awareness, which will help the seed of spirit to fructify in the coming age: astrology will inevitably play a dynamic part in this growth.

15. *A fifteenth century image of Sagittarius. The bow and arrow symbolize the half circle and cross which compose the glyph for Jupiter, the ruler over this sign of the zodiac.*

16. *The microcosm of Man in the centre of the macrocosm of fixed stars and planets. The posture of the body forms a five pointed star, which itself is a description of the periodic conjunctions which Venus makes with the Sun. This is probably why Venus is intimately linked with the human body.*

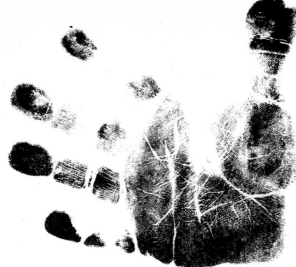

It is extremely difficult to determine the basic elemental nature of a child's hand, for although the lines change only slightly, the hand structure changes considerably.

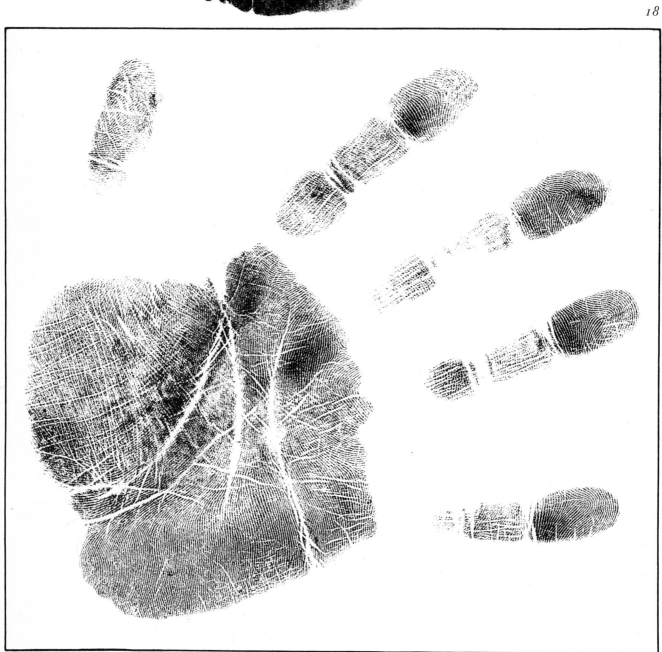

18. *The comparison of handprint*
19. *with the hand itself is very revealing: one observes how the 'feelings' exuded by both are quite different, though the elemental natures of each are quite easily grasped. It is essential that both prints and photographs be studied when linking the hand with the horoscope.*

19

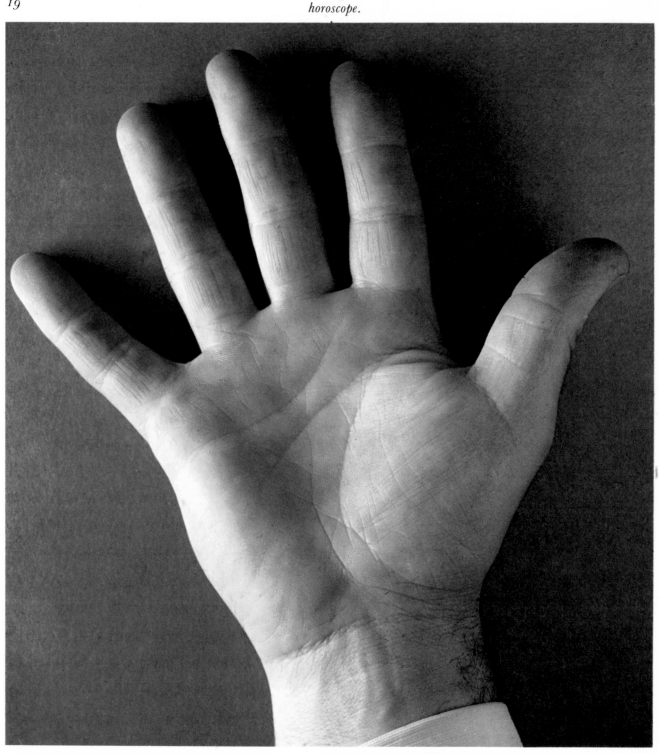

20. *The zodiacal man, from the
'Tres Riches Heures du Duc de
Berry' (Musée de Chantilly).*

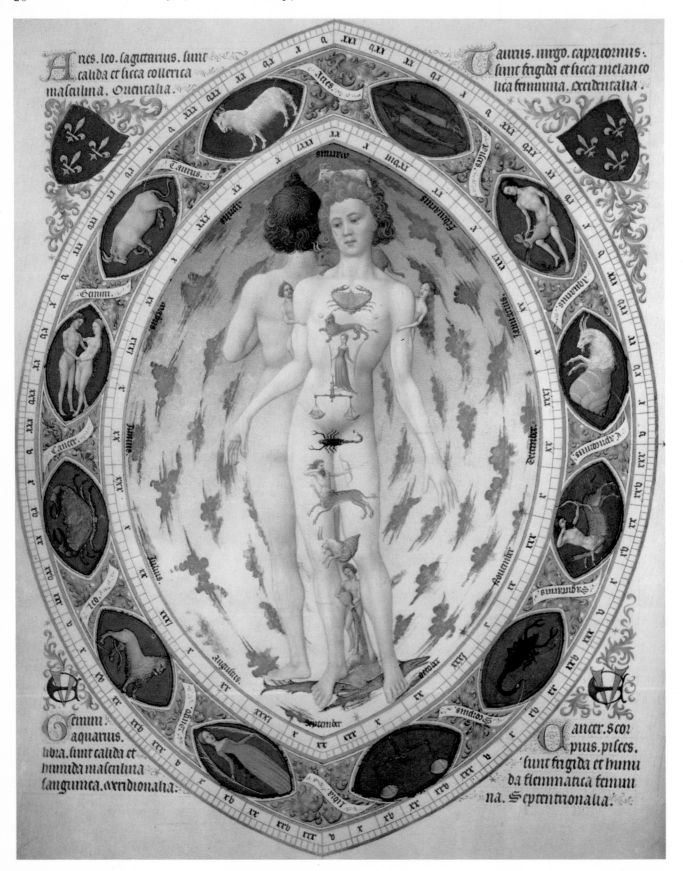

A SIMPLE OUTLINE OF ASTROLOGY

The basis of Astrology

The purpose of astrology is to place Man in some significant relationship to the cosmos, in order that he might apprehend and subsequently enact the full purpose of his planetary existence. To learn something of the basic doctrine behind astrology a few definitions must first be studied.

A *horoscope* is a symbolic representation of the positions held by the planets in the solar system at a given moment of time. Most usually this moment is the time of birth, in which case the horoscope is said to be a *natal* chart. The person for whom the horoscope is cast is usually called the *native*, sometimes the subject. In astrology it is usual to refer to the Sun and Moon as planets.

The Sun appears to move around the Earth once in a year, and the path of this apparent motion is called the *ecliptic*. The ecliptic is divided by astrologers into twelve equal segments of 30 degrees, called *signs*. Each of the signs is called by a name such as Aries, or Taurus: it is important to understand that although these names are the same as those of the constellations of the astronomers, they do not in fact mark out the same areas in the sky. The signs run from Aries to Pisces, in the order shown at figure 21. Each sign is symbolized by a meaningful glyph (figure 21) which must be memorized. The order and pictorial symbolism of the traditional zodiac is beautifully illustrated in figure 20.

All the planets have paths which, within a few degrees or so, follow the course of the ecliptic, and the positions of the planets are recorded by astrologers in terms of their positions against the ecliptic band. For example, the Moon may be said to be 12°

Taurus, which means to say that the Moon is in the 12th degree of that part of the ecliptic called Taurus. Each of the planets is symbolized by a meaningful glyph (figure 21) which must be memorized. Each planet has a particular influence in terms of its own nature – for example Mars has a particular influence on the energy and the sexuality of the native – and these influences vary in terms of the signs in which the planets are found. Thus, a Mars in Aries suggests a quality of energy and sexuality different from a Mars in Capricorn. The natures of the different planets as they manifest in the twelve signs are discussed in chapter 3.

Astrologers usually symbolize the phenomena of the heavens from a geocentric point of view, as though the solar system revolved around the Earth: in the horoscope the central point of the wheel symbolizes the Earth. Each day the Earth revolves on its own axis so the ecliptic and all the planets along the ecliptic band appear to be revolving around the Earth once in each day. Because of this, at any given moment in time a particular degree of a sign must be rising on the horizon, as in figure 23: since there are 360 degrees on the ecliptic and 24 hours in the day, to all intents and purposes it should take four minutes for one degree of the zodiac to rise over the horizon (figure 22). In a horoscope this rising degree is called the *Ascendant*, and is regarded by astrologers as the most important single point in the horoscope, to such an extent indeed that it is the Ascendant degree which is said to determine the type and personality of the native. The Ascendant is usually marked on the horoscope at the point indicated at

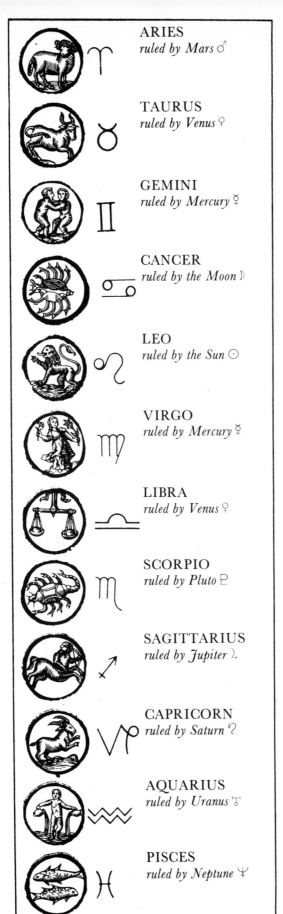

ARIES
ruled by Mars ♂

TAURUS
ruled by Venus ♀

GEMINI
ruled by Mercury ☿

CANCER
ruled by the Moon ☽

LEO
ruled by the Sun ☉

VIRGO
ruled by Mercury ☿

LIBRA
ruled by Venus ♀

SCORPIO
ruled by Pluto ♇

SAGITTARIUS
ruled by Jupiter ♃

CAPRICORN
ruled by Saturn ♄

AQUARIUS
ruled by Uranus ♅

PISCES
ruled by Neptune ♆

21. *The images, glyphs and planetary rulers of the twelve signs. The symbols for the signs and planets must be learned by heart.*
22. *The Ascendant point in the horoscope, sometimes called the 'East point'. This is the most important single point in a horoscope figure.*
23. *The Ascendant/Descendant line – the symbolic horizon. Below this line is the darkness of night, symbolic of the subconscious, whilst above the line is the light*

figure 22, and this point therefore represents the horizon to the east of the place of birth. Opposite this is the western horizon, where the corresponding degree of the opposite sign must be setting: thus, if nine degrees of Taurus is rising at the moment of birth, then nine degrees of Scorpio must be setting at that moment, (figure 23). This western horizon is called the *Descendant*.

The highest point which the Sun reaches in the course of the day obviously marks the highest point of the ecliptic in relation to the place of birth: this point is called by astrologers the *zenith*, sometimes the M.C.* Immediately opposite this highest point in the sky is the lowest point which is hidden under the Earth, and this is called by astrologers the *nadir* or the I.C.* The zenith and the nadir are usually marked on the horoscope at the points indicated at figure 24.

These four important points, Ascendant, Descendant, M.C. and I.C., are called the *angles*, and these mark the most significant focus points of the horoscope. They act rather like lenses (figure 57), magnifying the power and force of the degrees of the zodiac which fall upon them. The Ascendant is the lens through which all forces in the figures are concentrated, and it is thus an index and key to the whole personality of the native: it answers the question 'who is he?' The Descendant is the lens through which the striving of the native towards relationships is expressed, showing how he attempts to escape from self through channelling with another person: it marks what the person lacks and answers the question 'whom does he need?' The M.C. is the lens through which the native's status in life, the energies

*See glossary, p. 186.

of day, symbolic of the
conscious. The Descendant
point indicates the area of
freedom from the selfhood of the
Ascendant.

24. *The Zenith/Nadir axis. The*
    Zenith point indicates the
    symbolic area at which the Sun
    reaches its highest point; it
    therefore links with the
    aspirations and 'highest point'
    in the life of the native. The
    Nadir relates to the corresponding
    'beginning' of life.

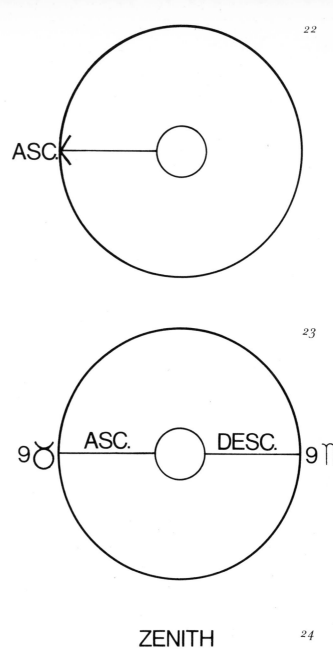

devoted to the expression of self in the outer world, are concentrated: it marks ambition, and answers the question 'where is he going?' The I.C. is the lens through which the personal, subjective energies of the native are brought to a focus, in particular regard to private home life and related matters: it marks the background of the native, and answers the question 'where did he begin?'

It will be seen that these four angles (figure 57) may between them furnish a great deal of information about the native, even without reference to the rest of the horoscope. Obviously, each of the angles will be designated in a horoscope in terms of the degree upon it at the moment of birth. The tables available to astrologers make it a relatively simple thing to calculate the zodiacal degrees on the angles. The influence of the sign on the angles is always magnified in the life of the native in terms of the phase or department of life which that angle rules: for example, a person with Leo on the M.C. will manifest an entirely different external life, career and status-seeking to someone with, say, Virgo on the M.C. These four lenses are so powerful that when a planet is located on or near them that planet will have much greater power and influence than it would normally: the planet is, so to speak, sucked into the vortex of forces around these nodal points. For example, Mars near the M.C. will mean that the energy of Mars will be intensified in the life of the native and given a force and impetus in regard to status-seeking and career (figure   ).

The four angles mark the basic grid of the horoscope, and also the basic nature of the

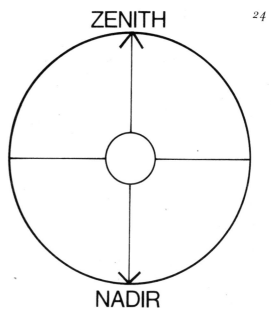

25

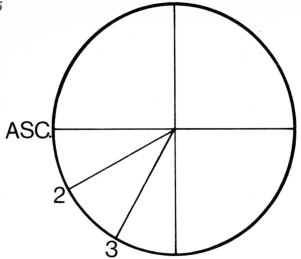

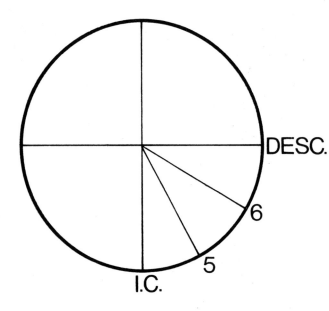

26

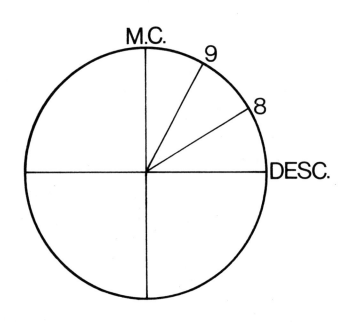

27

25. *The second and third houses which 'support' in a physical sense the demands of the Ascendant first house.*
26. *The fifth and sixth houses which are of an emotional quality, supporting the idea of 'relationships' implied in the Descendant seventh house.*
27. *The eighth and ninth houses which are of an objective nature, and support the idea of liberation and responsibility implicit in the tenth house.*

personality. Between each adjacent angle there are two other nodal points which give emphasis to certain other qualities in the native, though to a much lesser extent than the focusing force of the angles themselves. In between the Ascendant, or first house, and the I.C., or fourth house, we find two points called the second house and the third house (figure 25). The second house brings to a focus all the considerations in regard to the material support required by the Ascendant – it is the house which governs money, material well-being, and the ability to cope with money. The third house governs expression and communication, and brings to a focus the way in which the native relates to those in immediate contact with him. Both these houses, wedged between the self (Ascendant), and the home (I.C.), govern matters of a personal nature which expand into the fourth house question of 'beginnings'.

In between the I.C. and the Descendant (seventh house) are the nodal points of the fifth house and the sixth house (figure 26). The fifth house brings to a focus the creative energies of the native in their widest sense – it links with the power of the native to enjoy life, his capacity in love-making, in the constructive approach to life, and in the arts. The sixth house supports this fifth house, in a sense, for it brings to a focus the urge to clarify and sort out things, giving an idea of the way in which the native will bring order into his life. It is sometimes called the house of service, and is sometimes represented as the domain of the urge to clear up and organize the chaos engendered by the activities of the fifth house. Both these houses obviously govern matters of an emotional

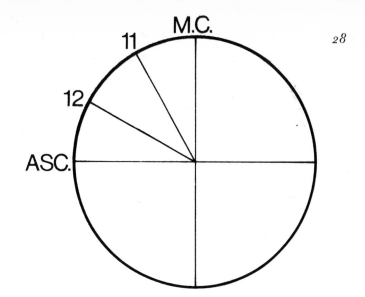

28

*28. The eleventh and twelfth
h.. es, which are of a
t. l:zed nature, and
t.. adaptability of
v.. terms of his
ability to relate to groups and
g..b tivities in the search for
...al identity.
ithin the horoscope figure the
.st single nodal points are the
four angles. In the example
given, the importance of the
influences (independent of the
planetary placings, of course)
would be Pisces, Sagittarius,
Virgo and Gemini, in that order.*

nature, which lead to the affairs of a seventh house nature of relationships.

In between the Descendant and the M.C. (tenth house) we find the eighth house and the ninth house (figure 27). The eighth house brings to a focus all those factors in the horoscope which relate to regeneration and deep inner striving. It is consulted by some astrologers as an index of the end of life – sometimes it is called the house of death. The ninth house brings to a focus all those things associated with deep thought, distant travel and the expansive qualities in the life of the native. It is an index of how the native will fare abroad, and in relation to foreigners, as well as in advanced education. Both these two houses are involved with the exploration of life, the eighth in a spiritual sense, the ninth in a physical and intellectual sense: one goes inwards, the other outwards, but both lead towards the complete fulfilment of the external ego, as represented in the tenth house.

In between the M.C. and the Ascendant we find the eleventh and the twelfth house (figure 28). The eleventh house brings to a focus all those factors which link with the native's ability to participate in group activities and social enterprise. The twelfth house brings to a focus all those factors in a horoscope concerned with the native's search for significance and life structure, and it is connected with the deeper questions of existence. These two houses are involved with the exploration of the search for meaning and identity in relation to a larger whole: in the eleventh house this exploration is in relation to visible society, in the twelfth in relation to the invisible inner world.

29

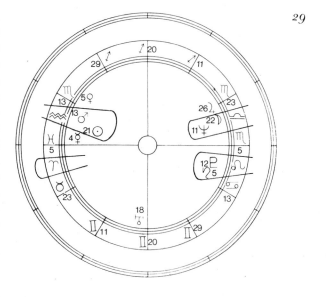

30

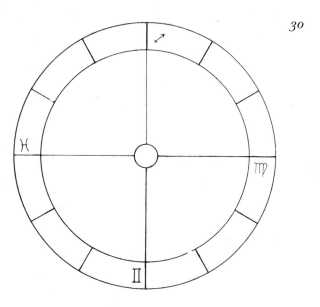

The degrees of the signs marked on the various houses are important, though there are several different ways of calculating them, all of which give slight variations. The beginner need not trouble himself too deeply about such differences in what astrologers call 'house systems', and he must merely note that while the planets in the different houses do manifest in particular ways, as set out below, the intermediate houses rarely give the same emphasis to the planets as do the angles.

The angles are of an altogether ·higher order of influence in the chart than the houses, but traditional astrology tends to incorporate the four angles with the eight houses, and study the effects of the twelve houses seen in a sequence, running anti-clockwise around the zodiac. Each of the twelve houses, as listed below, obviously carries something of the association of the sign linked with it – thus the nature of the first house is influenced by the nature of Aries, which is the first sign in the zodiac, and so on. The natures of the houses may be understood in terms of pairs of opposites, the lower part of the horoscope relating to personalized energies operating for the bene-fit of the ego, the higher part relating to a more free relationship which the native holds with the external world.

The First House marks the Ascendant, of course, and is the most personal of the houses, and consequently the most powerful in relation to the native. Everything in the horoscope, every planet, has ultimately to partake of the nature of the sign in the first house, the Ascendant sign. The first house may be conveniently described as a large lens, through which the Ascending sign will cast its light on all the activities governed by the other points in the horoscope. This is why the first house governs the appearance of the native, his or her disposition, the general psychic structure, and indeed the totality of the individual as a cosmic unit. The ruler is Aries.

The Second House is one remove from the personal first house, and in a sense lends physical support to the 'personality' of the first house. It governs possessions – those material forms which support physical life and make it more enjoyable. It is therefore a good index of finance in terms of earning and spending capacity, but it also shows the manner in which a person will gain or lose possessions. The ruler is Taurus.

The Third House governs relationships, and matters concerned with communications, such as letter-writing, telephone conversa-tions, and 'journeys of less than a day's length' as astrologers would say in other centuries, but in our speed-bound age this means journeys of short duration, involving motor-cars, bicycles and so on. Because this house deals with close or personal communi-cation, it is also consulted for matters of education. The ruler of this house is Gemini, the twins, and so by extension the house is representative of matters relating to brothers and sisters.

The Fourth House stands for the home, the place from which things start, and those things which are protected, secluded and withdrawn. We may understand this aspect through the connection with Cancer, sym-bolized by the crab, which carries its home on its back and protects itself under rocks. In

31. *Aries ancient and modern. The*
32. *natural house of Aries is concerned with the initiation of enterprises, and the sign rules the head. Aries is the pioneer and explorer, always wanting to be at the front, always seeking new experiences.*

33. *Taurus ancient and modern. The*
34. *natural house of Taurus is the one concerned with materiality and with support, which explains why Taurus is dedicated to what in earlier times was called 'the flesh'. In particular the Taurean likes beautiful appearance and good food. The link between Taurus and the body may be explained by the rulership of Venus over this sign (see figure 16).*

33

a horoscope the fourth house governs the conditions of early childhood, which is one reason why it is at the bottom of the horoscope, with the career, the opposite angle of status and aspirations, at the very top of the sky plan. It is sometimes called the house of beginnings. Like the other houses (notably the eighth) which are connected with Water signs, there is a link with mystical levels of awareness, and certainly it is the most mystical and ethereal of the four angles.

The Fifth House, being the natural house of the exuberant and creative Leo, relates to the general creativity of the native – his emotional attitude to the world which he enters after leaving the relative seclusion of the fourth house. The fifth house was consulted in times past for the elements of chance in the native's life. This has not perhaps changed a great deal, for it is now consulted on questions of courtships, sex, new undertakings, creativity, children and general pleasures – all businesses which have a great deal of chance, or apparently so. Its clearest indications are concerned with love affairs and related creativity – almost all the planets which are found in this house are permitted to use that side of their nature best suited for the creative purpose.

The Sixth House relates to the world of service to others, and finds expression through activities connected with cleansing, maintaining order and efficiency. Just as the materialism of the second house (ruled by Taurus) feeds the personality demands of the first house (Aries), this sixth house feeds the demands of the ego for pleasures ruled by the previous house – someone has to prepare the food and wash the nappies, so to speak.

34

35. Gemini ancient and modern.
36. Gemini has rule over dualities.
  We find expressed in Gemini
  the ideas which originated in
  Aries and found form in
  Taurus. Gemini is strongly dual,
  and usually aware of its duality.
  The house ruled by this sign
  governs communications, as well
  as travel – in modern terms it
  rules the telephone.

36

Thus, while the fifth-house pleasure impulses are self-expressive, self-indulgent, and tend towards disorder, the sixth-house urges linked with Virgo are controlled, repressive and conducive to order. The house might be termed 'the house of work', for to call it the house of service is to imply that the service is not willingly undertaken. The truth is that the urge to regulation and systematization expressed in this house accounts for the old name, so expressive of service and well-being, 'the house of health', and it certainly links with the native's attitudes to health, hygiene, cleanliness and so on. The house is a useful index of how the native will get on with employers.

The Seventh House marks the important Descendant angle, and rules partnerships, in particular marriage, the ultimate partnership. It deals also with what astrologers call 'open enmities' since quarrels and disputes do at least imply relationships of a clearly defined nature. The chief significance of the seventh house, however, is related to Venus, the ruler of Libra, whose proper domain is this seventh house, the area of good and harmonious relationships between people. Since this house is on the opposite side of the zodiac to the Ascendant it represents liberation from the egotistical demands of the native, the freedom to leave behind self interest through participation in the demands of another. The planets in the seventh house spark off the type and quality of relationships which are held with other people, and frequently they indicate something about the marriage of the native.

The Eighth House is connected with matters of deeper interest, with death, regeneration,

37. Cancer ancient and modern. The
38. protective shell of the crab is
supposed to symbolize the
protective nature of Cancer,
though this sign is altogether
more variable in nature and
quality than the average
astrological accounts would
suggest. Cancer is an impulse
productive of both mediocrity
and genius, and is therefore
extremely difficult to pin down in
simple descriptions. The sign
is concerned with 'beginnings'
and governs childhood.

37

legacies and hidden matters: and is connected with the idea of the results of relationships established in the previous house, and with immediate post-mortem influences of the native and his associates. The relations with others marked by this house are usually concerned with the idea of improving things – be they social conditions or personal life matters. The eighth house has an unfortunate association in traditional astrology, being sometimes called the 'house of death', but no good astrologer will examine this house merely in order to pronounce on questions of time of death, either of the native or his friends. The house is ruled by the intense and powerful Scorpio.

The Ninth House is best understood as an expansion of the opposite third house; it rules long journeys, deep explorations, and profound mental studies. It is therefore consulted by astrologers for matters concerning higher education, philosophy, and the native's relationship with foreigners as well as foreign travel. Certain of the ancient traditions concerning this house still linger on, but are no longer strictly valid. For example, in early times education was almost entirely restricted to ecclesiastical circles, so that the house was then properly associated with religion. Nowadays, however, it is difficult to condone the association of the mutable Fire of the ruler Sagittarius with religion, and indeed the native's attitude to religion is best studied through the eighth house. The ancient connection with prophecy which is often drawn for this house is however still valid, for seers and mediums frequently do have the ninth house emphasised. The planets in this house relate to the

38

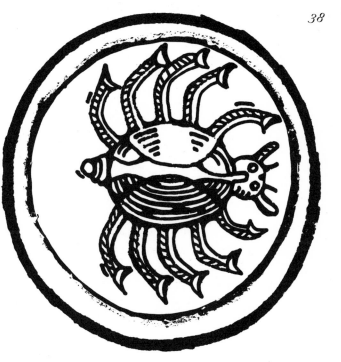

39

way in which the native will travel, and the nature of his philosophical interests and subjects of study.

The Tenth House, which marks the important angle of the M.C., governs the status of the individual, his or her social aspirations, and the actual position in society. The ruler is Capricorn. In the older forms of astrology this was called the 'house of the father' – and, of course, the father in a more patriarchal society than ours was very often instrumental in determining the career and status of the child. This old tradition lingers on in certain astrological circles, and sometimes the house is considered as relating to the father, with the opposite house (the fourth) relating to the mother. However, the house does not relate simply to father and to career, as such, but more to the aspirations of the native, and to his or her status, to the manner in which he will project himself upwards or downwards in the social hierarchy.

The Eleventh House relates to distant friendships, and to groups in which the native becomes involved through his family or professional contacts. It is the house natural to the sign of Aquarius, which is involved with ideals of mass reforms and humanitarian concepts of freedom. Since the house is on the opposite side of the zodiac to the fifth (which rules the intimate relationships of the native), the eleventh house governs relationships with people and things which are at a distance, far from the direct emotional contact offered by the Fire of Leo. The house therefore marks the attitude and reaction of the native to social events, clubs, political machinations, revolutionary urges, distant friendships, idealisms, and such

things as are in the background to his life. In traditional astrology the house was called the 'house of hopes and wishes', and it still covers the ideals held by the native, by which he attempts to impose his own personality on the world. While the native of the opposite sign Leo will require an immediate result for his labours, and an immediate adulation from the audience around him, the eleventh house force will create in a more general way, and will be happy with long-term results from certain labours. He will be satisfied with the creative work itself, not always requiring immediate adulation or praise, but being content in some idealistic way to 'go down as a name in posterity'. This is one reason why Aquarian artists can work well in group activities such as film making, whereas Leo artists can rarely do so without some inner tension.

The Twelfth House is the most spiritual of all, ruled by Pisces, and it is sometimes difficult to understand in ordinary terms those people who have the twelfth house emphasised in a chart. It has been called the 'house of sorrows' and the 'house of one's own undoing', and is quite rightly linked with the Piscean phase of Christianity (figure 327), with its belief in the renunciation of the material world in favour of the world spiritual. The house may be examined for the outcome of the spiritual forces gathered unwittingly or wittingly during the course of life: it marks the end-product of things, and has also been described as the 'house of the hangover', for the spiritual rewards and punishments which inevitably follow actions on the physical plane are symbolized by this house. It may be regarded as the house of spiritual debt, just as the one immediately below the Ascendant may be regarded as the house of material debt. The tendency in the past has been for astrologers to emphasise the importance of the twelfth house as marking the end of things, even the end of life – but it is more creative and satisfying to see it as relating to the new beginning which every end implies. It is this mystical level, the connection with beginnings, which reveals the house as relating to transition, be it from one phase of life to another, or from one particular incarnation to the next. In this sense it may be regarded as the house of *karma*.

We see from all that has been said above that the horoscope itself gives two different sets of information: it measures the positions of the planets against the zodiacal band, from which it is possible for the astrologer to determine how specific energies (the planets) manifest in intensity and manner (through the signs they occupy): at the same time it measures the position of the ecliptic in relation to the place of birth, from which the astrologer will determine how certain energies and drives (the planets and the signs) will manifest in certain areas of human endeavour (the angles and houses).

The interpretation of a horoscope is in itself involved with reconciling many conflicting tensions and apparent contradictions – for after all, every human being has many internal tensions and inbuilt contradictions. It is, however, possible to interpret the horoscope in terms of the two sets of information united in the horoscope. We may examine the significance of the various nodal points, the points of focus on the zodiacal band, taking into account such factors as the

41

42

29

43

43. *Libra ancient and modern.*
44. *Libra rules the house of relationships: the Libran frequently finds himself balanced between two possibilities, and not disposed towards action.*
45. *Scorpio ancient and modern.*
46. *Scorpio rules the house of regeneration, and the intense, powerful emotionality of the sign is aptly portrayed in the image of the dangerous scorpion, even though originally the sign was ruled by the spiritual-striving eagle.*

44

Ascendant and so on; and then we may examine the force of the planets, in terms of the sign placings and in terms of the interaction between the planets. The secret behind horoscope interpretation is in correctly assessing which are the most important factors operative in a particular chart. We have already noted that a planet will be emphasised when it is near an angle, but there are other factors in a chart which may lend emphasis to a planet or to a particular part of the zodiac. Because of this the next three sections will set out the rules for interpreting a horoscope and explain how these rules may be applied in particular figures. It will be understood, eventually, that the use of the hand in relation to astrology is one of the surest ways in which a beginner may learn to grasp the most salient and significant factors in a horoscope. For the moment, however, we shall study astrology without reference to the hand. We shall study first of all the influence of the signs, then the influence of the planets in the signs, and then the influence of the planets on or near the houses, and then finally the interesting and important influence on personality which the planets exert when they themselves hold certain angular relationships to each other. This line of study should not lead us to suppose that such a simple approach sets out completely all the factors which a serious astrologer will take into account when reading a horoscope: the potentials are as inexhaustible as life itself.

The student will appreciate that astrology is a far more complex subject than the present text will suggest, and that indeed there are many forms of astrology in use today.

The Significance of
the Twelve Signs

Each of the twelve signs has a distinctive set of characteristics which find outlets of expression whenever it is emphasised in a chart, as for example when it is found on one of the angles, or when one of the planets is found in it. We shall study first the basic structure and quality of these twelve signs, and note in particular how they manifest when on the four angles of the horoscope. Obviously there is an interaction between the four angles because of the opposite pulls they set up – for example a Taurean Ascendant will always have Scorpio on the Descendant which means that the Taurean personality will tend to establish relationships (seventh house consideration) in a particular way, and indeed sometimes it is difficult to determine to what extent it is one astrological factor which gives rise to a particular manifestation and to what extent it is another factor. Thus the Taurean is usually possessive and jealous in his relationships, and it is difficult for one to determine to what extent this is due to the basic Taurean nature, which is possessive in the sense that the bull is possessive of his field and cows, and to what extent it is due to Scorpio (a notoriously jealous sign) being on the house of relationships for all Taurean Ascendants (figure 23). The astrologer has to attempt to draw a picture which reconciles these different pulls, as well as the other directions set up by the four angles. The way in which the twelve signs manifest through the planets which represent specific outlets of energy will be discussed on page 38ff.

The twelve signs consist of different combinations of elements and qualities. The element is a measure of being, the quality a measure of action. There are four elements:

45

46

47

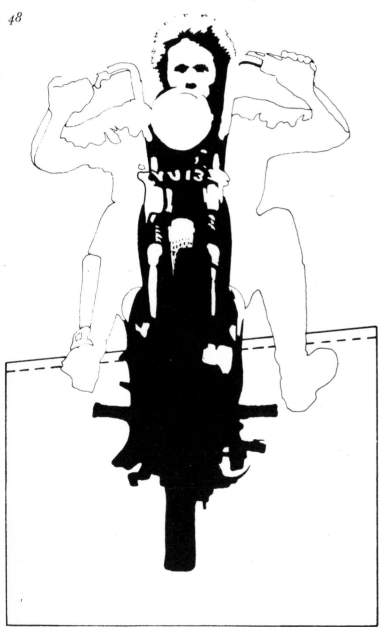

48

47. *Sagittarius ancient and modern.*
48. *The sign is very much involved with travel, as the material expression of the aspiration of Jupiter.*
49. *Capricorn ancient and modern.*
50. *Capricorn is given to moods, obsessions and worries.*
51. *Aquarius ancient and modern.*
52. *Aquarius pours two kinds of water on to the Earth – one refreshing, the other poisonous. In modern terms it is concerned with humanity and with the destruction of humanity.*

Fire, Earth, Air and Water, and the nature of these are discussed more fully on page 67ff. in the section on hand types, since the form of the hand is most usefully classified in terms of the four elements. There are three qualities; Cardinal, Fixed and Mutable, the meaning of which we shall shortly examine. For the moment we must consider how the four elements in some ways resemble the natures of the phenomena after which they are named.

Fire burns, warms and consumes. Fire types warm and consume others: they are exuberant, enthusiastic, positive in regard to life, creative in attitude, often rather exaggerative, and with a developed sense of self-importance. The Fire signs are Aries, in which Fire energy is harnessed to the assertion of self and individuality; Leo, in which Fire energy is harnessed to the expression of self; and Sagittarius, in which Fire energies are harnessed to the improvement of self and individuality.

Earth is heavy and dry, and yet in a sense it supports the spiritual world, for from its constituents life derives its physical vehicles. Earth types are the physical backbone of society; they are often slow and ponderous, as though weighted with form, and yet they are practical in the sense that they can both supply and use material forms. Earth types sustain the other types, and have a sense of practical materiality. The Earth signs are Taurus, in which Earth energy is brought towards the practical manipulation of material; Virgo, in which Earth energy manifests in a mental way, and concerns itself with the refinement and classification of materials; and Capricorn, in which Earth

energies are put towards the end of the domination of nature through the urge and ability to organize.

Air is pervasive, and through its constituent oxygen is the main source of our continuing life, as well as the means by which we communicate. Air types are, like air itself, difficult to pin down; they are the great explainers of the world around, those who are anxious always to be communicating and establishing relations with others. The Air signs are Gemini, in which Air energy is concerned with explaining and expounding individual truths in an unemotional manner; Libra, in which Air is devoted to relationships and comparing truths; and Aquarius, in which Air energies are applied to understanding the universal truths behind the phenomena of our world.

Water is a source of refreshment and, although colourless itself, reflects the colours of the world around it: our bodies are largely composed of its element. Water types are sensitive to their surroundings, constantly searching for some containing form to give an identity and meaning: they are the sensitive souls of the human world. The sensitivity of the type often makes them cautious, and they feel the need to sustain and refresh others which sometimes makes them extremely self-sacrificial. The Water signs are Cancer, in which the Water energies are used to preserve emotional sensitivity; Scorpio, in which Water energies are used to preserve emotional intensity, and a sense of self discipline; and Pisces, in which the Water energies are used to preserve emotional fluidity, often to the detriment of self-survival.

The qualities are descriptive of polarities of motion: the Cardinal is pure movement, the Fixed is static, while the Mutable is caught between the two, the mediator, so to speak, which may move or may not move depending upon the influences around it. In regard to the influence of the signs we find that the Cardinal puts the emphasis on the physical, and is active, purposive, restless, and enterprising: its fault is that it is domineering. The Fixed puts the emphasis on feeling, and is reserved, conservative, slow, stubborn, while the fault is that it tends to be tyrannical. The Mutable puts the emphasis on thought: it is flexible, unreliable and changeable, and though intellectual in outlook, is bad at accepting responsibility. The qualities may be represented by imagining the Cardinal as an arrow pointing upwards, the Fixed as a heavy dot and the Mutable as a combination of these – movement pulling against fixity, and creating a state of tension (figure 55).

55

Since each of the twelve signs incorporate different combinations of the elements and the qualities, it is possible to see these combinations in the signs and, from what has been said so far, gain a fairly accurate picture of the natures of the twelve signs. Each sign combines one element with one quality, and, though much of the nature of the signs may be grasped from a proper understanding of the elements and qualities, it is a little easier for the student to see how they interact by making a study of the 'identity' of the signs themselves. The following notes summarize the characteristics of the twelve signs. A full understanding of the fascinating diversity they present may be gained from a wide

reading of astrological books and from experience: the bibliography at page 184 will be found particularly useful, for it sets out those books which are recommended for their sections on the signs.

Aries is Cardinal Fire. The influence is outgoing, pioneering, self-reliant, idealistic, enthusiastic, exaggerative. The type tends to be insensitive to the needs of others.

Taurus is Fixed Earth. The influence is constructive, strong-willed, conservative, slow, practical and sensuous. The type makes a faithful friend but an implacable enemy.

Gemini is Mutable Air. The influence is versatile, clever, restless, intelligent, contradictory, volatile and eloquent. The type tends to be superficial.

Cancer is Cardinal Water. The influence is emotional, sensitive, unstable, clannish, romantic and imaginative. The type is sometimes very original and gifted.

Leo is Fixed Fire. The influence is passionate, sincere, pleasure-loving, creative, proud, good at organizing, generous and authoritative. The type tends to be egocentric.

Virgo is Mutable Earth. The influence is discriminative, quiet, exacting, nervous, shrewd, cool, dignified and methodical. The type tends to be over-critical.

Libra is Cardinal Air. The influence is harmonious, elegant, orderly, comparative, peaceful, changeable, helpful, and gifted in the arts. The type tends to be lazy and sensuous.

Scorpio is Fixed Water. The influence is shrewd, magnetic, determined, secretive, dignified, self-confident, masterful, sensitive and critical. The type tends to be dogmatic and violent.

53. *Pisces ancient and modern.*
54. *Pisces, for all its wish to belong to a group – to swim in shoals, so to speak – in modern times often finds itself isolated*
55. *The Qualities symbol.*
56. *The important angles of the*
57. *horoscope, the self manifesting through Aries, outer aim through Capricorn, relationships through Libra, and inner drives through Cancer.*

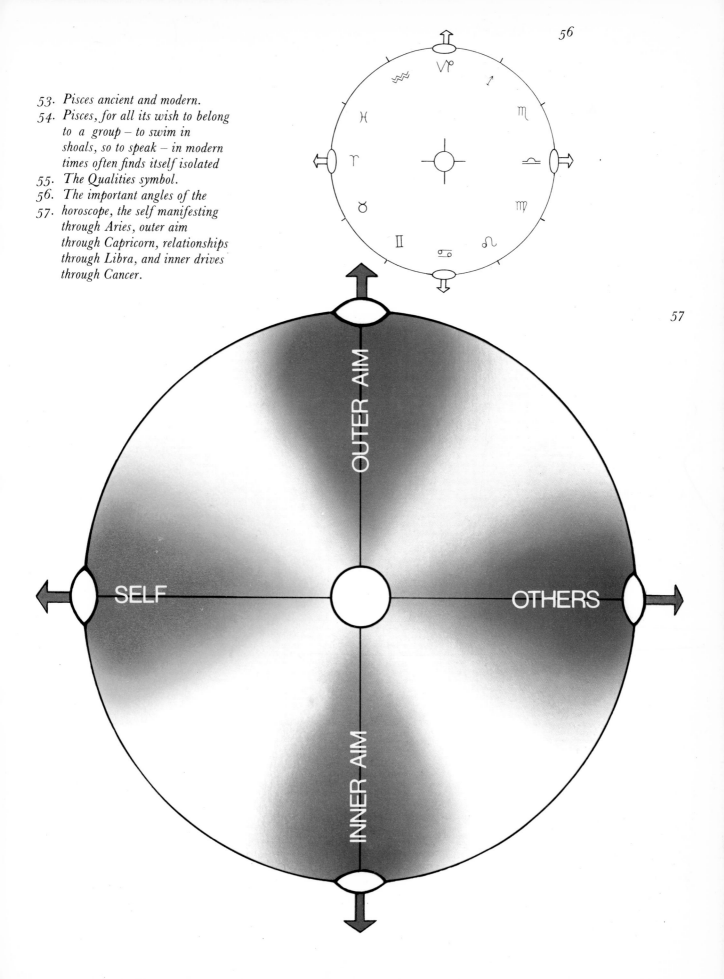

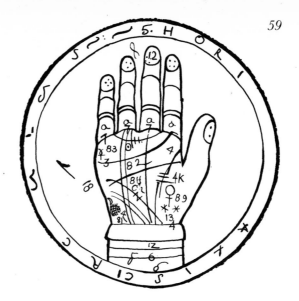

58. *The twelve signs of the zodiac, with their basic colour associations, from a fifteenth-century book on popular astrology. With the exception of Cancer, which is now a crab, the associations are much the same today.*

59. *A diagram of signs and lines on the hand, from a seventeenth-century treatise on palmistry. The breaks on the life line in those days were taken to portend death and destruction.*

Sagittarius is Mutable Fire. The influence is independent, enterprising, open, kind, honest, dignified, intuitive, optimistic, expansive. The type tends to be prodigal.

Capricorn is Cardinal Earth. The influence is industrious, practical, prudent, persevering, diplomatic, cautious, melancholy, methodical and ambitious. The type tends to be cold, suspicious and parsimonious.

Aquarius is Fixed Air. The influence is erratic, artistic, refined, tenacious, perverse, magnetic, intuitive, independent and original. The type tends to be wayward and sceptical.

Pisces is Mutable Water. The influence is emotional, sympathetic, impressionable, friendly, benevolent, apprehensive, untidy and extremely sensitive. The type tends to be despondent and vacillating.

The drives, energies and forces of the twelve signs are, of course, contained as potentials in everyone: we are all, potentially at least, complete models of the universe. What distinguishes people one from another in terms of astrology is the particular grouping of these potentials which determine how they will actually manifest in their personalities and life patterns, because certain parts of the zodiac form nodal points at the moment of birth. A part of the zodiac may become a nodal point because a planet is placed in it, or it may be a nodal point because it is on an angle. The angles are, therefore, extremely important, and we may assume that the areas of life to which they relate (the Ascendant relating to self-awareness, the tenth house to status and aspiration, the seventh house to relationships, and the fourth house to background)

will be strongly influenced by the signs upon them. For example, Aries on the Ascendant will make a type entertaining and assertive because the Cardinal Fire of Aries will manifest through self: Aries on the tenth house will make the native enterprising in forging a career for himself, will make him ambitious, as the Cardinal Fire manifests through status seeking.

It is best for beginners to attempt the interpretation of angles in a simple way, and to think in terms of the signs which are emphasised on them in a particular chart. The following keywords should be memorized with this aim in mind. Aries is enterprising; Taurus is practical; Gemini is versatile; Cancer is sensitive; Leo is creative; Virgo is discriminative; Libra is reconciling; Scorpio is intensifying; Sagittarius is explorative; Capricorn is cautious; Aquarius is unconventional; Pisces is imaginative. The fuller list of keywords at page 38 gives further help in interpreting the angles. It is only by experience that one can learn to balance the four often contradictory pulls which the angles establish in a personality.

The student could do no better at this point than attempt to build up a mental picture of each of the twelve zodiacal 'types', realizing the while that no such types exist save as ideals. All human beings participate in the whole of the zodiac, with different characteristics emphasised or retarded due to the moment of birth. The best way of forming such pictures in the mind is through reading about the zodiacal types, and attempting to test these against known horoscopes of friends and those of famous people.

The Significance of the Planets

The planets can never be studied in a vacuum because they are always set against some part of the zodiac, and therefore by astrological definition are always transmitting some influence or another. However, experience shows that they are not merely moving lenses which transmit the zodiacal light according to their natures; planets do have qualities and characteristics of their own, and they do influence human beings by their own intrinsic nature when they are emphasised in a chart. It is important that the beginner should learn something about the nature of the planets, because they are not only of great importance in astrology but are also related to various palmistic teachings concerning the meaning of the hand structure.

The Sun rules the creative self-expression of the personality, and is an index of the life force, creativity and spiritual being of the native. A Sun which is emphasised in a chart is usually an indication of artistic creativity, physical dignity, self-reliance, a strong animal spirit and a generous, affectionate, commanding nature. A badly placed Sun, or one badly aspected (see page 49), tends towards excesss, and the native may be rather showy, ostentatious, over-confident and egotistical.

In a male chart the Sun often links with the father, in a female chart with the husband. The Sun manifests itself in each of the signs in the following way:

Sun in Aries gives an assertive nature, a drive towards individuality, and a conscious aim involved with energetic leadership.

Sun in Taurus gives a conservative, rather fixed nature, a drive towards possessiveness, and the conscious aim involved with the realization of material security.

Sun in Gemini gives a quick, changeable nature, a drive towards a versatile development of self-awareness, and a conscious aim involved with intellectual communication.

Sun in Cancer gives a retiring, moody nature, a drive towards romantic attachment to others, and a conscious aim involved with sensitive enfolding of a rich emotional life.

Sun in Leo gives an exuberant and proud nature, a drive towards vivifying creativity, and a conscious aim involved with dignified or exuberant self-expression.

Sun in Virgo gives a conscientious practical nature, a drive towards thoroughness in service, and a conscious aim involved with the establishment of just principles.

Sun in Libra gives a gentle, discriminative nature, a drive towards the enjoyment of harmony and stability.

Sun in Scorpio gives an intense, strong-willed nature, a drive towards regeneration, and a conscious aim involved with the exercise of power, usually over others.

Sun in Sagittarius gives a dignified, restless nature, a drive towards the exploration of ideas, and a conscious aim involved with the attainment of wisdom.

Sun in Capricorn gives a cautious though ambitious nature, a drive towards the practical expression of duty, and a conscious aim involved with being dependable.

Sun in Aquarius gives an unconventional, humanitarian nature, a drive towards a detached, if original, pursuit of truth, and a conscious aim involved with the expression of useful knowledge.

Sun in Pisces gives an imaginative, highly

60

60. *The Sun rules the right hand side of the body, the Moon the left. Such rulerships may be understood only on the deeper levels of occultism, which portray man as caught between two forces, each equally destructive of the true human condition: the urge to be purely spiritual (solar) may be as destructive of real growth as the urge to be purely material (lunar). True man must find the middle way between these two urges.*

emotional nature, a drive towards the sympathetic understanding of others, and a conscious aim involved with a search for emotional balance.

The Moon reflects the Sun, and in astrology it stands for the imaginative, reflective side of self, and is sometimes linked with the sub-conscious. It governs the receptive, with-drawn, secluded and sensitive side of the personality. When the Moon is strongly placed in a chart, it makes the native highly sensitive, impressionable, sentimental, changeable, and indeed, subject to change. Sometimes the native may be surprisingly shrewd and practical. When this planet is badly placed, the sensitivity or imagination is limited or felt to be under stress, and the subject tends to be untidy, withdrawn, prejudiced, morbidly concerned with the self, or strangely subject to misfortune. The Moon reflects in a very sensitive manner the quality and nature of the planets linked with it by aspect (see page 49). A study of the Moon placing is useful for determining what the native will absorb in life. In a male horoscope it usually affords some hint as to the nature of the wife, in a female horoscope it is usually linked with the mother. The Moon manifests itself in each of the signs in the following way, but it must be understood that very frequently the 'deep need' which the planet represents is hidden to the native:

Moon in Aries gives a restless personality, with a deep need for independence, and emotions which are easily aroused.

Moon in Taurus gives a conservative, posses-sive personality, a deep need for a placid existence, and emotions which are in them-selves refined, though sensuous.

Moon in Gemini gives an alert, rational per-sonality, with a deep need for physical and mental activity, and emotions which, though tending to be superficial, are in constant need of stimulation.

Moon in Cancer gives a sensitive, changeable personality, with a deep need for environ-mental security, and strong emotions which are romantically inclined.

Moon in Leo gives a confident, pleasure-loving personality, with a deep need for recognition and admiration, and emotions which are rich and passionate.

Moon in Virgo gives an industrious, unassum-ing personality, with a deep need for order and clarity, and emotions which are usually well hidden, or even repressed in expression.

Moon in Libra gives a gentle, hospitable per-sonality, with a deep need for companion-ship, and emotions which are delicate and refined.

Moon in Scorpio gives a magnetic, moody and determined personality, with a deep need for the development of self-control, and emo-tions which are intense and passionate, though sometimes hidden behind a cool and deceptive front.

Moon in Sagittarius gives a restless, cheerful and frank personality, with a deep need for mental and physical freedom, and emotions which are spontaneous, though sometimes superficial.

Moon in Capricorn gives a cautious, prudent, sometimes rather cold personality, with a deep need to exercise austerity, and emotions which are not easily aroused or sensibly bestowed.

Moon in Aquarius gives a humane, indepen-dent and friendly personality, with a deep

need to help others in a detached way, and emotions which are often eccentric in expression, and which sometimes appear to be indifferent.

Moon in Pisces gives a highly sensitive, sentimental personality which tends to be emotionally lacking in balance, with a deep need for a social life, and emotions which are deep though often inconstant.

Mercury governs the ability of the native to communicate, and is a useful index of his mentality, although it is usually concerned more with details than generalities (which are the domain of Jupiter), more with the day-to-day demands of brain work than with profound or metaphysical thought. When Mercury is strongly marked in a chart it makes the native quick in mind and expression, and often also in body. He may be a fluent and witty talker, and will almost certainly find himself involved with work connected with communication: he will be of a volatile disposition. Mercury is often vacillating in its action. When this planet is badly placed, the speech and curiosity may be exaggerated in one way or another – the native may be talkative, untruthful or sarcastic, or he may be completely obsessed with details. Mercury in excess tends to be exaggerative, and the personality may sometimes be given to theft and slander. Mercury will take rather than give: one studies this planet in a chart in order to determine how a person expresses himself. Mercury manifests itself in each of the signs in the following way:

Mercury in Aries gives an alert mentality, with a need to communicate in a slangy, even argumentative or exaggerated manner.

Mercury in Taurus gives a slow, opinionated mentality, with a need to communicate in a conventional, reiterative though practical manner.

Mercury in Gemini gives an inventive mentality, with a need to communicate in a logical, voluble and witty, if selfish, manner.

Mercury in Cancer gives a clear, imaginative mentality and a retentive memory, with a need to communicate in an emotional and loquacious manner.

Mercury in Leo gives an authoritative, creative personality, with a need to communicate in a warm, positive, dignified and very expansive manner.

Mercury in Virgo gives a sensible, critical mentality, fond of working within a framework of facts. There is a need to communicate in a business-like, precise and categorical manner.

Mercury in Libra gives a comparative, well-balanced mentality, with a need to communicate in a friendly, personalized yet rational manner.

Mercury in Scorpio gives a shrewd, critical, rather probing mentality, with a need to communicate in a positive, assertive and perhaps sarcastic manner.

Mercury in Sagittarius gives a restless, aspiring mentality, with a need to communicate in a direct, truthful, and sometimes argumentative manner.

Mercury in Capricorn gives a dry mentality, cautious but clever, with a need to communicate in a conventional though often eloquent and witty manner.

Mercury in Aquarius gives an inquisitive, original and synthesizing mentality, with a need to communicate accurately, abstractly and in a detached manner.

61. *Mercury, who rules the two*
62. *extremes of healing (love of spirit) and money (love of matter). The planet gives an index of the native's relationship to matter.*
63. *Venus who rules over love-making, music and the body in general.*

Mercury in Pisces gives a somewhat confused, illogical, though often creative mentality, with a need to communicate in a voluble, confused but humorous manner.

Venus stands for the spiritual side of the native as manifest through the physical life, and it represents the ability of the native to enjoy beauty and to co-operate with others, which is why it is traditionally regarded as the planet of love. It governs the higher emotions, the understanding and the general refinement of the individual. When Venus is strongly placed it brings to the fore the beauty of the native, as well as his love for beauty: it tends to emphasise the need for a social life, makes the native popular with members of the opposite sex, and generally indicates happiness and harmony in the emotional life. A strong Venus also indicates a love for the arts, especially for music. When the planet is badly placed it tends to restrict the urge towards co-operation, and the native will lack confidence, or will be un-practical and lazy. An afflicted Venus often makes the native opportunist. A study of the Venus placing is useful for determining what the native loves in life, how his affections are expressed and where his centre of balance lies. Venus manifests in each of the signs in the following way:

Venus in Aries gives a strong, easily aroused affection, and a love of romantic involve-ments and enthusiasm. Tends to give a restless and inconstant nature.

Venus in Taurus gives strong, earthy affections which are slow in developing, and there is usually a love of the arts, especially the art of music. Tends to give a sociable, generous nature.

Venus in Gemini gives spontaneous though changeable affections, and an interest in intellectual activities. Tends to bestow a youthful and exuberant nature, and an urge to travel.

Venus in Cancer gives protective, sympathetic and romantic affections and there is a ten-dency towards romantic idealization. Fond of family life, the woman with Venus in this sign tends to be over-motherly.

Venus in Leo gives complete committal of affections in a generous display of emotions, and there is usually some involvement in artistic affairs. Tends to be dramatic in expression of emotions, and to be given to a love of luxury.

Venus in Virgo gives discriminating, rather exacting and controlled emotions, and there is a tendency towards avoidance of emotional contact with others. Tends to be detached and pure in relationships, appearing almost selfish or cold.

Venus in Libra gives tender affections which require another to act as a partner: is said to be 'in love with love'. The affections are usually easily expressed, and often there is a pursuit in an artistic field which permits of romantic contact.

Venus in Scorpio gives passionate and posses-sive emotions, and the native is usually highly sensitive to lack of regard in others. There is a penchant for luxury and secrecy. Pride rather than affection usually sets the keynote of a relationship with the opposite sex.

Venus in Sagittarius gives impulsive, affec-tionate, though fickle emotions, and there is usually a penchant for adventure, especially involving travel. Tends to be changeable,

and does not wish to be chained down by circumstances or persons.

Venus in Capricorn gives lasting and sincere emotions, and a conventional wish for domesticated life. Tends to be snobbish in choice of partner, and slow to develop relationships.

Venus in Aquarius gives a rather idealistic, impersonal use of emotions, and a longing for an intellectual kind of relationship which is at root unconventional. Tends to be unselfish in dealing with others.

Venus in Pisces gives indiscriminate, tender and easy-going emotion and a love for romantic entanglements, as well as for music and poetry. Tends to be lazy, and unprepared to make effort on behalf of self.

Mars stands for the physical side of the native as manifest in life; it is an index of his energy, his ability to endure, and the positive go-getting quality of the native. It is directly linked with the sex drive. Mars always wants to be doing something or going somewhere. It governs the excesses to which the native is subject. When Mars is strongly placed it makes the native enterprising, courageous, confident, active and proud, though sometimes openly quarrelsome: always it bestows great energy and an ability to construct or destroy. Sometimes there is a general lack of refinement: Mars always seeks to be independent and free. When badly placed, the explosive and disruptive side of the planet is emphasised; the native will be rough, destructive and reckless, sometimes involved with violence or crime. A study of the Mars placing is useful for determining what the native is aiming at, and the direction and manner in which his

physical and sexual energies are applied. Mars manifests in each of the signs in the following way:

Mars in Aries gives a vigorous supply of energy, a positive and perhaps domineering attitude to life, and ardent desires. Sexuality strong and ardent.

Mars in Taurus gives a steady supply of energy, a persevering and rather stubborn attitude to life, and earth-bound desires. Sexuality is earthy and sensual.

Mars in Gemini gives an uneven supply of energy, which manifests itself sporadically, and an attitude to life which drives the native to act mainly by intuition, which he may do brilliantly. The desires, though quickly aroused, may disappear just as quickly. Sexuality sometimes superficial, sometimes deep: generally requires more than one partner.

Mars in Cancer gives an emotional fount of energy, which tends to make the native subtle, moody and tenacious. The attitude to life is sympathetic and protective towards near friends, while the desires tend to be sensuous. Sexuality refined.

Mars in Leo gives powerful, hot-tempered and impulsive emotions, which find their expression in dramatic outbursts. The attitude is independent and given to being authoritarian, while the desires are impulsive and usually find an outlet through some distinctly creative channel. Sexuality warm and expressive.

Mars in Virgo gives a methodical application to energies, though there is a tendency to be carping towards others. The attitude is calculating, critical and painstakingly efficient. Desires are sometimes controlled almost to

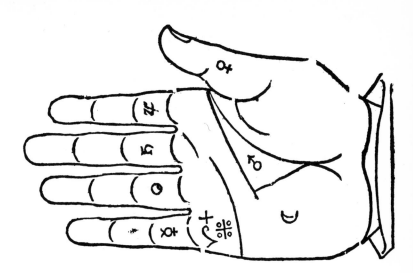

64. *Mars, like all the other planets, has a dual nature – though essentially active and warlike, he may be constructive as well as destructive.*

65. *The horoscope for the United States of America shows Mars in the aggressive Aries, on the house concerned with materiality. The two possibilities for the development of the nation are evident from this placing.*

66. *In earlier forms of palmistry Mars had rule over the centre of the hand, through an area called 'the plain of Mars'.*

the point of extinction. Sexuality idealistic: favours gentle relationships, though by no means always platonic.

Mars in Libra gives a relaxed source of energies which are used in an easy going way. The attitude reflects this relaxed condition by being amiable, yet it is easily influenced by external stimuli. The desires are refined and cultivated. Sexuality sensuous and refined.

Mars in Scorpio gives an intense supply of energy which is usually well disciplined, co-ordinated towards some purpose, and used for augmenting the native's sense of power. The attitude is dignified at best, restless at worst, though persistent in both cases. The desires are powerful, strong and sensuous, though often hidden from others. Sexuality very strong and permeating.

Mars in Sagittarius gives a rather fitful, un-disciplined supply of energy, though it may be used, under the pressure of enthusiasm, for achieving quite remarkable results in a speculative or exploratory capacity. The desires are sensual and passionate. Sexuality expansive, exploratory and deep.

Mars in Capricorn gives a well-controlled supply of energy which is thrust into ambitious projects involving organization and persistent effort. The desires are strong, even sensuous. Sexuality is strong and earthy.

Mars in Aquarius gives an erratic supply of energy which is thrust into group activities, often involving humanitarian aims. The desires are strong but rather detached. Sexuality strong, but often more than one partner is required, one being peripheral.

Mars in Pisces gives a sensitive supply of energy, though the native tends to be restless.

He is sometimes the victim of deception. Sexuality involved with romantic notions of others, though sensuous.

Jupiter represents the deeper side of the mental plane: it stands for the speculative thought of the native, and for the expansive side of his nature. It governs the moral nature, and the degree to which the native will respond enthusiastically to life and to responsibilities. When Jupiter is strongly placed in a chart it makes the native generous, optimistic, loyal, popular, friendly and generally highly successful in life and business. When badly placed, the expansiveness and self-control of the planet are limited, with the result that the native will often run to excess of optimism, and become self-indulgent, prodigal or particularly reckless in the use of energies and assets. A study of the Jupiter placing is useful for determining the expansive quality of the native and for gauging what spiritual growth the person requires from life. Jupiter manifests in each of the signs in the following way:

Jupiter in Aries gives a wish for freedom, and an enthusiastic approach to active occupations.

Jupiter in Taurus gives a wish for indulgence in material pleasures, and an enthusiastic approach to the gathering of possessions.

Jupiter in Gemini gives a wish to improve methods of communication, and an enthusiastic urge towards constant change of situation or mental occupation.

Jupiter in Cancer gives a wish to become more sympathetic towards others, and to improve the emotional quality of the native's being. There is usually a need for domesticity.

Jupiter in Leo gives a penchant for dramatic

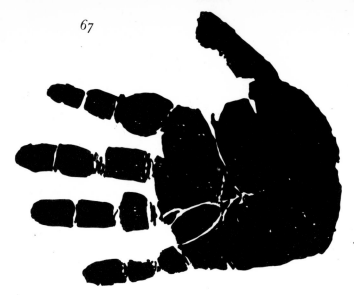

Deloue domino genituræ.

show, an emphasis on vitality, often expressed artistically, and gives a wish to be the leader in most situations. There is an enthusiasm for good living.

Jupiter in Virgo gives a wish to increase critical faculties or technical skill. There is usually a quiet enthusiasm for research or service to others.

Jupiter in Libra gives a wish to be surrounded by harmony both in social life (which is preferably artistic), and in environment, which must be quietly beautiful, though not showy. There is a craving for partnership.

Jupiter in Scorpio gives a wish to exercise will-power over others, and to indulge the passions. There is an enthusiasm for all matters involving regeneration, or the testing of resources.

Jupiter in Sagittarius gives a wish to be in a position to be generous, free and magnificent. There is usually a strong urge to follow a sport, or towards reckless speculation, or towards the exploration of a subject.

Jupiter in Capricorn gives a strong sense of ambition, and a conscientious sense of self-control towards achieving ambitions. There is a strong urge towards the fulfilment of duty, in terms of what the native takes this to be in his own life.

Jupiter in Aquarius gives an urge towards sociability, a wish to study or actively engage in some philosophical or sociological system of ideas, and an enthusiasm to see wrong punished and right rewarded.

Jupiter in Pisces gives a somewhat over-emotional, easy-going nature, usually with few admitted ambitions other than the increase of public good. There is usually a refined aesthetic sense.

Saturn represents the restrictive side of the native, and it stands for the way in which the native is prepared to pay for things given, and demand payment for things received: it is the planet of justice. It governs the practical and material elements of life as related to the personality; the ability to work hard, concentrate and persevere, as well as the general reliability of the native. When Saturn is strongly placed in a chart it emphasises the sense of the material and control, with the result that the subject tends to be very practical, patient, reliable, prudent and honest. Saturn always believes that everything must be earned, and that effort is often in itself a reward. When the planet is badly placed the limitation experienced by the native is great indeed, and energies are dammed up so that a narrow, conservative, emotionally cold and very despondent outlook is adopted. A study of the Saturn placing is useful for determining the fears and limitations which beset the native, what bounds are set to his life, and what disappointments and delays he may expect. Saturn manifests in each of the signs in the following way:

Saturn in Aries The underlying fear is of being frustrated. The character tends one minute to be powerful, the next rather retiring, and all the time the personality appears to lack real depth.

Saturn in Taurus The underlying fear is connected with a sense of insecurity; the feeling that he or she will run out of material resources. The character otherwise gives every impression of being secure, for it is determined and deliberate, if solidly materialistic. It tends to be selfish and slow.

67. *Attempts have been made in the past to describe hand forms which correspond to the planetary activities. A particularly interesting system is that put forward by Georges Muchery (see bibliography). This is the Jupiter hand form.*
68. *The expansive Jupiter, from a fifteenth-century textbook.*
69. *The hand form of Saturn according to Muchery. Note its thin and long structure in comparison with the expansive hand of Jupiter.*

Saturn in Gemini The underlying fear is connected with the idea of restriction: the native cannot bear to be restrained either physically or intellectually. The character is adaptable, rational and appears rather cold.

Saturn in Cancer The underlying fear is of being emotionally vulnerable to others. The character tends to be withdrawn, timid, pessimistic and rather clannish.

Saturn in Leo The underlying fear is of appearing mediocre, either to oneself or to others. The character is proud, autocratic and given to organization, but there is usually a feeling that full creative self-expression is not being achieved.

Saturn in Virgo The underlying fear is of the unknown, of that which cannot be categorized. The character is itself well organized, being careful, conscientious and discriminating.

Saturn in Libra The underlying fear is of being passionately involved either in an occupation or in a human relationship. The character tends to be serious and gentle, yet there is an element of intolerance in the nature.

Saturn in Scorpio The underlying fear is of emotional dependence, which is felt to offer a threat to the proud egotism of the type. The character appears forcefully relentless, cold and inflexible of purpose, but there is considerable energy and will-power which permits excellent executive ability.

Saturn in Sagittarius The underlying fear is of being tied down to one place. The character is dignified and honourable, though independent in thought and action. The native is often interested in philosophy or the occult.

Saturn in Capricorn The underlying fear is of making effort to no material purpose, of going unrewarded. The character is materially ambitious, limited in outlook, possessed of integrity and caution.

Saturn in Aquarius The underlying fear is of becoming emotionally committed. The character tends to be original, humane, detached and often opinionated. The native will sometimes work for some humanitarian ideal.

Saturn in Pisces The underlying fear is of being isolated from other people. The character tends to be sad and moody, noticeably changeable, and possessed of a highly sensitive imagination.

The preceding seven planets all clearly relate to the personal world of Man, and link with Man as an individual; each of the drives and dispositions they represent is found in every human being. There are however three other planets which do not work in quite the same way – these are the ones discovered in relatively modern times, Uranus, Neptune and Pluto. These three planets do have distinctive natures of their own, and they do transmit influences from the zodiacal band in the way that other planets do, but they are not always personal in their influences. One reason for this is that they are relatively slow-moving and therefore, in terms of sign placing at least, they affect whole generations of people rather than particular individuals, and their manifestations are consequently noted in historical rather than in personal terms. However, the influences of these three planets do find strong personalized outlets when they are on or near the angles, and very often their effects when so placed produce

69

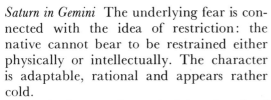

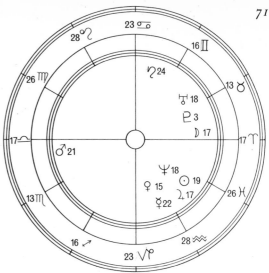

quite remarkable personalities, sometimes of genius, depending on the forces in the rest of the chart in terms of ordinary astrology. For this reason, it is advisable to interpret the influences of these three planets in terms of angular forces rather than in terms of sign placings. Anyone who wishes to pursue their influences in terms of signs is referred to the bibliography at page 184 where some of the most satisfactory books are listed.

Uranus, Neptune and Pluto relate to spiritual vibrations rather than material ones and it is usually possible to see from their placing in a chart whether or not the native is able to respond to the spiritual vibrations offered. Most often the force is induced by the planet being on an angle, though sometimes it is given prominence by a strong aspect (see page 49) from an important planet in the chart.

Uranus rules the originality and disruptiveness of the native, as well as his attitudes to authority. The planet is said to have the energy of Fire, the emotion of Water, and the intellect of Air: it is therefore an extremely powerful planet and its manifestations for good or evil are particularly observable in charts. When Uranus is on the Ascendant or on the M.C. (since energies are poured into manifestation of self or into ambition) it indicates originality, tremendous force of character, and suggests that the native will be something of a rebel: it seeks to exert power over others and the planet appears to lift the native into a spiritual vibration of a very high order (figure 194). A badly-placed Uranus manifests as though energies are being frustrated, with the result that the native may be malicious, dangerous, eccen-

tric and even criminal, as a result of sinking lower into the trough of the material world. At all events a strong Uranus, whether good or bad in the chart, is productive of a strong personality in which the ego works as though vested with almost superhuman energies. A study of the placing of Uranus enables one to determine to what degree the native may respond to genius.

Neptune rules the spirituality of the personality and marks the level of his relationship to his own inner world. The planet is an index of the response which a native will make to higher vibrations and his ability to make direct contact with highly spiritualized energies, such as music, the arts, and all extra-sensory energy sources. The force of Neptune is to open the personality to new experiences, and to allow that personality to grow as an outcome of these experiences: the result of this is that it sensitizes the spirit, and sometimes renders it extremely restless in its incarnate phase. Nowadays most drug-taking is a direct result of Neptunian influences in which heightened sensitivity and release from bodily experiences is sought gratuitously and without a sense of responsibility to self. The higher spiritual experiences which are governed by Neptune, and which are sometimes touched upon by drugs, are not intended for Man in his ordinary phase of incarnation; they may normally be experienced only after much preparation, when the person is in a position to accept the responsibilities to which such experiences lead. This truth veils much of the real tragedy of drug taking. When Neptune is emphasised in a chart the native is invested with a sensitive inspiration, and an ability

70. *The Martian hand form,*
    according to Muchery.
71. *The horoscope of General Booth,*
    founder of the Salvation Army,
    showing Mars on the Ascendant,
    always indicative of militancy
    and the urge to begin new and
    energetic enterprises.
72. *The Lunar hand form,*
    according to Muchery.
73. *The Earth hand form,*
    according to Muchery.
74. *The Mercurial hand form,*
    according to Muchery.

72

73

74

to communicate and transmit high quality vibration into life: there is often some involvement with music or mediumship, though the native is often unconventional in the way in which he expresses his sensitivity. The type is always highly emotional. A badly-placed Neptune tends towards deception, illusion, misunderstandings and confusion, as though spiritual forces are being perverted and rendered useless. Neptune is an extremely sensitive planet, subtle in its actions, and its influence will pervade the whole life of any native who has it strongly placed on an angle or conjunct with either of the luminaries.

Pluto rules the disruptive and regenerative side of the personality, and it is an index of how the native is able to use his energies for the redemption of self and others. A Pluto which is emphasised in a chart is extremely powerful, indicating even in highly evolved people an undercurrent of violence or uncontrolled energy. It is suggested that the planet governs qualities and urges in Man which have not yet been recognized by most people and to which few human beings can yet respond. Certainly, Pluto is concerned with the idea of control: its energy has been likened to that of the atom, which may be used to regenerate our social structure or to destroy it. Badly placed, Pluto tends to emphasise criminality in a chart, and the native may be violent, intense, magnetic and powerful, yet dedicated to criminal activities.

The influence of these three planets when they are upon or near the four angles of the horoscope is quite remarkable, and this can be clearly seen from the charts for several men of genius in this book.

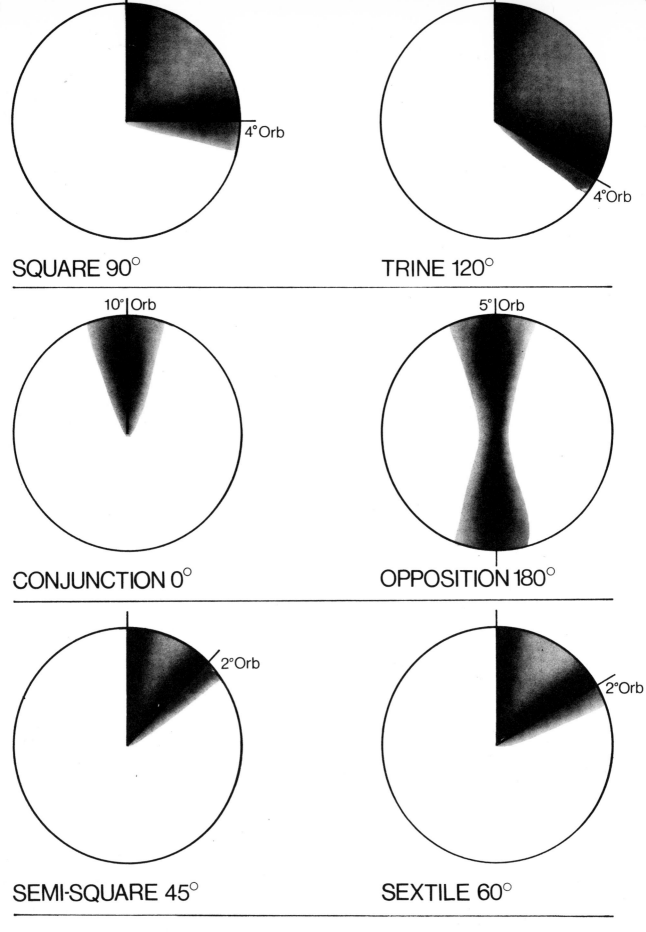

SQUARE 90°

TRINE 120°

CONJUNCTION 0°

OPPOSITION 180°

SEMI-SQUARE 45°

SEXTILE 60°

75. *The six major aspects.*

The Significance of the Aspects

We have seen how the influences of the planets change in terms of the sign placings and positions they hold within the frame of the horoscope, especially in relation to angles. However, these are not the only conditions which change the influences of the planets on the personality of the native: there are other influences at work which arise from the angular relationships which the planets hold to each other. These angular relationships are called *aspects*, and they have a great effect on the influence of planets. Two planets separated by 90° are, for example, said to be in square aspect to each other; planets separated by 120° are said to be in trine aspect to each other. There are, in fact, many such aspects used by astrologers, but the scope of this book requires that we study only the six basic aspects. These are the conjunction, the opposition, the trine, the square, the sextile and the semi-square. The degrees which these represent are illustrated in figure 75.

ASPECT	DEGREE	SYMBOL
Conjunction	0°	☌
Opposition	180°	☍
Trine	120°	△
Square	90°	□
Sextile	60°	✳
Semi-square	45°	∟

It is not necessary for an aspect to be exact for its influence to be manifest in a horoscope. For example, it is possible to allow what astrologers call an orb of 5° deviation on either side of the actual aspect for opposition and conjunction, and 4° for a trine or square. Thus, two planets separated by, say, 115° may still be regarded as being in trine to each other. The figure at plate 75 shows the orbs permitted for each of the aspects, though it will be appreciated that the more exact the aspect, the stronger the influence exerted by that aspect.

The theory behind aspects is that planets which are in signs of the same element will obviously have much in common – for example Jupiter in Leo will tend to work very well with Venus in Aries, since they represent the expansive principle and the affections respectively, working through the same element. At the same time planets working through elements which do not relate well, such as Fire and Water, may be expected to to have little harmony, and to manifest through conflict and tension. Venus in Aries and Mercury in Taurus, for example, would suggest a conflict between the affections and the ability to express affections. If we apply this theory to the simple diagram at figure 78 we will see that the planets in trine to each other are working through the same element, whereas planets in square to each other are working through elements which do not in themselves harmonise very well. The study of aspects is a long and rather complicated business (see bibliography at page 184), but for our purposes here it is necessary to understand only the principles at stake. A thorough grasp of the elemental natures and their interpretation is needed to understand the essential teaching behind aspects. It is normal for astrological text books to list the different forces encountered through all the interrelationships of planets for each of the different aspects. However, it is more important from a student's point of view that the essential philosophy underlying

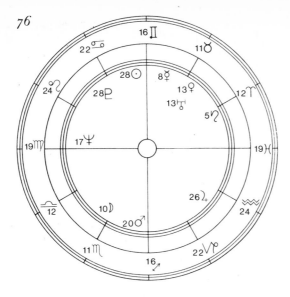

76. The horoscope of an English painter. Neptune on the Ascendant gives extreme sensitivity, whilst Jupiter in the fifth house makes for expansion in the arts.

77. The horoscope of an architect. Saturn on the Ascendant gives a concern for structure and form. The energy of Mars in Capricorn intensifies this urge to construct material shells.

78. The triangle which links together the three Fire signs demonstrates the elemental basis of the trine aspect. Figure 77 shows a trine in the Air signs.

the aspects be understood, and therefore it is not my purpose to list the different combinations of the aspect, but to consider the theory of aspects in general. It must be clearly understood that the aspect itself, whether working for good or bad, cannot be separated from the sign and house placings, and so in this particular field the astrologer often has to balance conflicting pieces of evidence.

The good aspects tend to expand the natures of the planets and to bring benefits to the native. They usually imply an ease of working, a certain beauty of manifestation. The bad aspects tend to limit and frustrate, even when they involve planets which are normally expansive in working. The bad aspects point to the fears of the native, whereas the good aspects point to his hopes and aspirations. Planets aspected by the Sun or the Moon tend to be brought into prominence and the nature of that aspect is emphasised. The Sun tends to vitalize and stimulate, while the influence of the Moon is a little less powerful.

Conjunction This strong placing brings energies to a focus through one sign, and therefore through one element and quality. Here the power of two or more planets fuse and interpenetrate each other. It cannot be regarded as being either a good or bad aspect, but more as an *intensifying* aspect. If one of the bad planets is involved then the intensification will be towards tension; if on the other hand a good planet is involved, such as Jupiter, then the intensification will be towards expansion. One has to think of planets in conjunction as combining their rays for good and bad in terms of their essential natures.

Opposition Planets in opposition to each other are separated by half the zodiac, and must be regarded as pulling against each other, implying a tension or a need to reconcile the divergent urges of the planets involved. Once again, planets in opposition cannot really be considered in terms of whether they are manifesting for good or bad; one has to think of them in terms of pulling against each other with the essential force of their own nature. Saturn in opposition to the Moon, for example, will imply difficulties because of the dark nature of Saturn, whereas Jupiter in opposition to the Moon will bestow benefits. With opposition there is usually much more tension manifesting in the external life of the native than with conjunction, which often links with the inner side of the personality. Oppositions are always very obviously manifest in the life of the native.

Trine This aspect implies that two or more planets are working harmoniously through the same element but stimulated by operating through different qualities. The force is always beneficial and expansive, usually helping the native towards material and spiritual benefits, but there may be too much ease of working in this particular direction, and in terms of a life structure it may point to a weakness in the person – though usually a weakness which manifests gracefully or easily, even pleasantly in life. At all events, the trine suggests an easy flow, and an easy interpenetration of the energies represented by the planets involved.

Square The square represents planets working inharmoniously through elemental conflicts, and marks strong obstructions and difficulties between the energies of the

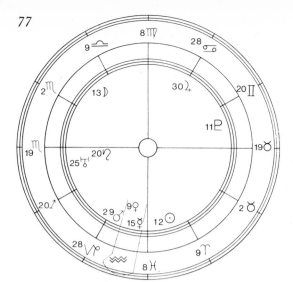

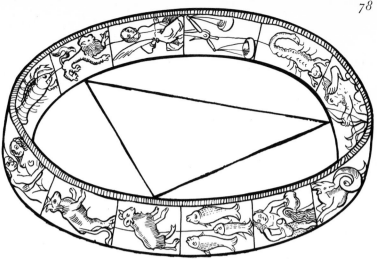

planets involved. It is generally held that a square represents a cross to be borne – something the native must struggle with in order to refine his spirit more distinctly. On this level, therefore, a square may be useful to the native, even though it is unpleasant in his life. Certainly, an understanding of the square in a horoscope, and its influences on the life of a native, is often useful in helping the native to understand his own inner world, in regard to his deep-seated needs and requirements from life. The square represents difficulties and tensions.

Sextile This is a beneficial influence, since the planets involved will be operating through elements not too inimical to each other. It may be regarded as being roughly half the force of the trine itself, though sometimes, when a planet is particularly prominent in a chart by being near an angle or otherwise strongly placed, the sextile may be strengthened, but it is rarely as strong as the trine. Always the sextile works for good, in the same manner as the trine.

Semi-Square This partakes of the nature of the square itself and may be regarded as being of roughly half the force of the square, though the notes in regard to the sextile are applicable here. The semi-square always suggests difficulties, though more easily overcome than with the square, and perhaps with less reward at the end of the struggle.

The implications contained in the natures of the elements themselves must be studied for a correct understanding of the background to aspects. Fire is fed by Air, and Air is refreshed, made lighter or more diffused by the heat of the Fire. So although Fire consumes the oxygen of Air, Air itself benefits

from the relationship; in personalized terms one sees that the Fire ego receives adulation from the Air audience, and the Air ego is vivified by the exchange. This is, of course, the precise relationship exchange offered by the sextile from these elements. Fire scorches the Earth it rests on, and we might say that an intense Fire will change the chemical composition of the Earth, and make it even harder. The relationship between Fire and Earth may therefore be regarded as potentially destructive, yet only Earth can provide a support for Fire. The relationship is somewhat akin to that of a feudal society, in which the Earth peasantry supports a Fire elite. This dangerous situation is like that which results from the tension of a Fire-Earth square. Fire makes Water boil and Water will put out Fire; it might therefore be said that Fire and Water combine explosively, and once more there is a tension engendered between planetary influences in square from these elements – even more dangerous than those in square from Earth to Fire.

Earth and Water combine very well, since Water refreshes Earth and turns it into life-giving mud, while Earth itself lends Water a direction, mobilizes its fluidity, and hence gives a meaning to its nature. On a personalized level we may see that the hardness and austerity of the Earth ego is softened and rendered more sensitive by the presence of a Water ego. This is, of course, the precise relationship exchange offered by the sextile from these elements. Earth and Air scarcely interpenetrate, and the stability of Earth is quite opposed to the diffused fluidity of the Airy nature. Planets combined in Air and Earth will not as a rule interpenetrate their

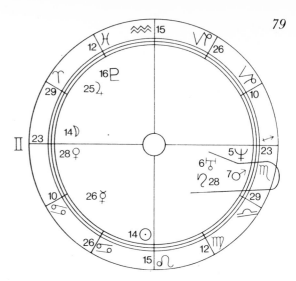

79. The horoscope of Alfred, Lord Tennyson. Note the exact sextile between Sun and Moon, the conjunction of the Sun with the fourth house cusp, and the proximity of the Moon and Venus to the Ascendant. Such contacts with the angles are generally productive of genius, or of great spiritual strength.

rays harmoniously, though one would scarcely expect anything either explosive or particularly beneficial from the combination. The square aspect offered to this relationship will create a tension in the personality which will manifest more as a rift in the nature (figure , for example) than as an explosive tension. Underlying the numerical background to the theory of aspects there is always the elemental nature to be taken into consideration.

The planets themselves are expressive of a particular elemental nature: the Sun, Mars and Jupiter are of a Fire nature. The Moon is of a Water nature; Saturn is of an Earth nature, while Mercury takes on the elemental nature of the sign in which he is placed. These elemental natures largely account for the way in which planets manifest in certain signs: Fire planets are especially strong in Fire signs, and so on. Such considerations must be borne in mind when evaluating the force of planetary aspects.

The natures of the planets themselves are of course intimately bound up with the interpretation of aspects. The Sun and the Moon will strengthen and vitalize, so that good or bad aspects to either of these luminaries will always be important in a chart. The conscious aim of the individual will be more affected by the Sun, while the general personality and nature of the native will be affected by planets involved with the Moon; there is always an influence on changeability and susceptibility when the Moon is involved in an aspect. The aspects to Mercury almost always affect the nervous system and the more superficial mentality, such as the ability of the native to com-

municate. Mercury is said to be a neutral planet, which is to say that it is influenced very strongly by the planet aspecting it. Mercury receives rather than gives. Aspects to Venus influence the affectionate side of the native's life: the good aspects intensify the native's ability to be happy, the bad aspects emphasise the tendency to be unhappy. Even bad aspects to Venus soften the workings of the harsher planets. Aspects to Mars usually influence the quality of the sex energy of the native: the bad aspects render the native harsh in terms of the qualities of the planets aspecting, while the good aspects enliven and direct in a useful way because both influences and creativity spring from martial sex energies. Aspects to Jupiter are involved with the expansive side of the native, and influence his ability to be successful and to benefit those around him. Even bad aspects to Jupiter are often mitigated by the expansive nature of that planet. Aspects to Saturn influence and direct the limitations which beset the native: the good aspects tend to add a degree of order and ambition in regard to the nature of the planets aspecting, the bad aspects to Saturn intensify the limitations inherent in the aspecting planets. Even the good aspects to Saturn usually limit the native in some way. Aspects between Uranus, Neptune and Pluto operate over such long periods that they are generally regarded as affecting whole generations rather than individuals. These 'long term' aspects do however receive emphasis through one of the involved planets being on or near the angles. In such cases the effect on individuals *is* noticeable, and is usually productive of extremes.

Casting a Horoscope

Casting a horoscope appears to be much more difficult than it really is: in fact, after a little practice it is possible to cast and tabulate a horoscope accurately in about fifteen minutes. The most common question in regard to casting a horoscope is what is meant precisely by the 'moment of birth'. To all intents and purposes one may take the first cry as marking the moment of birth but there are several rather complicated astrological devices involving computation used for determining the exact moment of birth, which does not always correspond with the first cry. Such devices are called 'rectification techniques', and need not concern us here: they are mentioned only because they indicate that there is a certain degree of latitude in regard to what an astrologer means by the 'moment of birth'. Very few birth-times are in fact given accurately, and rarely so within three or four minutes. It is possible to calculate the horoscope exactly to the nearest second, but this general inaccuracy in the known moment of birth means that usually it is not worth while taking into account seconds of time. The following instructions are intended as a guide to casting a horoscope which will be accurate to the nearest minute or so. As one's proficiency in astrology progresses one will in any case learn techniques by which it is possible to determine to the second the moment of birth and therefore construct an absolutely accurate horoscope. For our purposes, however, a horoscope cast to within three or four minutes will be more than adequate. The bibliography at page 184 sets out some excellent instruction manuals for more complex horoscope casting.

The beginner who does not specifically want to spend a lot of time and effort in learning how to calculate horoscopes would be well advised to have one cast by a professional. Most magazines dealing with astrology or the so-called 'occult' contain advertisements in which professional astrologers undertake to cast horoscopes for a small sum. The expense involved in having a professional cast the figure will be minimal in relation to the actual cost of buying the books and tables needed for casting horoscopes. Since the majority of libraries do not stock all the books required, the beginner is nearly always compelled to invest a fair amount of money in the purchase of information tables in order to calculate even one horoscope. It would be best for anyone who wants to study only his own horoscope or those of his close friends, to have them cast by a professional. This will not only mean that the chart is likely to be more reliable, but much cheaper in the long run.

In order to cast a horoscope two basic books are required. The most important of these is an ephemeris, which is a table of planetary positions, generally marked for each day in a particular year. The most commonly available ephemeris for recent years is that published annually, a year in advance, by Foulsham, called *Raphael's Ephemeris*, which gives the planetary placings for noon on each day in each year. A separate booklet must be bought for each year. The best compact accurate ephemeris is the *Deutsche Ephemeride* published by Otto-Wilhelm-Barth-Verlag, and distributed in Britain by Fowler and Co. Ltd. The set comes in six volumes, incorporating data

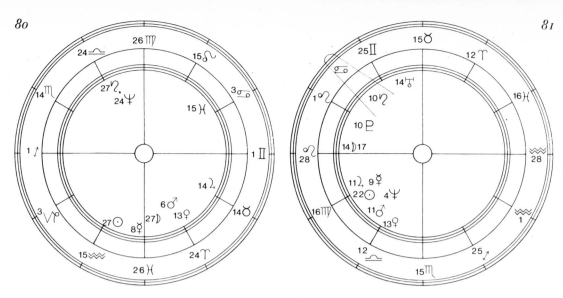

from 1850 to 1980, though volumes may be purchased separately. These ephemerides give accurate planetary placings for midnight at the beginning of each day. The second publication which is required for the casting of horoscopes is called a 'Table of Houses'. This tabulates material which enables one to cast horoscopes for different latitudes throughout the world. The standard ephemerides usually give tables of houses which include all the places along latitudes near London, Liverpool and New York, but it is possible to purchase a special booklet which gives tables suitable for calculating latitudes from the Equator to 50° north, and 50° south, and also for Leningrad which is nearly 60° north. This material supplements that given in the standard ephemerides and the beginner is strongly recommended to purchase such a book. With these two books, the ephemeris and the table of houses, it is possible to calculate the degrees on the angles and, of course, the intervening houses, for any moment of time in the past hundred years at any latitude and longitude. When such calculations have been made, it is very easy to work out the exact positions of each planet at that particular moment of time, and insert them in the framework of the horoscope.

The first requirement for casting a horoscope is to ascertain the sidereal time, the time by the stars, by which we may determine the exact position of the zodiacal band in relation to the place of birth at the moment of birth. This is done by consulting the ephemeris for the day and year in question. The sidereal time is listed in *Raphael's Ephemeris* in the third column in the lower

two thirds of the left hand page. In the *Deutsche Ephemeride* it is given in the second column in the upper two thirds of the relevant year and month. It is important to realize that the sidereal time as given by Raphael is for noon, while sidereal time given by the German book is for the beginning of the day, at midnight. Thus, if one compares the sidereal times given for 1 January, 1944, one finds in Raphael that it is 18 40 06, and in the German book it is 6 38 08: this must be borne in mind when calculating a horoscope. The sidereal time in both cases is given for Greenwich, and it is a fairly easy matter to calculate from this moment of time precisely what the real time was at the moment of birth. If the birth was before the noon time given in Raphael, one *subtracts* the difference: if it was after noon then one *adds* the difference. Clearly, all births for a given day must be after midnight, and therefore with the *Deutsche Ephemeride* one simply needs to *add* the time as given. For example, if the birth were at 10 p.m. one would add 10 hours to the time given by *Raphael*, or add 22 hours to the time given by the *Deutsche Ephemeride*. If the time were given as 10 a.m. one would subtract 2 hours from the time given by *Raphael*, or add 10 hours to the time as given by the *Deutsche Ephemeride*. Someone born at 10 a.m. on the morning of 1 January, 1944, would, according to the *Deutsche Ephemeride*, have been born at the sidereal time of 16 38 08. Information derived from the sidereal time of birth is used in order to find the degrees of the signs of the zodiac on the angles and on the intermediate house cusps. In order to do this the latitude for the place of birth

80. *A horoscope which illustrates the major aspects of conjunction, trine, square, semi-square and sextile. This is the horoscope of a female student of physiotherapy.*

81. *The horoscope for a twin, whose brother's figure is reproduced at figure 130. The hand structures and line patterns (figures 131 and 132) are very similar, as indeed are the horoscopes, in which there are only a few minutes' difference.*

82. *The Sun god, Apollo. The Ascendant is a symbol of the rising Sun, which is why it is so important in a chart.*

must first be found from a gazeteer. Then one turns to the relevant latitude given in the table of houses, and looks down the column headed 'sidereal time' until the time nearest to the sidereal time for the moment of birth is seen. If we presume that the birth at 10 o'clock in the morning of 1 January, 1944, is the one we are wanting to calculate, and if we presume that it took place in London, we would take the table of houses for the latitude 51° 32′ north, which is the latitude of London, and find 16 38 08 under the sidereal time. In fact the nearest time listed is 16 37 42, a few seconds' error which for our purposes we may ignore. We look along the line of figures opposite to the relevant sidereal time and we see that the Ascendant is given as 15° 26′ of Aquarius. This is, then, the Ascendant for the moment of birth. As horoscopes are rarely accurately cast for precise minutes or seconds, it is best to think in terms of the Ascendant being a whole degree, and since 15° 26′ is in the 16th degree of the relevant sign it is better, and certainly a lot simpler, to round up and think of the Ascendant as being 16° rather than 15° 26′. We write this figure on the cusp of the Ascendant angle (figure 83). Under the 10th house we see that 11° of Sagittarius is placed and accordingly this degree is written on the cusp of the tenth house angle. From these two figures it is possible to determine the degrees on the opposite angles, since these are precisely the degrees on the opposite signs of the zodiac. Opposite the tenth house the I.C. will have 11° Gemini and on the seventh house or the Descendant one will find 15° 26′ of Leo, which is rounded up to 16°. The degrees on the intermediate cusps are calculated in a similar manner by taking the figure along this line in the relevant columns. The eleventh and twelfth house columns give the signs and degrees which are to be marked on the appropriate cusps, and opposite these will be the signs and degrees which will be found on the fifth and sixth house cusps. Similarly the degrees found on the second and third house cusps will correspond to the degrees of the opposite signs on the eighth and ninth house cusps. Sometimes one finds that two, or even four, signs do not find a place on one of the house cusps. These intercepted signs are given a position between the cusps, in their appropriate zodiacal order, as for example in figure 84.

So far it has been assumed for the purpose of explanation that the time and place fit closely with the information given in the ephemeris and the table of houses. We have assumed that the time of birth corresponds to Greenwich Mean Time, and we have assumed that the place of birth is near the longitude of Greenwich and the latitude of London. However, it is not always as simple as that; very often the time of birth is given in Greenwich Mean Time, but sometimes it is given in the 'zone time' or the 'standard time' of the country of birth. It is important to determine which of these is intended, for one must calculate in such a way as to render the time in terms of Greenwich Mean Time, so that it is related directly to the information given in the ephemeris. If the standard time for the country of birth is ahead of Greenwich, then clearly the number of standard hours must be subtracted from the moment of birth to

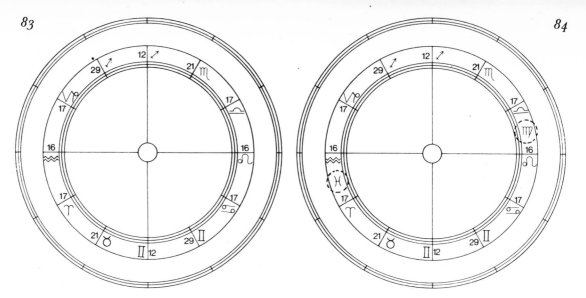

give Greenwich Mean Time. Several of the books mentioned in the bibliography on page 184 gives an up-to-date list of standard times. Another difficulty is Summer Time. If the moment of birth is given in Summer Time, then one must subtract from the given birth time the one hour which Summer Time is in advance of Greenwich Mean Time. In the years during and just after the Second World War, double Summer Time was in operation, and for such dates it is necessary to subtract two hours in order to reduce to Greenwich Mean Time. The figure obtained through the above calculations is, of course, the sidereal time for birth at Greenwich, and we wish to convert this to local sidereal time. Towards this end one has to bear in mind that each degree of longitude may be converted in time by allowing four minutes for each degree. If the birth is west of Greenwich then the calculated figure (at four minutes of time per degree of longitude) will be added to it, and if the place is east of Greenwich then the figure must be subtracted from it.

The final task in constructing the chart is to place the planets in the correct positions within the zodiacal figure which has so far been established. The positions for the planets are given for midnight and for noon in the German and English ephemerides, and it is a relatively simple matter to calculate which degree a particular planet is in by working out how far it has moved in the preceding 24 hours, and then taking the fraction of time it has moved from the ephemeris position to the time of birth. If, for example, the time of birth is 4 a.m., and one finds that the Moon has moved 14 degrees during the day of birth, from say, 8 degrees of Cancer to 22 degrees of Cancer, then one calculates that in one sixth of a day (four hours) the Moon will have moved 2 degrees and 20 minutes. This figure is added to the original position of the Moon, 8 degrees of Cancer, to give 10 degrees 20 minutes as the position of the Moon at birth. In our 'rounding up' system, we would then consider the Moon to be in 11 degrees of Cancer. The symbol for the Moon, followed by 11, must then be written in at the appropriate place within the horoscope figure. If 2 degrees Cancer happens to fall on the fifth house cusp, then the Moon will be a few degrees further on from this cusp. In astrological terms this Moon will be in the fifth house. The Moon is the fastest moving body in the geocentric system of measurement, which is why it requires calculation to determine its degree placing: the other planets do not move very quickly, and one may determine the degree which they occupy merely by glancing at the row of planet places given for the day of birth, and comparing this with the following day. The calculated position for each planet is recorded in the same way as the Moon, as illustrated in figure 85. The only planet with which the beginner may experience difficulty is Pluto. This planet was not discovered by astronomers until 1930, and consequently none of the ephemerides of earlier date list the placing: a table of Pluto's positions may be purchased, while the ephemeris contained in Herbert T. Waite's *Compendium* (see page 184), gives the monthly positions of Pluto for the past seventy years. The German ephemeris gives the daily positions of Pluto from

83. *The angles and house cusps inserted into the horoscope, directly from the table of houses relevant to the latitude of birth.*

84. *The 'intercepted signs' inserted. These are the signs which are not located on an angle or upon a house cusp.*

85. *The planets are inserted into the zodiacal framework constructed from the table of houses. The zodiacal framework is rather like the numerals on a clock face, whilst the planets are like so many pointing hands.*

86. *A fifteenth-century zodiacal man.*

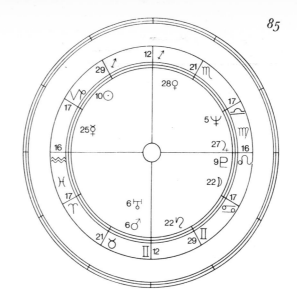

1960, though the symbol for Pluto differs from the English – it is a semi-circle containing a dot (☉).

The rules for determining the angles and the intermediate house cusps may be summarized as follows:

1. Take the time of birth and note whether this is already in Greenwich Mean Time, or in some other time.

2. Allow for any zone or standard time, subtracting the difference if it is to the east of Greenwich or adding if it is to the west.

3. Subtract one hour if Summer Time was in operation at the time of birth, two hours if double Summer Time was used. This gives the time of birth in Greenwich Mean Time.

4. Calculate the interval from noon or midnight, depending upon which ephemeris is being used, and add or subtract, as appropriate, from the figure given as sidereal time in the ephemeris. The figure obtained is the time of birth in sidereal time. (Sidereal time does not flow like ordinary clock time and this is taken into account in *accurate* casting: such precision is not required here.)

5. Adjust for longitude, at the rate of 4 minutes for each degree. Add if the place is east of Greenwich, subtract if west of Greenwich. The figure obtained is the time of birth in local sidereal time.

6. Calculate the degree placings of the planets.

7. On a horoscope sheet, complete the entries for the angles and houses, and then insert the planets in the appropriate positions.

86

Interpreting the Horoscope

The astrological symbol of the human being, the horoscope figure, is extremely complex, and this in itself makes interpretation a difficult matter. It cannot be too much emphasised that serious interpretation is involved with considerable responsibilities, and itself demands experience and knowledge, neither of which may be acquired easily. This is why there are so many people who profess to be interested in astrology, and yet few people who actually practice genuine astrology in a responsible way. However, a start must be made somewhere and, provided it is remembered that this is merely a beginning, the information contained in the following pages will be helpful, for it sets down the most important rule-of-thumb methods by which charts may be interpreted.

Chart interpretation is not a result of building individual fragments and items of interpretation into a whole, in the manner as one might read a book, sentence by sentence: genuine interpretation works the other way round – it starts with a general picture of the figure, and then proceeds to refine upon this. Much as a painter brushes in the salient forms of his composition, then begins to work in the broad masses, then the inter-action of forms, and finally the details, so does the astrologer work from the larger issues down to the smaller. This is, in fact, the only way to interpret a chart correctly, yet it is a difficult thing to do, for it is involved with making a kind of inner somersault. One has to see the figure as a whole – and yet to the beginner this is a difficult thing to attain, for at first he sees only details. This is where palmistry often proves so useful, even for those who have only a simple grasp of the rules of the hand interpretation. In many respects, a palm print is a useful guide for a beginner who finds himself confused by a particular chart, for it is usually a relatively easy thing for him to determine at least which elements are interacting within the palm, and then attempt to discover these reflected within the horoscope, along the lines set out on pages 38 and 49. In this way he will begin to grasp intellectually at first, and later instinctively, the most salient and important elements in a horoscope, and from this will grow an ability to interpret a chart without the necessity for a print.

However, there are a few fairly simple rules which may be considered as forming the very basis of chart interpretation, allowing the astrologer to gain a quick grasp of the underlying nature of the subject – a sort of thumb nail sketch which may later be worked into a full length portrait. It is important that the beginner should attempt to work in this way – to learn how to grasp the essential forces at work within the figure, for all the other interactions of forces will serve only to refine, or render more complex, the essential nature represented by the basic massing of forces. The following rules, although by no means exhaustive, will serve towards this end of producing an accurate thumb nail sketch. Once more, the bibliography at page 184 will help towards a selective reading which will render chart interpretation more reliable.

The first aim is to assess the nature of the Ascendant, both in itself, and in relation to the twelfth house cusp and the second house cusp. The signs on these two house cusps mark respectively the attitude of the native

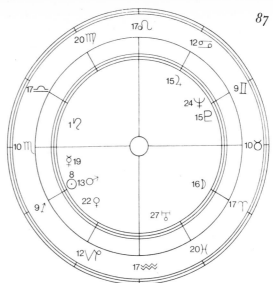

87. The horoscope of Mark Twain, the American author.

88. The handprint of Mark Twain, made by the palmist Count Louis Hamon, better known as 'Cheiro'.

to spiritual matters and material matters: his invisible self is at once the product of these attitudes, as well as a product of the sign and degree on the Ascendant. The tendency is for this important degree to reflect one of the strong elemental forces in the psychological make-up of the native, to such an extent that it is often possible to speak of a person being of such and such a type (say, Leo) because the Ascendant is in that sign. However, we must not be tempted to take the Ascendant degree, even where there is a planet in it, as being in itself indicative of the 'type', for although it is always important, it is not always the most important representative of an elemental force. To gain experience in this matter, the beginner should refer to a hand print, or to the hand itself. For example, we might assume from the horoscope of Mark Twain that he was a Water type, because he has a Scorpionic Ascendant, with both Saturn and Mercury in that sign, but when we look to his hand (figure 88), we see that the hand is basically of the Fire nature (see page 67). A glance back at the horoscope will confirm this, for we see the Sun, Venus and Mars in the Fire of Sagittarius, Moon in the Fire of Aries, and Leo on the M.C. Twain is obviously more of a Fire personality than a Water personality.

The second step is to find the location of the ruling planet. Technically, the ruling planet is that which rules the Ascending sign.

In the horoscope example, we find that Scorpio's ruling planet, Pluto, is located in Gemini, in the eighth house. This would of course mean that much of Twain's Water nature would find expression through eighth house activities, as well as through Geminian

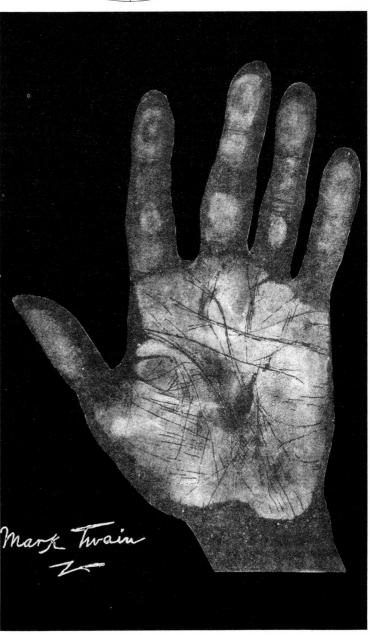

Mark Twain

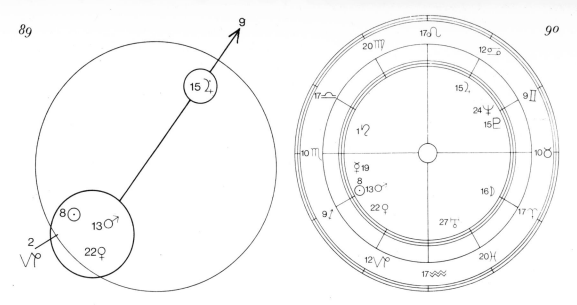

activities. In fact, he was impelled by a love of the curious, the hidden and the mystical, as we might expect from an eighth house emphasis. He was deeply interested in astrology and palmistry – he is reported to have said 'I was born with Halley's Comet, and I expect to die upon its return', which he did – and it is due to his interest in the work of the palmist Cheiro that we owe the existence of his hand print (figure 88). When a sign is given emphasis through the presence of several planets, as in the case of Sagittarius, which has Sun (conscious aim), Venus (love and arts) and Mars (energy) all gathered around the material second house, we would expect the house placing of the planet ruling this sign to play an important role in the life of the native. This would be another 'ruler'. In the example of Twain's chart, we find Jupiter, the ruler of Sagittarius, on the cusp of the ninth house, the area which deals with exploration, deeper thought, and publishing, the house which is indeed proper to the expansive Jupiter. In view of this it is not surprising that Twain should become involved with writing – particularly in writing about the results of his exploration of life. As in this case, it is not unusual to find horoscopes with a 'ruling planet' which is not the technical ruler.

The third step is to consider any planet which is on, or near, an angle. Any planet near an angle is *always* emphasised in a chart. When this happens, the force, drive, and indeed the associations of that planet play a very important part in the life of the native, manifesting through the 'lens' of the particular angle on which it is found. In the case of Twain, there is no close proximity of a planet to an angle, though Saturn and Mercury are equidistant from the Ascendant. It is significant that he spent much of his time writing and lecturing (Mercury) in order to balance his losses (Saturn) through financial speculation. Fire types, and Sagittarians in particular, are given to excess in regard to speculation. It is evident that with such a strong planetary influence on the second house, Twain would have to work for a living: the living would rarely work for him. Unfortunately, the presence of Jupiter on the ninth house tends to expand the Sagittarian urge towards gambling, for the ninth governs speculation – whether it be mental (philosophy) or physical (competitive sports) or emotional (publishing, financial speculation).

The fourth step is to consider the placing of the Sun, both in sign and in house, and the aspects to it. This is important, for the Sun position relates to conscious aim, and it is possible to see to what extent it harmonizes, or is in discord with, the factors so far established. Looking back over what has so far been established in the case of Twain, two patterns emerge: one, the transfer of energies (Sun, Mars and Venus) through the expansive Jupiter into the ninth house (figure 89); and, two, the transfer of the conflict between Saturn and Mercury into the eighth house (figure 93). These two manifestations of Fire energies and Water energies are contained in the linear markings of the hand, for there is a curious line which runs from the Watery domain of the Mount of Moon right through the hand up to the base of the finger of Jupiter (figure 88), suggesting that the energy of Jupiter (Fire) is linked with

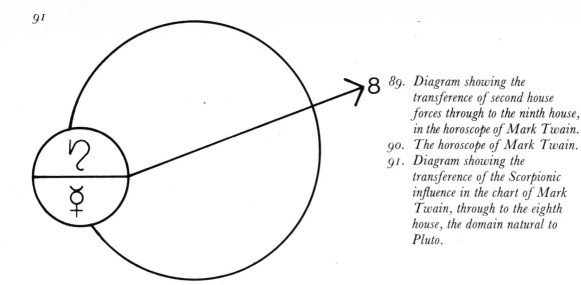

89. *Diagram showing the transference of second house forces through to the ninth house, in the horoscope of Mark Twain.*

90. *The horoscope of Mark Twain.*

91. *Diagram showing the transference of the Scorpionic influence in the chart of Mark Twain, through to the eighth house, the domain natural to Pluto.*

the energy of the Moon (Water), as an important aspect of the conflict behind the personality. However, if we return to our examination of the Sun, we see that it strengthens the Fire side of the nature, and will therefore intensify the Sagittarian expansiveness and love of life through a conscious aim to express self by means of a Fire activity, manifest through Sagittarius. Thus, we see two sides to Twain's nature – first the exuberant and creative Fire (Sagittarius is famous for its sense of humour) which will find an outward expression through a ninth house activity; and secondly, a more subdued though intense nature, which will attempt to balance communication and restriction (Mercury and Saturn) through an eighth house channel. These were indeed the two sides of Mark Twain. The Sun placing by sign gives the creative urge, and its placing by house indicates through which realm of activity the creative urge will manifest most directly. The second house rules money and material affairs, and Twain was constantly writing books in order to recuperate his financial losses through speculations. Besides the placing of the Sun, we have to look into the condition of the Sun in terms of the aspects it receives. In fact, there are two important aspects to the Sun – the most important being from the Moon in Aries, which gives a splendid harmonic trine, and thus supports the expansive, genial and creative force of the Sun – indeed of all the three planets in Sagittarius. The orb of 8° is not too wide when the Sun and Moon are involved. The opposition between Pluto and the Sun is 7° out, and this orb tends to weaken the force of the aspect, though the

tension engendered between a ruler of a Water sign (Pluto) and the ruler of a Fire sign (Sun) will colour the background and personality of the native. It is this aspect which accounts for the quality of pessimism in the life and writings of Twain, a quality which was all the more unexpected in a person so creative and exuberant. The force and influence of the Sun, both in sign and house placing, and in aspects, tends to increase as the native gets older and although there are other factors of considerable importance which contributed to his increased pessimism with age, it is mainly the aspect between the Sun and Pluto which accounts for its presence in the first place. The strain of pessimism and melancholy, which conflicts so strongly with the general quality of the chart, may be seen in the hand by the presence of the long line of Fate (figure 88), which runs upwards from between the Mount of Venus and the Mount of Moon to join the curious Moon-to-Jupiter line, just under the finger of Saturn. Such a line in a Fire hand is always indicative of a tendency to depression, as though the initial energy of the creative Fire impulse cannot be maintained.

The fifth step is to note the position, by sign and house, of the Moon, and evaluate the aspects to it. The Moon represents the subconscious level of the personality, and therefore must be linked with the Sun if one wishes to understand how its forces will manifest. The Sun governs the spirit of the native while the Moon governs his physical life, the formation of the spirit's instrument which is the body, with all the reflexes the body contains. Just as the Moon takes its

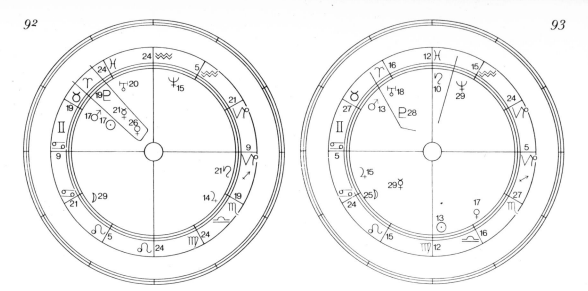

form from the light of the Sun – is adapted to the Sun, so to speak – so is the body and psychic life of the individual adapted to the conscious spirit of the Sun within him. The simplest way to study the Sun-Moon relationship is not by means of the technical aspects, but by means of the elements. In the case of the Mark Twain horoscope (figure 90) there is no conflict, as both are manifesting in Fire Signs, but it is obviously more common to find some kind of conflict or tension due to the luminaries being expressed through different elements. The nature of such conflicts or tensions may be established by considering the notes at page 49.

The sixth step is to study the placings of each of the planets in their signs and houses, and thus form an estimate of the way in which various energies (the planets) will receive direction and impulse (the signs) and in which mode of human existence (the houses) they will manifest. The list of interpretation for sign placings at page 38 will be of considerable use to beginners in respect of this level of interpretation. It is important to remember that the force of a planet may be increased by being on an angle, or by being strongly aspected by one of the luminaries, or by being in its own sign, or in its own house – as for example, Venus and Jupiter in their respective houses in Twain's chart partly account for the importance of these two here. The natures of the planets and the qualities of the signs must be thoroughly understood for a reliable analysis to be undertaken in regard to evaluating and balancing the many apparently conflicting elements in the make-up of the individual. A strict

balance is not always required: one must remember that all people are full of contradictory impulses and conflicting emotional strains. It is the work of the astrologer to determine which forces will be called into play under what circumstances.

The seventh step is involved with attempting to draw up an integrated picture of all the forces within the personality which have been observed as operating within the chart. When this has been done one has a thumb nail sketch as a basis for serious astrology.

Astrology is not a guessing game, and while the expert practitioner will observe facets of the personality which the native himself may not be aware of, it is usually a good thing for the beginner to commence on pragmatic lines, and to compare his readings with the native's own understanding of himself. In this way both the beginner and the native will learn a great deal, and the beginner will approach an understanding of astrology in the light of practical experience.

Our study of astrology has so far been determined by the context in which we are working: we are studying the relationship between hands and natal charts, and because of this we have examined only the simple elements of astrology mainly insofar as they relate to palmistry. This should not in any way disguise the fact that astrology is itself an extremely complex science, the complexity of which may be grasped to some extent when we observe that the natal chart itself should not be looked upon as a fixed element, but as something with a growth potential. It is not a static symbol, but a dynamic growth. The horoscope, like the human spirit it symbolizes, is a kind of seed,

92. *The horoscope of Tchaikovsky. Figures 92–94 show how a similar Ascendant may give rise to different personalities.*

93. *The horoscope of Jesse James. The opposition between Sun and Saturn on the angles, and the square thrown by Pluto on to both Mercury and Moon, account for his criminality.*

94. *The horoscope of Byron.*

95. *A fairly typical seventeenth-century book on palmistry: This titlepage shows how astrology and palmistry were regarded as quite separate art forms.*

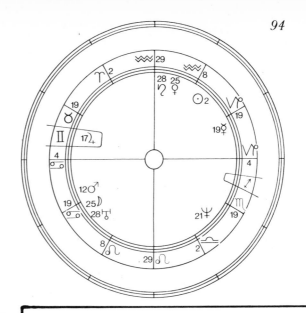

95

and the serious work of astrology is involved with studying, elucidating, and even predicting the growth and nature of the plant which will emerge from this seed.

No astrologer worth his salt will look at a horoscope simply as a fixed symbol. In order to understand the native in terms of his life pattern he will 'progress' the chart in one way or another, according to clearly defined rules, and from this he will begin to see the native as a living being, evolving in space and time. Obviously the scope of this book precludes a study of even simple progression techniques, and so the bibliography at page 184 has been designed to help students who wish to familiarize themselves with the 'growth' of the horoscope, which must accompany all serious attempts to study astrology and mankind. Beginners are urged not to attempt progression techniques until they feel themselves to be competent at interpreting the static figure. This is necessary because a valid interpretation of a progressed figure depends absolutely on the correct interpretation of the basic horoscope figure, the natal chart, which represents the potential of the native in its seminal form. The points at which potentials will be realized and experienced in a life time cannot be established until they have been fully understood as potentials. The warning is necessary only for those who wish to take the study of astrology further, into deeper levels: it does not concern the present study which is exclusively concerned with interpreting the static natal chart, and relating this to the hand structure, which for the sake of our own purposes may be regarded as a static, though living, symbol.

PALMISTRY,
The SECRETS thereof
DISCLOSED,
Or a *Familiar Easy,* and New
Method, whereby to *Iudge* of the
most *General* Accidents of Mans *Life*
From the *Lines* of the Hand, withal its
Dimensions and *Significations.*

Also many Perticulars added, Discovering the *Safety* and *Danger* of Women in *Child-bed.*

VVith some choice *Observations* of *Phisiognomy,* and the *Moles* of the Body.

As also that *Most Useful Piece* of *Astrology* (long since promised) concerning **ELECTIONS** for every *Particular* Occasion, now *Plainly* Manifested from *Rational Principles* of ART.

The Second Time *Imprinted.*

And much Inlarged by the Author,
RICHARD SAUNDERS,
Author of the Former Book of *Chyromancy* and *Phisiognomy.*

Cuiq; sua est tempestas, & tempus cuique voluntati sub Cælis, Eccle. Cap. 3. verse 1. to 12.
Tempus est potentius Legibus.

LONDON,
Printed by H. *Brugis* for G. *Sawbridge,* at the Sign of the *Bible* upon *Ludgate Hill,* 1664.

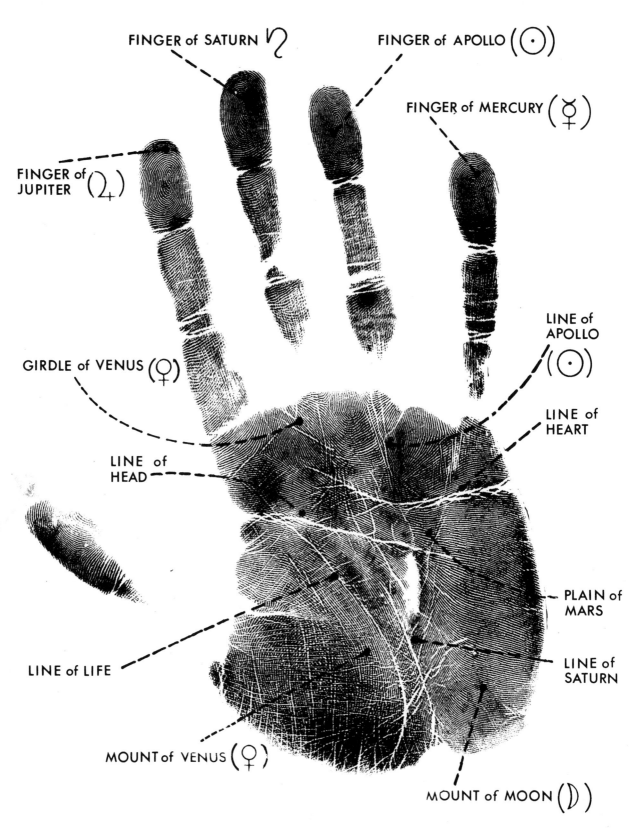

FINGER of SATURN ♄

FINGER of APOLLO (☉)

FINGER of APOLLO (⊙)

FINGER of MERCURY (☿)

FINGER of
JUPITER (♃)

GIRDLE of VENUS (♀)

LINE of
APOLLO
(⊙)

LINE of
HEART

LINE of
HEAD

LINE of
HEAD

PLAIN of
MARS

LINE of LIFE

LINE of
SATURN

MOUNT of VENUS (♀)

MOUNT of MOON (☽)

96. The traditional nomenclature in palmistry.

THE RELATIONSHIP BETWEEN ASTROLOGY AND PALMISTRY

The basis of Palmistry

In astrology it is necessary to construct a complex figure in order to look into the personality and life pattern of the subject; with palmistry the 'complex figure' is ready made, in the form of the hand itself. This is in some respects something of a disadvantage, for the actual business of casting a horoscope is a useful preliminary, since it allows one to 'tune in' to the subject. Building up the figure is itself an exciting process of discovery, by which one progressively notes developments, subtle or obvious, in the nature of the person for whom the horoscope is being cast. With the hand there is rarely such a moment of respite for one is dealing not merely with the hand but with that strange appendage to the hand – a human being. This can be a problem, especially as few people can keep quiet, and most feel impelled to ask questions even as the palmist tries to tune in to the more subtle vibrations of the personality. This is one reason why hand prints are so useful – they politely remove the human element. At the same time, prints are useful in that they reveal details of the hand, in its *chiromantical** aspect, which would probably go unnoticed save by the most experienced palmist. One must, therefore, establish a practice of taking prints of all those for whom readings and chart comparisons are required, even though an analysis requires the hand itself, as well as, finally, the human subject (see page 59).

As with the study of astrology, it is necessary to learn the basic grammar before beginning a study of palmistry. With this in mind, one must study the hand chart at figure 96 and learn the various terms with-

in the traditional nomenclature before proceeding further. It may also be a convenient point to study the scheme at figure 157 which is the basic diagram relating astrology to palmistry, within the framework of the system expounded in this book. In this system we find that the traditional rulership of the planets over certain parts of the hand is adhered to, with certain important exceptions. The most important change in this scheme is that the traditional Plain of Mars has been dispensed with, and the planet Mars is taken as ruling the ring finger, traditionally ruled by the Sun. The beginner may not concern himself at this point with how the scheme has been arrived at – the logic within the system will reveal itself in due course, when he finds it possible to apply it in his theoretical and practical work. It will be seen immediately that the planets of astrology are also used in palmistry, and this fact might in itself suggest that the two systems are related. Astrology and palmistry are certainly related, but they are not related by the 'planets' which they appear to have in common. It is extremely important that this be understood at the outset – the Jupiter of astrology is not, for example, the Jupiter of the palm.

The study of the hand has, for historical reasons, as well as for practical reasons, been divided into two separate areas: the palmist will study the form of the hand, from this attempting to assess the basic personality group, and individual traits, of the subject; and then he will study the lines of the hand, from these attempting to assess the underlying drives, qualities of energies, particular qualities, and so on. The really accomplished

*See glossary, p. 186.

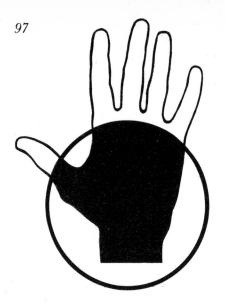

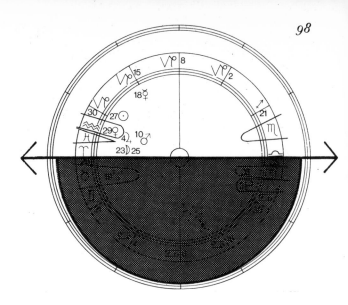

palmist will relate the two groups, the morphological and the linear, and from these draw up an image of the personality in terms of its inner drive, conflicts, and externalized aims.

There are very many different systems by which the structure of the hand may be classified and interpreted, but the one evolved by the writer is particularly useful in the present study, for it was initially based on a study of the relationship between astrology and palmistry. Several of the other systems suggest that their descriptions of hands relate to astrology, but in fact they tend to be more confusing than helpful. The normal procedure, as with Muchery, was to describe a particular distinctive hand form, and relate this to a planet. This method produced 'systems' which were extremely difficult to use in actual practice. The system here, which has the distinction of being extremely simple as well as theoretically sound, is in no way confusing, and is very helpful in practical terms.

The system, in its elementary form, is based on the idea that the fingers represent one quality of being, while the palm represents another. One may compare the basic structure of such a division to the basic structure of the horoscope, which presents the conscious life of the native as being above the earth (the Ascendant-Descendant axis separates that part of the sky which is under the earth from that which is above the earth), 'in the light of the Sun', and the unconscious life of the native as being below the Earth, 'in the light of the Moon'. Of course, we may relate the fingers and the palm of the hand to a similar, deceptively

simple, theory. The fingers represent the domain of the forces which differentiate the man, making him special, and thus they relate to the conscious domain of the human being, to personality. The palm itself represents the domain of the forces which contribute to the sense of individuality only insofar as they link with group activities, social pressures, and those qualities and energies which unite one man to another. The palm is a reservoir of energies which may be visualized as surging upwards and manifesting through the fingers (figure 99).

From another valid point of view it could be maintained that, in simple theory at least, the fingers represent the domain of the spirit, and the palm represents the domain of matter. The solar force in astrology promotes spiritual growth, whilst the lunar force supports material growth: the two together maintain life. As we shall see, there is a special and important area in the hand which links together these two 'spiritual' and 'material' areas. This area is dominated by the thumb, which itself appears to belong to neither group: it is rooted in the Mount of Venus, which is clearly demarcated from the rest of the palm by the line of Life. Above the thumb, yet linked to it, is the finger of Jupiter. This complex of three forms (figure 146), which I call the *triad of palmistry*, forms an important link between the spiritual world of the fingers, and the material world of the palm, as well as being in itself an important index of the basic nature of the individual.

In terms of hand form, then, we shall concern ourselves with the two areas and their relationship: that of the fingers, and

97. *The lower half of the hand corresponds to the lower part of the horoscope, which itself is*

98. *related to the 'dark' side of Man, to the subconscious elements, which manifest through the 'light' half in social activity.*

99. *Each of the fingers individualize and channel certain of the energies which are undifferentiated in the 'dark' half of the palm.*

100. *A seventeenth-century nomenclature.*

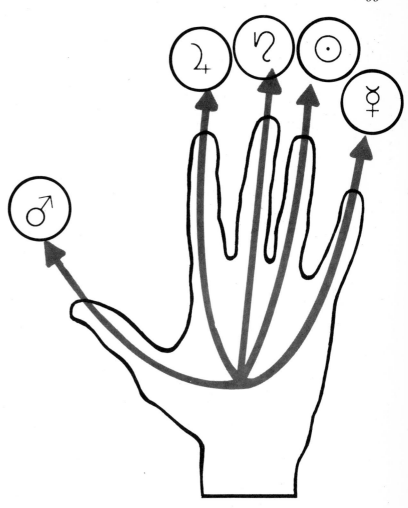

that of the palm. Experience shows that every hand must consist of a combination of long or short fingers with a square or long palm, and it is on the strength of such combinations that the present basic division of hand forms has been established. There is a Fire hand, which consists of a long palm with short fingers (figure 102). There is an Earth hand, which consists of a square palm with short fingers (figure 106). There is an Air hand, which consists of a square palm with long fingers (figure 112). There is a Water hand, which consists of a long palm with long fingers (figure 120). This fourfold classification must be studied in more detail to give an understanding of chirognomy.

The Fire Hand
The Fire hand consists of a long lively palm and short fingers (figure 102). The combination of these two results in an energetic, impetuous emotional type who is more intuitive than intellectual. Judgements are made quickly and are often arrived at through hunches, the conclusions being expressed dogmatically or dramatically. The virtues of the sign spring from the warm emotions, which are usually creative, frank, outspoken and optimistic. The type is usually creative in a very practical way, though enthusiasm runs out and things are best done quickly. The faults spring from excessive emotion, which may be associated with the combination of short fingers and a long palm: thus the type is impatient, sometimes exhibitionist, usually egocentric, tending to be changeable and irresponsible. He is, however, always exciting and excitable. All Fire types are impetuous, which is to say that they are capable of throwing themselves

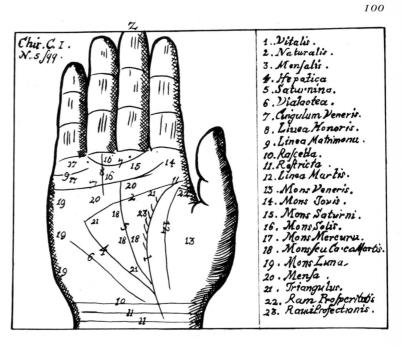

100

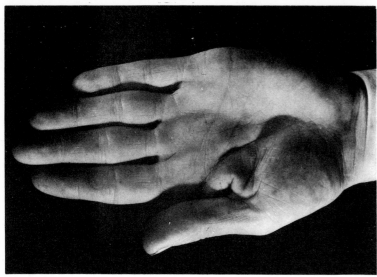

101

101. *A typical Fire hand, with a
long palm and short fingers.*
102. *A Fire hand of a female
painter.*

102

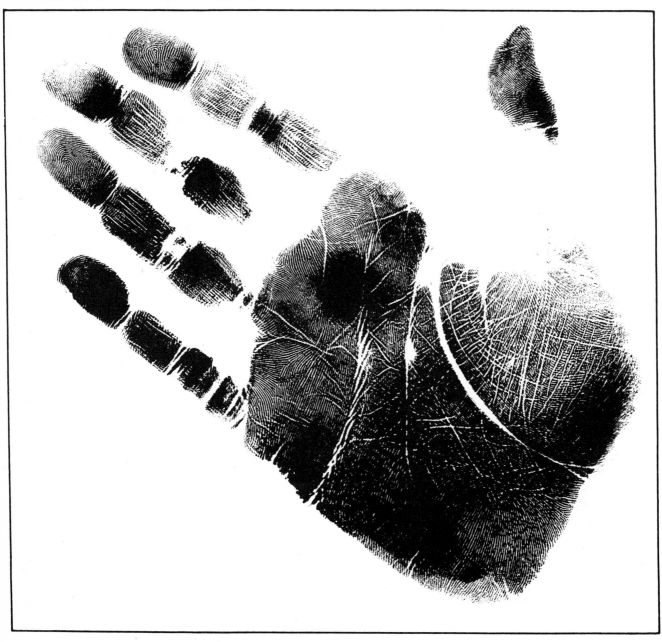

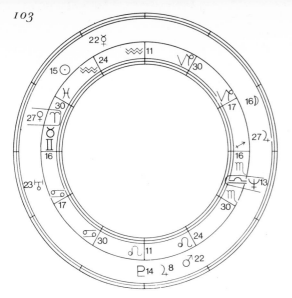

103. The corresponding horoscope
*103. The corresponding horoscope
for the hand at figure 102. Note
the trine in the Fire signs.*

immediately and fully into any situation which interests them. The fingers of the type reach to grasp at emotional expression. The Fire type manifests in terms of the astrological Fire element (page 32).

The most common Fire hand has a number of lively, quite deeply-marked lines on the palm. Usually the four main lines of Head, Heart, Life and Fate are well marked, and surrounded by a variety of lively subsidiary lines. The presence of a Simian line usually indicates that the Fire type is particularly creative, and must indeed be involved in some creative form of development. More will be said about this important line on page 147, but for the moment it is necessary to understand that the Simian line is always an indication of an emotional tension which, in the personality as represented by the Fire type, can only result in a predisposition for the emotions to be too highly charged for normal human commerce.

The female Fire hand is a little softer in appearance and much more rounded, usually not quite so heavily lined as the print at figure 102 demonstrates. With the female hand there is still the same tendency for the palm to have lively lines, though the papillary ridges are a little more refined. Any Fire hand which possesses few lines, suggesting Earth characteristics, or a great number of lines, suggesting Water characteristics, must be regarded as being of a very complex type (see page 183). The particular way in which the complexity will disturb the emotional versatility of the Fire nature must be determined by other factors in the hand such as through distinctive papillary formations on the fingers, or the length of fingers.

As we might imagine, the major characteristics of the Fire hand manifest themselves in the hands of those who are strongly Fire through influences operative at the moment of birth. The female hand at figure 102 is of a strong Fire nature, and her horoscope at figure 103 indicates a strong Fire polarity. The relationship between horoscope and hand links with creative Fire. The subject is a painter. The strength of the element manifests itself through the five planets in Fire signs, but an extra emphasis is given to the Fire quality by the presence of the remarkably strong trines between Venus in Aries, Mars in Leo, and Jupiter in Sagittarius. The hand print at figure 317 is also strongly Fire, and the corresponding horoscope shows two planets, including the Sun, gathered around the Leo Ascendant. It has already been noted that a Fire hand which manifests only a few lines, such as one would expect to find in an Earth hand, will be of a complex type. This tends to suggest that there will be a conflict in the nature. The conflict in the chart is not between Fire and Earth as we might expect but between Fire and Air, for the subject shows five planets in the Air signs, four of them in Libra.

The three astrological signs linked with the Fire nature have in common the fact that they are all involved with projecting their personalities into the world, imposing the stamp of their own ego on material conditions. As a result, the influences are towards the creative manipulation of the material by investing it with spiritual qualities, and most undertakings of Fire types are in some way constructive as well as productive.

Each of the three Fire signs, Aries, Leo and

104. A typical Earth hand, with a square palm and short fingers. Note the very simple linear structure.

Sagittarius, seek development of their personalities through active involvement with life, and this usually means that there is no real compromise with either the spiritual or the material: the type tends to live in a state of tension between the two. When the spiritual predominates the type is usually creative, but when the material predominates the type is rather sensuous.

Aries is extremely self-assertive, the most impetuous of the signs. The ego is indomitable, through the aggressive instincts channelled towards useful aims, and the type may often be very sociable. The major problem which Aries faces is that of learning self-control through achieving a balance between emotional and physical needs.

Leo is the most directly creative of the Fire signs, being thoroughly optimistic, constructive and magnificently extrovert. When under pressure the urge towards exhibitionism usually gets out of control. The type is generous with its energies, if not with its possessions, working best when allowed to impress its own vibrant personality on situations and materials – Leo is therefore a good organizer, as well as being artistic. The major problem which the type faces is that of learning to control the wish to dominate others emotionally – of learning to put exhibitionist tendencies in the right place.

Sagittarius manifests Fire burning with a purpose. It is expansive, usually highly evolved, and seeks to organize people and things in such a way as to allow the potentials in these to find unfettered expression. When under pressure the type will become like the other Fire types, profligate, though the urge to control others becomes more

pronounced, and the type may be rather tyrannical. The major problem which Sagittarius faces is involved with learning to control, or direct, its own expansive urges so that it will not damage other people.

The Earth Hand

The Earth hand consists of a heavy square palm and short, usually quite thick fingers (figure 106). The combination of these two results in a well-balanced and reliable type who is more intuitive than intellectual. Judgements are arrived at slowly but held tenaciously. The dependence on emotions and the rigidity of the general outlook means that there is an unusual resistance to change, and this is often expressed in strong determination and a conservative outlook. The virtues of the sign spring from the reliability offered by the square palm, for this brings a good balance, backed by a certain self-control. Thus the Earth type is generally honest, practical and dependable, and under certain circumstances may be creative. The faults spring from the inertia associated with the square palm, which is not easily stirred into activity by the emotional life indicated by the short fingers: thus the type may be stupid, is almost always slow to start, and may be very obstinate, unimaginative, and even violent. All Earth types are reserved, which is one way of saying that they are capable of keeping themselves to themselves; on an emotional level this means that the type possesses integrity. The fingers grasp at emotional security. The Earth type manifests in terms of the astrological Earth element (page 32).

The most common male Earth hand has few lines on the palm. Usually the three

70

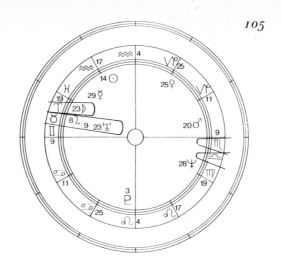

105. *The horoscope for the hand reproduced below in figure 106. Note the powerful trine aspect in the Earth signs.*

106. *A typical Earth hand in form and linear structure. The finger patterns are of an Air nature, which is perhaps understandable with Sun and Mercury in an Air sign (see figure 105).*

106

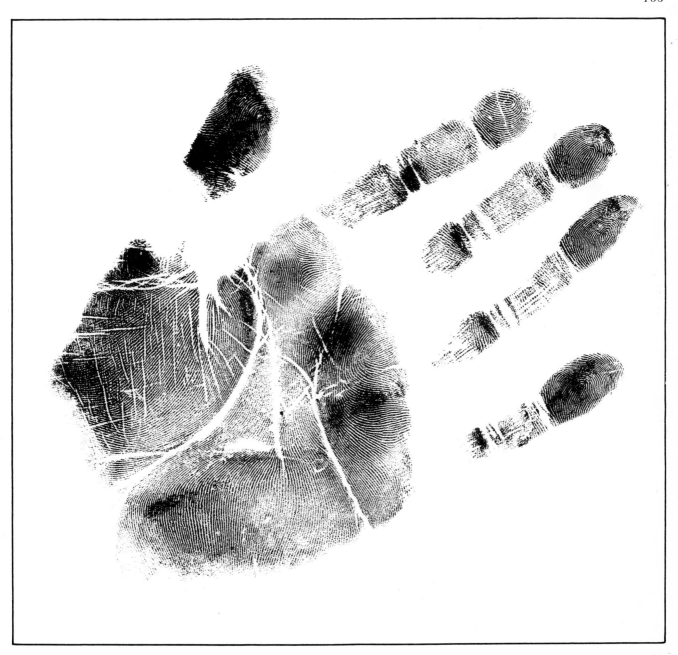

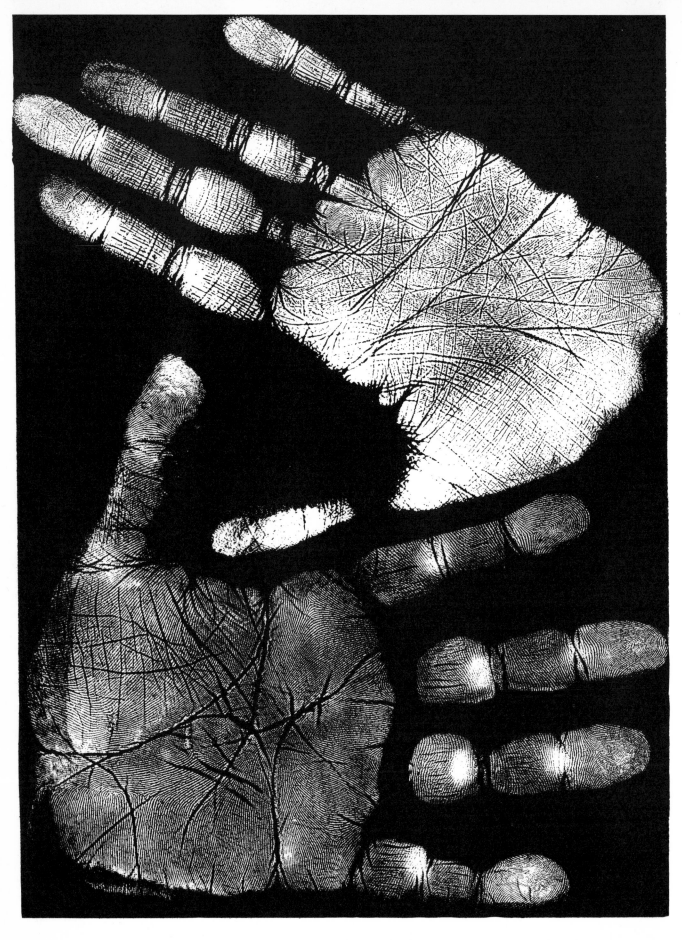

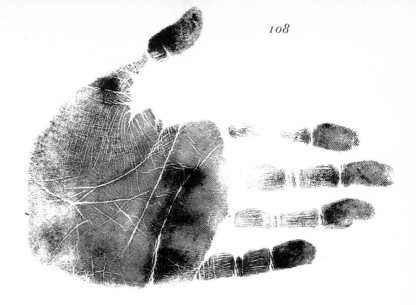

107. *Two hands to facilitate
comparison. The top female
hand has long fingers and a long
palm, the lower male hand a
square palm with short fingers.
Both personalities are well
known in the field of popular
music.*

108. *A female Earth hand.
Sometimes, when the palm is
particularly broad, the fingers so
incline together to give the
impression of the hand being of
the Fire proportion: the
beginner must be careful when
determining the basic nature of
such a hand.*

main lines of Heart, Head and Life are deeply marked, and carry few hair lines or subsidiary lines. It is not uncommon for the Earth hand to manifest a strong Simian line: this is the line which runs right across the hand print at figure 317 is also strongly Fire, and the corresponding horoscope shows two relation to the type considered here it is necessary to understand that the Simian line is, superficially at least, an indication of an emotional tension which throws the personality off balance, emphasising the Earth predisposition to either violence or creativity.

The female Earth hand is altogether softer in appearance and much more rounded, as the sample print at figure 110 demonstrates. With the female hand, however, there is still the same tendency for the palm to have a limited number of lines, though the papillary ridges are more refined. Any Earth hand which possesses more than three or four subsidiary lines in addition to the main three must be regarded as being of a complex type (see page 187). The particular way in which this complexity will disturb the essential simplicity of the Earth nature must be determined by other factors in the hand, such as the papillary ridges or the marking of the mounts.

As we might imagine, the major characteristics of the Earth hand manifest themselves in the hands of those who are strongly Earth through influences operative at the moment of birth. The male hand at figure 106 is of a strong Earth nature: the corresponding horoscope at figure 105 indicates a strong Earth polarity. The relationship between this horoscope and hand is dis-

cussed on page 163. The female hand at figure 110 is also of a strong Earth nature: the corresponding horoscope at figure 109 shows Sun and Mercury in Taurus, Mars and Saturn in Virgo, and the M.C. in Capricorn.

The three astrological signs linked with the Earth natures have in common the fact that they are all involved with, if not actually weighed down by, the physical. Each of the three signs, Taurus, Virgo and Capricorn, seek for release from the physical by attempting to manipulate matter, and in some way· produce a material record of emotions and thoughts, in order to give expression to self.

Taurus is practical, physical and extremely slow to react emotionally. When under pressure the type may be violent, though normally he is peaceable, and has a good, if bawdy, sense of humour. Sometimes the type is creative through a sheer delight in tactile and physical energies and is often musical, with an instinctive grasp of rhythms. He is often creative through the constructive handling of materials involving physical contact. The major problem which Taurus faces is that of giving emotional expression, and yet maintaining a sense of integrity.

Virgo is practical, discriminative, and slow to express emotions. When under pressure, the type may become merely carping, though otherwise he is creative in elucidation and by virtue of constructive criticism. He works best by analysing and breaking down the big structures into component parts. The major problems which the types faces is involved with bringing order to chaos, and learning to discriminate in emotional matters.

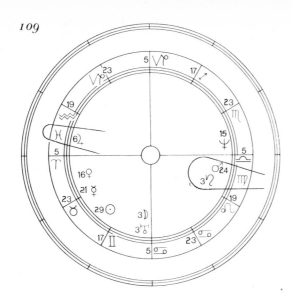

109

110. *A female Earth hand with strong Water lines.*
111. *Such a print as this is extremely hard to evaluate, since it consists of extremes. The line structure is patently of an Earth nature, the patterns on the fingers of Jupiter and Apollo of a Fire quality, whilst the general form might suggest an Air nature. However, an examination of the hand itself reveals it to be strongly Earth.*

Capricorn is practical, given to imposing formal order into situations, and slow to reach decisions of an emotional kind. When under pressure the type becomes unreasonably obstinate, and will break rather than give in to circumstances. He is sometimes creative in the building of complex structures and forms from minute units, as for example in writing. The major problem which the type faces is involved with adaptability, of learning to be more fluid in order to combat the essential rigidity of his nature.

The Air Hand

The Air hand consists of a square palm and long, usually quite flexible, fingers (figure 114). The combination of these two results in a well-balanced, reliable type who is more intellectual than intuitive, though some Air types do have quite a brilliant intuitive sense. Judgements are arrived at quickly, but by means of a rapid intellectual effort, the conclusions being expressed clearly and with a view to informing. The dependence on intellect, as opposed to emotion, means that the type is often profoundly mistrustful of the emotional values held by others, and even of his own. The virtues of the type spring from the reliability offered by the square palm – a reliability which is usually of a spiritual nature, or expressed in the intellectual world. The type is generally truthful, an accurate reporter of facts, usually excellent at organizing things, has a factual, discriminating yet original mind, and generally may be trusted in most matters. Under certain circumstances the type may be creative, though more usually in a manner involved with direct personal communication, on a verbal level rather than visually.

110

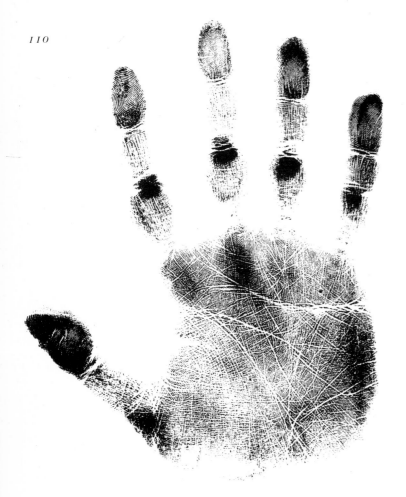

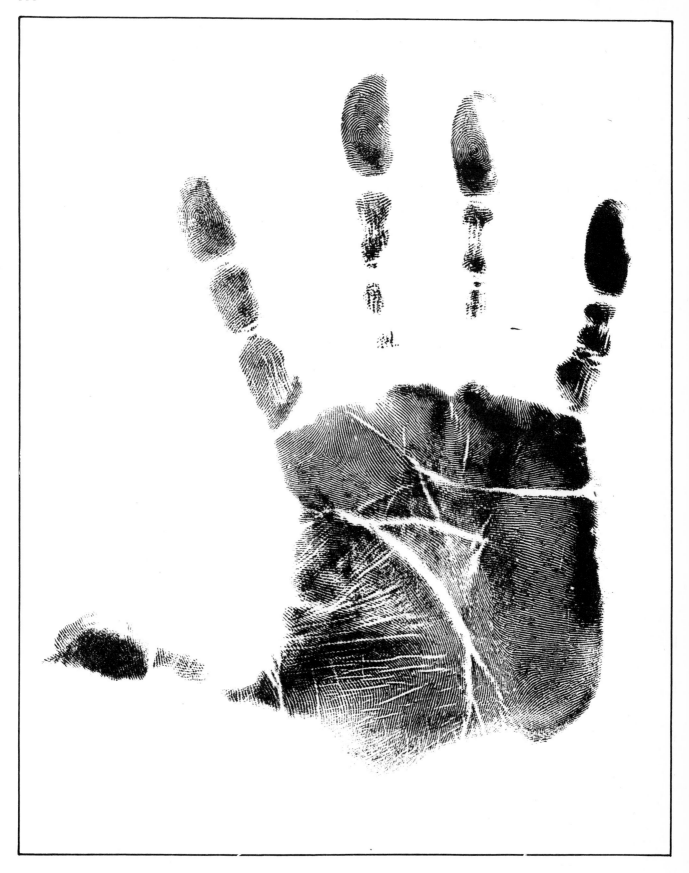

113

112. *Strong Air hands, with the typical fleshy palm and long fingers.*
113. *A female Air hand.*
114. *A typical Air print. Note the rich loops on the finger ends and the fleshy quality of the square palm.*

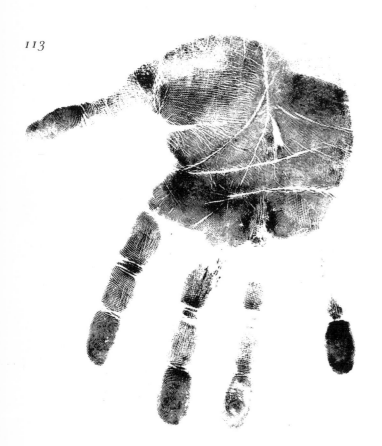

The faults spring from the meeting of intellect with inertia, which means that the type tends to seek only a cerebral level of understanding and, not being easily stirred into emotional activity, there is a tendency to appear superficial, even when this is not the case. The type may have such an acute mind that he is in a position to take advantage of other people: hence, the person with an Air hand may sometimes be opportunist. He is rarely violent. All Air types love freedom, are inquisitive, quick-witted and need desperately to communicate. The fingers of the type reach out for intellectual contact with others. The Air type manifests in terms of the astrological Air element (page 33).

The most common Air hand has a number of lines on the palm (figure 114). Usually the three main lines of Head, Heart and Life are well marked in a lively way, carrying few hair lines or subsidiary lines in themselves, but are supported by many very lively lines over the palmar surface. It is not uncommon for the Air hand of a creative person to manifest a strong Simian line as in figure 114. This line (see page 147), is always an indication of an emotional tension which in an Air personality will tend to 'soften' the intellect, and open the personality to a wider framework of experience, with the result that the person may be creative, though usually in a literary manner.

The female Air hand is altogether softer and more rounded in appearance, as the sample print at figure 113 demonstrates. With the female hand, however, there is still the same tendency for the palm to have a lively quality of line, while the papillary ridges may

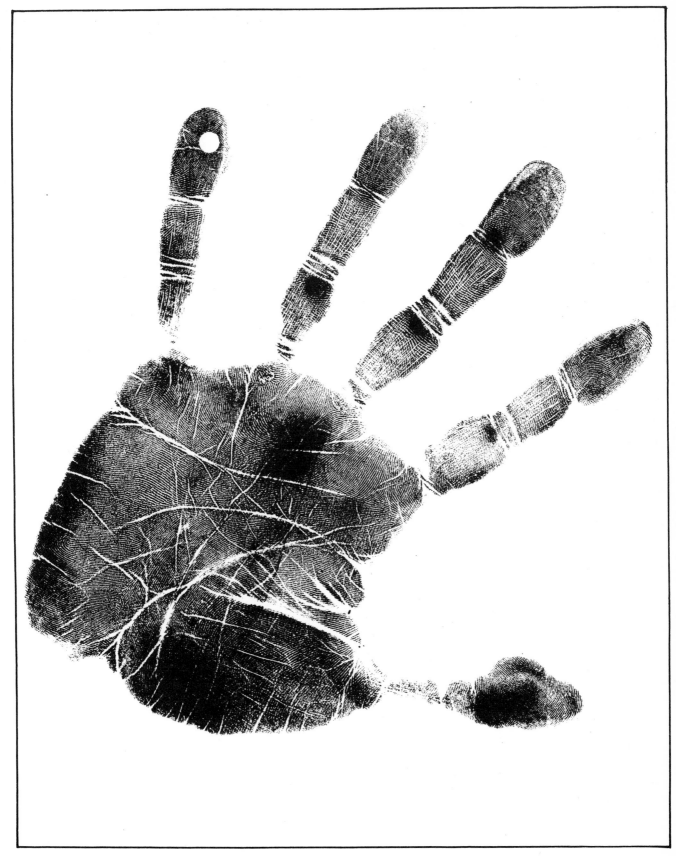

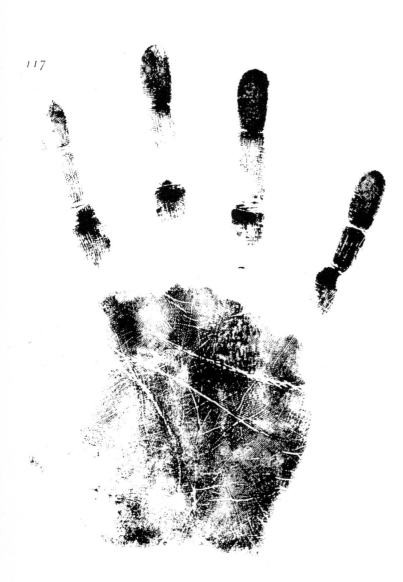

117

De Saturno domino genituræ.

be more refined. Any Air hand with lines that are remarkably different to those indicated in the two figures at 114 and 117 may be regarded as a complex type. The particular way in which the complexity will disturb the communicative intellect of the Air nature must be established by looking at other factors in the hand, such as the papillary ridges on the fingers or through the markings of the mounts, though it is most usual to find the complex Air personality disturbed by emotional problems with which he cannot cope.

As we might imagine, the major characteristics of the Air hand manifest themselves in the hands of those who are strongly Air through influences operative at the moment of birth. The female hand at figure 119 is of a fairly typical Air nature; the corresponding horoscope at figure 118 indicates a strong Air polarity, for Sun and Uranus are in Gemini, Jupiter and Neptune in Libra, and the Moon in Aquarius. The relationship between the horoscope and the hand is discussed more fully on page 157, but it is worth noting at this point that the open fingers are characteristic of an Air print, whilst the lively and distinctive linear markings are also typical. The male hand at figure 112 is also of a strong Air nature.

The three astrological signs linked with the Air natures have in common the fact that they are all involved with, if not actually dominated by, the intellectual world. Each of the three Air signs, Gemini, Libra and Aquarius, seek for intellectual communication and expression by attempting to release ideas, and in some way communicate ideas and thoughts to others,

115. *Arch patterns on all the fingers. These formations must be considered as being of an Earth nature, more specifically under the dominion of Saturn.*

116. *The repressive Saturn, which rules frustrations, limitations and fears.*

117. *A female Air hand: one of the most significant characteristics is the wide finger spread, both in prints and in photographs.*

118. *The horoscope for the native whose hand is shown below. Note the strong Air emphasis.*

119. *The print for the horoscope right. The Fire lines are manifest in the strong Leo force of the horoscope.*

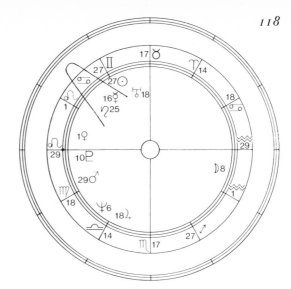

118

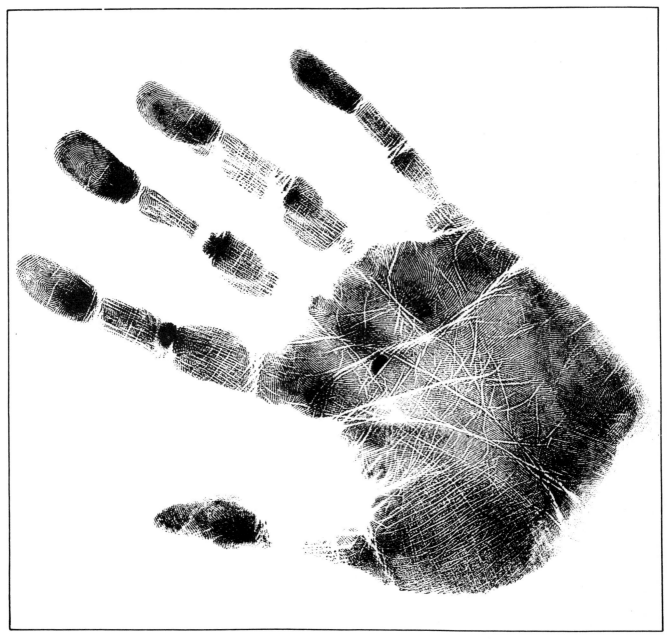

119

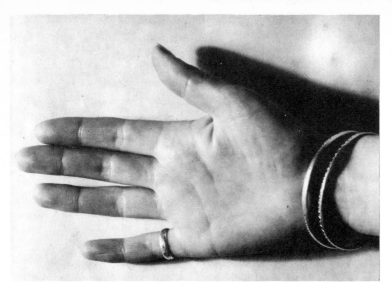

120. A female Water hand, with long palm and long fingers. It is not uncommon for the fingers on such a hand to cling together. A ring on the finger of Mercury is often a sign of sexual difficulties.

partly as a means of self-expression, and partly as a means of making contact, for all Air types need people.

Gemini is quick, sociable, generally clever, versatile and witty, but tends to be rather superficial. When under pressure the type may become criminal as a result of an inability to accept responsibility, yet even in this phase he often possesses a good mind and a sense of humour; he is the 'brilliant' criminal, capable of talking his way out of situations, the arch con-man. Sometimes the type is creative through a facility with words. The major problem which Gemini faces is that of remaining serious or deep, for since there is always a strong tendency to skim over the surface of things, or to treat things in a superficial or humorous way, much of real meaning is missed or ignored.

Libra is gentle, inclined to be rather indolent, and although the type often has a good intellect he is usually reluctant to develop it. Personal effort and decision-making do not come easily to the Libran: he will make decisions for others but finds it difficult to act on decisions in connection with himself. When under pressure the type may become merely fanciful and evasive, though with remarkably little but uncharacteristic effort he may be creative in his ability to introduce harmony into places and situations. He works best through harmony on a decorative basis – that is to say, he will accept existing frameworks, and yet render them more agreeable by re-arrangement or representation of the surface of existing materials. The major problem the type faces is an emotional inertia which induces a tendency to lose himself in dreams concern-

ing beauty, harmony and equilibrium, rather than attempt to introduce these factors into life by real effort.

Aquarius is clever and sometimes intellectual, though usually quite undisciplined with the result that the intellect is very rarely brought to bear on situations, and there is generally an inability to reach decisions or to effect decisions in life. When under pressure the type may become rather unrefined, unsociable, and even rather objectionable, wishing merely to disturb or destroy existing orders. Under these circumstances he is at best eccentric, at worst antisocial. The type is frequently creative in its ability to communicate through a wide variety of artistic means: the Aquarian has a rather special way of looking at life, and is often able to communicate this to other people. The major problem which the type faces is that of learning to control the wish to be different and the urge for freedom, in order to fit harmoniously into the framework of society: he has to understand that freedom has its own responsibilities.

The Water Hand

The Water hand consists of a delicate long palm, and long, almost sinuous, fingers (figure 122). The combination of these two results in an insecure and over-charged emotional type, who usually has a good intellect. The forces of the strong emotional energies discharging through the fingers tend to make the type highly imaginative and extremely sensitive to external conditions. Judgements are arrived at quickly and intuitively, but are not adhered to with any great certainty. The type tends to be emotionally insecure about his own position

121. *A female hand which is Water by form, though Fire in linear characteristics, as the print below demonstrates.*

122. *Although the lines on this hand are not characteristic in quality of a Water type, the descent of the head line into the Mount of Moon is typical, for it emphasizes the sensitivity of the type, and renders the imagination more powerful than usual.*

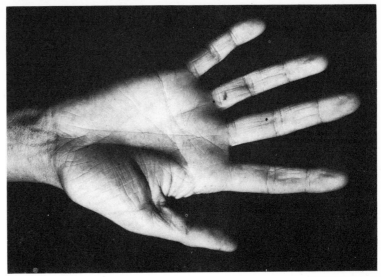

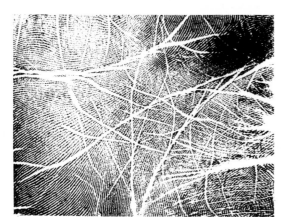

123

124

123. *Typical Fire lines.*
124. *A male Water hand, typical both in form and linear structure. The creative whorls on the finger tips render the type especially sensitive.*
125. *Typical Earth lines, set in the coarse papillary skin ridges.*
126. *Typical Water lines. The female hand tends to be even more flaccid and mesh-like in distribution.*

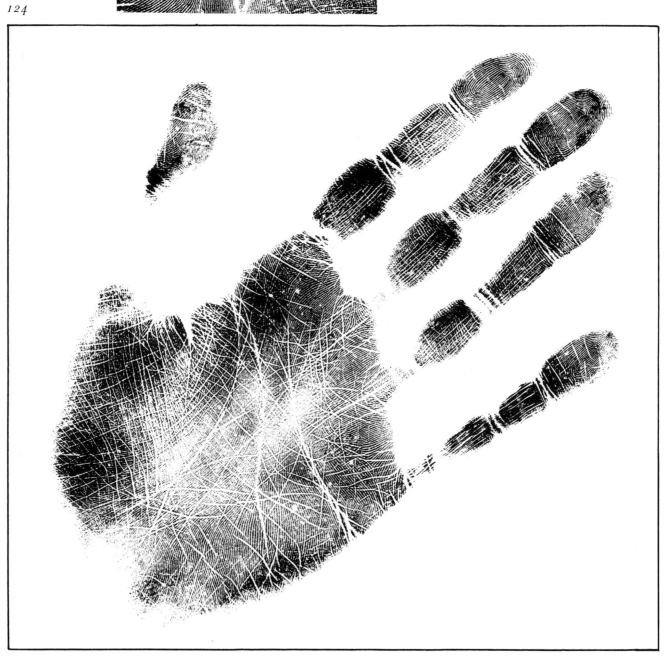

in life. The general high key to the emotions and the remarkable sensitivity to outer impressions is such that there is an unusual fluctuation in the personality for he tends to reflect the moral, emotional and physical shades of those around him. The virtues of the sign spring from the extreme sensitivity which renders him sympathetic to others. Sometimes this sensitivity leads to creativity, and then the type is not quite so emotionally lost. The faults spring from lack of practicality, and the inability to fit into normal life due to a morbid, over-imaginative or unreal grasp of life; he is secretive and tends to be withdrawn. Water people are of a rather unstable emotional nature, though often give the appearance of being fairly self-contained. The major characteristic is that they tend to reflect the world around them, and thus they are constantly searching for support from other people, for some containing form which will give shape to their Watery nature. They need a unifying aim so strongly that they will follow almost any direction pointed out by another person. The fingers of the type grasp at emotional direction. The Water type manifests in terms of the astrological Water element (page 33).

The most common male Water hand is weak or delicate in appearance and is covered in a mesh of delicate lines over the palm surface. All the major lines of Heart, Head and Life are evident though usually almost hidden under the bewildering confusion of minor and subsidiary lines. The hand is extremely soft, receptive and pliable. A strongly marked Girdle of Venus, (figure 124), or a strong Simian line (figure 285), is always an indication of an extremely high emotional tension which will throw the personality, already somewhat precarious and highly-charged, completely off balance, emphasising the predisposition of the Water type towards retreat into fantasy and imagination. The female hand is altogether more delicate in appearance, a little more rounded, and even more soft, as a sample print at figure 128 demonstrates. With the female hand, however, there is still the same tendency for the palms to be covered in a mesh of delicate lines, which almost hide the major lines. It is extremely rare to find a Water hand which is not covered in many lines. If the lines are noticeably different in quality from those one would associate with a Water type (see figure 126) then the type must be regarded as complex. The particular way in which the complexity will disturb the emotional charge of the Water nature must be determined by other factors in the hand, particularly in terms of the element suggested by the structure of these unusual lines. One must imagine the basic Water nature being affected by the element indicated – as for example in the way the Fire energies would make the Water energy of the type boil, should the line structure be essentially of a Fire nature. Sometimes the papillary patterns on the fingers suggest what direction the neurotic forces will take when the Water structure is disturbed.

The major characteristics of the Water hand manifest themselves in the hands of those who are strongly Water through influences operative at the moment of birth. The hand at figure 138 is of a strong Water nature: the corresponding horoscope at

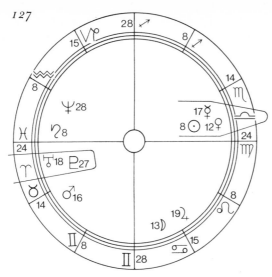

127

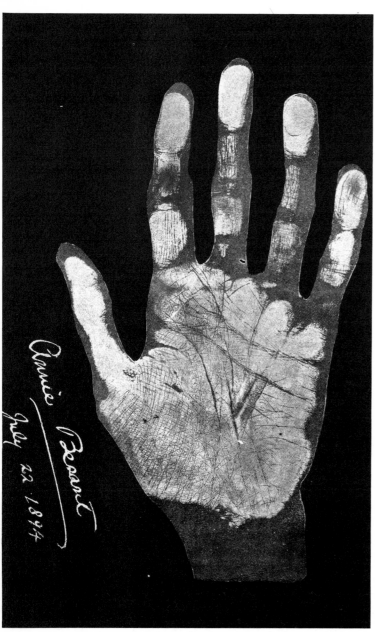

128

127. *The horoscope for Annie Besant, the Theosophist.*
128. *The hand print of Annie Besant, made by 'Cheiro'.*
129. *The hand of a modern English writer, whose horoscope is figure 133.*
130. *The horoscope for the hand at figure 132, the twin of figure 81. Figures 131 and 132 are virtually identical.*
131. *The hands of a pair of male twins. See figures 81 and 130.*

figure 37 indicates a strong Water polarity for not only is the Ascendant in Cancer, but also the Moon and Uranus are placed in this sign, Mercury and Mars are in Scorpio, and the M.C. is in Pisces. The sensitivity of the linear structure on the hand of Mrs. Annie Besant, one of the founders of the Theosophical Society, indicates a strong Water polarity (Moon conjunct Jupiter in Cancer, Saturn in Pisces) on a hand which is of an Air form, reflecting the Air nature of her horoscope (figure 127). Her Ascendant is Pisces, but she has Sun, Venus and Mercury in Libra.

The three astrological signs linked with the Water nature have in common the fact that they are all involved with spiritual development in one way or another. As a result the influence is towards the spiritual, as opposed to the material, and most undertakings of Water types have the aim of improving the psyche or the imaginative faculties, though this sometimes becomes involved with morbid fantasies. Each of the three signs, Cancer, Scorpio and Pisces, seek development of their emotional life by the exercise of their deep sensitivity. This usually means that there must be either a compromise with the material or a retreat from the physical: in the first case there is often a material expression of the sensitive nature, a delicate physical record of emotion, as in the form of a poem or a painting; in the second case there is often a retreat from the physical, sometimes into a well-regulated contemplative withdrawal, as in religious life, or into emotional instability (resulting from an inability to deal with the material world), often with attendant psychological blocks and difficulties.

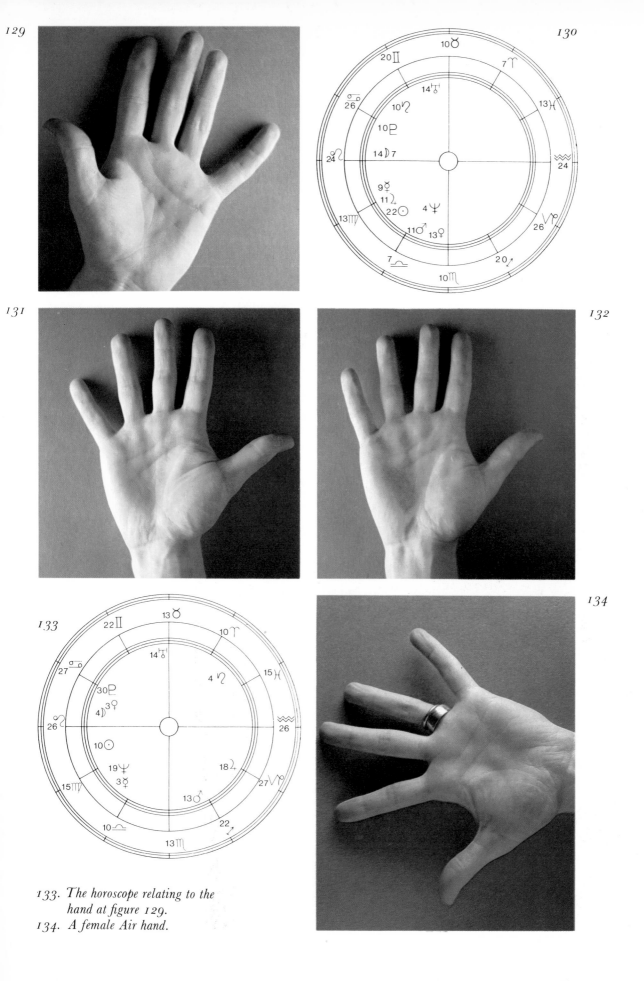

133. *The horoscope relating to the hand at figure 129.*
134. *A female Air hand.*

135. *The triad of palmistry.*
136. *The fourfold division of the hand, linked with the fourfold division of the horoscope, and at the same time according with palmistic traditional theory. The bright red area represents the outward conscious movement towards life, dominated by the thumb. The orange area represents the creative conscious expression of feelings, dominated*

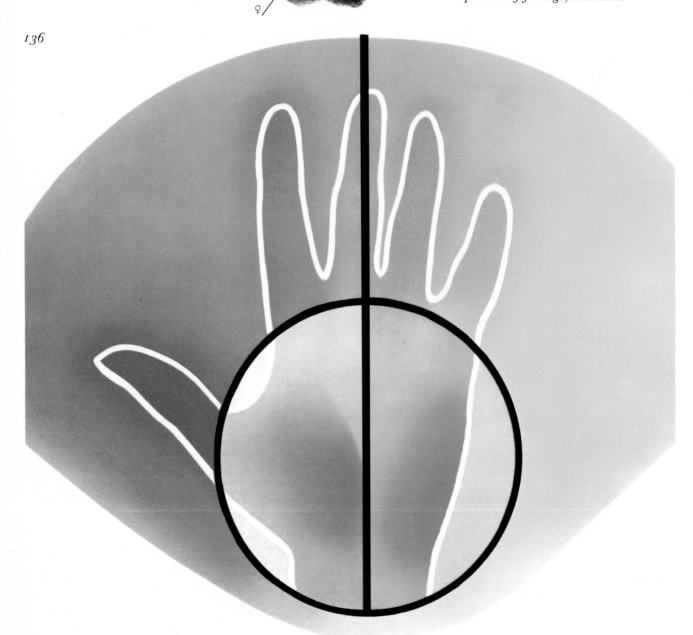

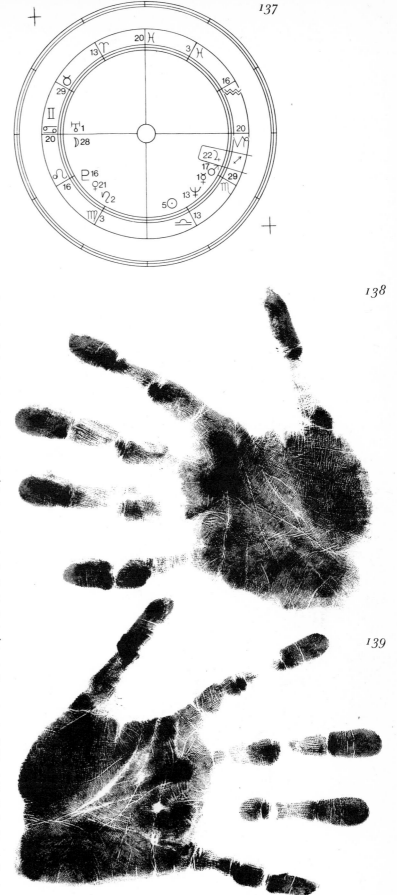

by the finger of Apollo. The blue area represents the reservoir of physical energies associated with Venus, and of easy access to the conscious expression of material ideas. The green area represents the reservoir of psychic energies, associated with the Moon, and of easy access for creative and sexual concerns.

137. Related hands and horoscope,
138. showing strong Water influences.

Cancer is highly sensitive, and reflects more than any other sign the qualities, whether good or bad, of those around. They are extremely sympathetic, and often find a position in life through helping and serving others. For a rather complex astrological reason, great strength of personality and even genius is sometimes manifested in Cancerian types, and when this happens they escape the morbid limitations which are normally associated with Water types. The genius can show itself in a variety of different ways. The major problem which Cancer faces is that of achieving a spiritual growth through emotional contact with others.

Scorpio is the most practical of the Water signs, is extremely deep and magnetic, and when under pressure the wish to dominate others is usually exhibited. The type is extremely penetrating, lucid and works best by investigating conditions and structures with a view to regenerating them. The major problem which the type faces is that of achieving emotional development through the powers of regeneration and control, as for example through medicine.

Pisces is emotional, and often spiritually refined, and bases all its decisions on emotional factors. When under pressure, the type will withdraw either literally, in a physical sense, or emotionally, into the imagination. All Water types tend to require a form, and look for this form to other people, in order to channel their emotional energies. The major problem which faces Pisces is that of fitting in its own deep emotional sensitivity into a world which now values most highly the material qualities which surround human beings.

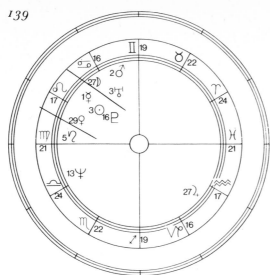

139

140

139. *Related hand and horoscope.*

140. *The hand form is basically Fire, with a rich quality of lines which suggest strong Water propensities. The horoscope, which gives four planets in Leo and three in Cancer, supports this division.*

141. *The finger of Saturn has a papillary pattern of the loop variety, but the other fingers have whorls. This is one way in which a finger may 'stand out' from the rest, and thus indicate a particular intensification or conflict in regard to the energies it represents.*

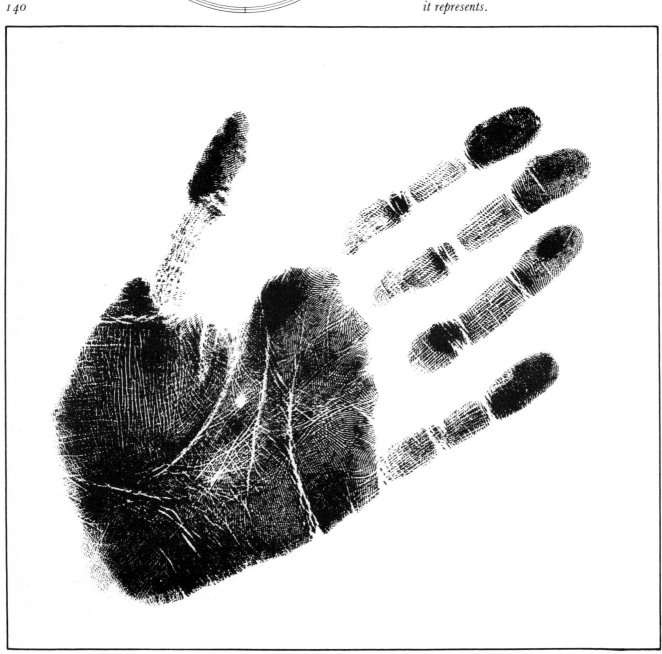

The Fingers and Mounts

Before examining the individual fingers and mounts from a point of view of their palmistic significance, we must note something about the way in which fingers and mounts are to be interpreted. Long fingers extend what the occultists call the 'mental' plane, which means that the type is extremely sensitive, though tending to be withdrawn from the physical world. Short fingers strengthen the involvement with the 'vegetative' world, and imply considerable practicality. On reflection one realizes that it is partly the length of the fingers which influences the psychological traits associated with the four hand types: both Water and Air types are removed from direct need to manipulate materials, and find themselves handling emotions or ideas; Fire and Earth types are always involved with the material world, one in a creative way, the other in a manipulative way.

The prime rule for interpreting individual fingers is that the finger should 'feel' right in relation to the hand as a whole. If it stands out in any way – either literally (figure 141), or by appearance, then it may be regarded as having particular influence in the life of the subject. As one becomes more accustomed to looking at hands, the more one will begin to sensitize oneself to fingers which are in some way different or wrong. Perhaps the most common way in which a subject will isolate the force of a finger, and subconsciously draw attention to that field of energy represented by the finger, is by wearing a ring: thus a ring on the finger of Mercury is a certain indication of difficulties in adjusting to relationships, especially in sexual matters. Fingers which do not fit in to

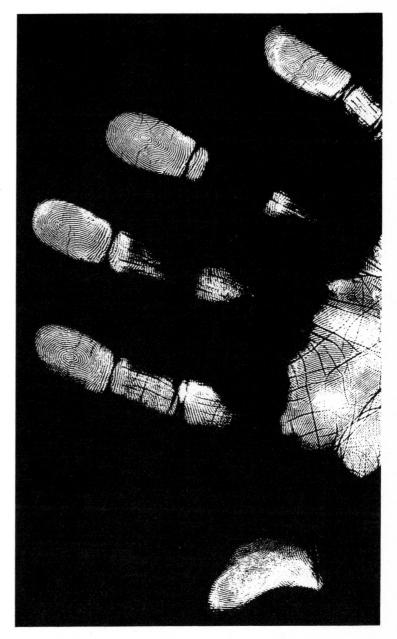

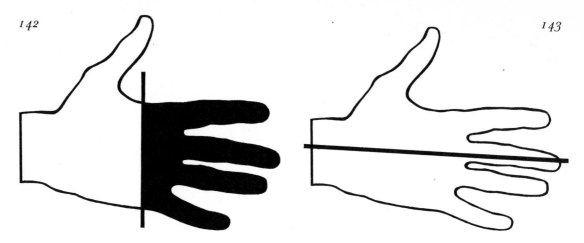

the hand as a whole indicate that the energies and drives ruled by those fingers are not integrated harmoniously in the life and personality of the subject. For example, deep-set fingers, or bent fingers, are fairly clearly discernible, and usually indicate a strong tension in the field represented by the finger itself: a long finger will suggest too strong an emphasis on the relevant field, and so on. This is why a deep-set finger of Mercury is regarded as a sign of sexual block, which manifests itself commonly in terms of compensation through a preoccupation with money. We may understand this as a move from the spirituality of sex to the extreme of materiality, so to speak, since the sex of Mercury, its wish to communicate, is being pulled down into the material palm of the hand. This is why a long finger of Jupiter is regarded as an important sign of a strong ambition which tends to mar the human dignity of the native by throwing him off balance in regard to life itself.

There are virtually no hard and fast rules which may be applied to finger interpretation, for it is so much a matter of balancing one finger, its quality, appearance, length, texture and so on, against the rest of the hand. It is essential however, that the theoretical and practical background to each finger be thoroughly grasped before the significance of any deviation or excess may be properly understood in the life of the personality concerned. The most important considerations in the interpretation of fingers are the finger patterns themselves, for each pattern indicates a particular mode of being in such a way that it is possible to interpret, from a pattern on a particular finger, how the

energies of that finger will manifest in life.

Sweeping aside all the half-baked traditions concerning the link between palmistry and astrology, the diagram at figure 157 may be taken as the basic key for understanding the relationship between the two systems. This correlates the traditional planets of astrology with the planets of palmistry. At a later point the signs of astrology are related to palmistry and it will be seen that each human hand is a miniature zodiac in itself.

Fundamentally the diagram at figure 136 is based on a division of the hand into four quarters, which themselves are a result of two divisions. The first division is that which runs across the middle of the hand below the fingers and above the Mount of Venus and the Mount of Moon (figure 142). The top area is clearly the domain of the fingers and their so-called mounts, and this represents the active side of the personality, which may be seen manifesting in the world. All the obvious personality traits of all external activities are assessed from this top part of the hand. The lower part of the hand contains the passive side of the nature, and from this area one judges the hidden side of the personality, that which is not visible in the outer world. This domain is the world of the subconscious, of latent energies, and in terms of psychology it would be related to the *id*, that nest of undifferentiated, unformed and undisciplined energies which all people have in common, waiting to manifest diversely through the fingers above (figure 99). It is this division which perhaps accounts for the fact that the upper part of the hand differs in every individual (particularly the top part of the papillary patterns),

142. *The first division of the hand gives 'activity' and 'passivity', as does the horizon division of the horoscope.*

143. *The second division gives 'objective' and 'subjective' domains, as does the vertical division of the horoscope.*

144. *Superimposed, the four areas link directly with the four quarters of the horoscope created by the angles. See 136.*

145. *The palmist examines the hand used by the subject for all questions concerning the present lifetime.*

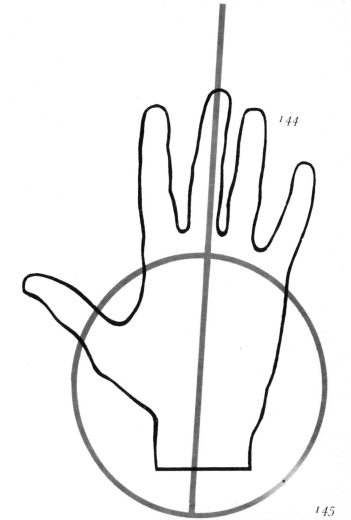

144

145

and is thus expressive of personality, of the 'mask' of conscious forms which the character and temperament make from the underlying subconscious. As the diagram at 99 suggests, the fingers reach out to give expression to certain modes of being – the fingers seek identity, whilst the palm of the hand remains an anonymous reservoir of energies. The lower parts of the hand, the Mount of Venus and the Mount of Moon, show few remarkable differences between individuals.

The second division is vertical, technically running through the finger of Saturn and along the line where the line of Saturn would ideally run, as in figure 143. The thumb, or radial, side of this division links with the external, objective life of the native, the ulnar side links with the internal and subjective. Superimposing these two divisions, as in figure 144, gives four areas which between them cover all the different levels within the personality of man (figure 136).

In the top left of this figure, there is an active and externalized energy in which is placed the finger of Jupiter (bright red). Jupiter itself is in astrology the planet of expansion, and is studied in a chart by astrologers in order to assess the degree of power, the degree of expansion in the personality, as well as the extent to which the personality is able to grow in all fields, whether physical, mental, or moral. This planet of Jupiter was traditionally the ruler of that most sensitive of zodiacal signs, the Water Pisces, which has had rule over western civilization for the past two thousand years, and is connected with the spiritual world immediately above Man. The finger is an index of ambition in its widest sense, of

146

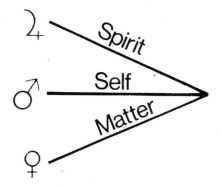

146. *The simple 'triad of palmistry' which is, of course, linked with*

147. *the Ascendant, twelfth house and second house relationship in the horoscope figure, presents the easiest system of analysis which may be superimposed on the preliminary classification in terms of 'elemental type'. The triad reminds us that certain Indian systems of palmistry are reputed to be based on an analysis of the thumb alone.*

148. *The horoscope of Dante. The presence of so many planets above the Ascendant, and in the domain of Jupiter would*

147

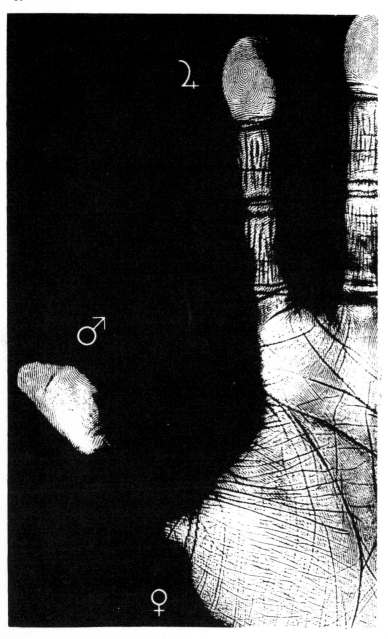

the degree to which the personality may slot into the outer world around, and expand within that context. The finger of Jupiter is examined by palmists who wish to study the ambition, self-confidence and world-orientation of the subject which springs from definable spiritual drives within the native: ambition is merely the physical manifestation of spiritual drives. Clearly then, there is a link between the Jupiter of astrologers and this part of the hand. This does not mean to say that from this part of the hand one can necessarily determine the quality, nature, aspects or sign-placing of Jupiter in the natal chart. The only thing which does not fit into the linear pattern outlined above is, of course, the thumb. Whilst the tradition varies from system to system, most palmists would agree that the thumb is an indicator of power and energy, and they therefore take the rulership of the active Mars as being the most appropriate. Properly speaking, therefore, the thumb belongs to the upper part of the divisions – relating to 'energy made explicit and given form'. Accordingly we must think of the divisions of the hand not so much in terms of a four quarters divider but more as a circular divider as in 136. This is the energy reservoir, which contains those two powerful mounts ruled by the feminine planets Venus and Moon.

The thumb presents something of a problem to palmists. Traditionally the thumb has always been an index of the power of the personality, though specifically linked with the will power, and the rulership of Mars is usually bestowed upon it. As we have seen, from its placing in the active objective area of the hand it certainly does link with the

suggest a highly spiritualized
personality.

149. *A well-balanced triad of
palmistry, in which the thumb is
not too dominant, the mount of
Venus too fleshy, nor the finger
of Jupiter excessively long, short
or bent. The bend inwards of the
finger of Jupiter is to be
taken as an indication that the
spiritualized energies are being
transferred to the domain of
Saturn: the subject is materially
ambitious.*

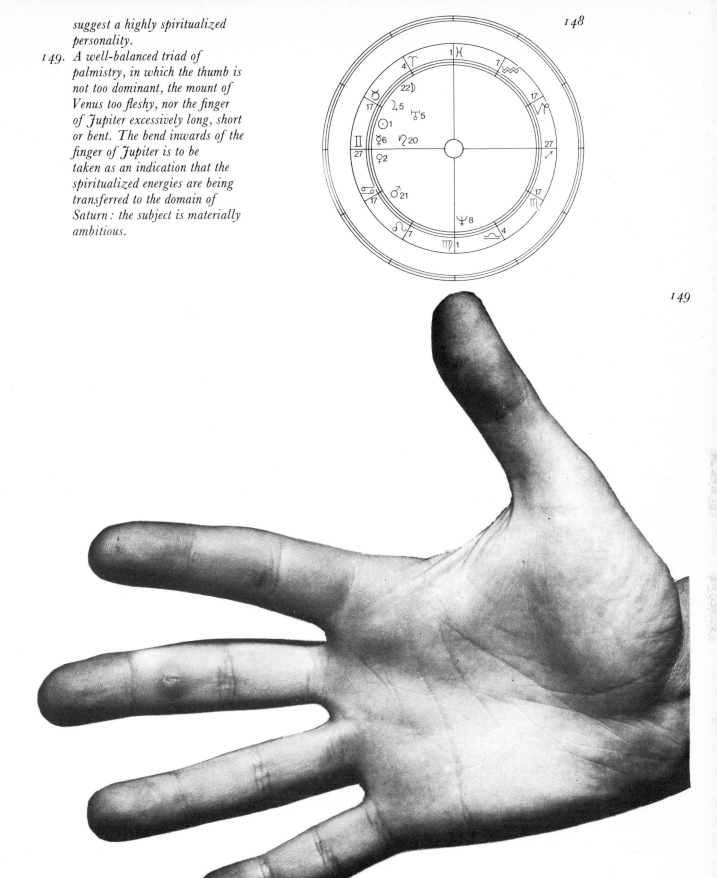

148

149

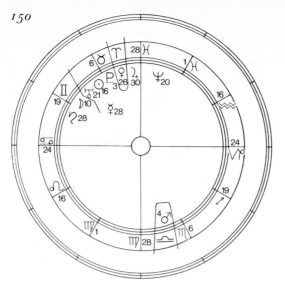

planet, but in accordance with our wish to disassociate the actual planet of astrology from a strict rulership over a particular area of the hand, we must observe that the thumb is an index of more than merely the relationship and influence of Mars. The thumb in a sense is that part of the hand which accumulates the combined energies of all the active planets, particularly the Fire planets (the Sun, Mars and Jupiter) and it acts something like the lens of the Ascendant, in colouring and polarizing all the conflicts and drives in the personality. This part of the hand, is, therefore, the best index of the strength of personality, tenacity, courage, sense of enterprise and even physical strength of the native. One never finds a weak thumb on a strong personality.

It is interesting that the thumb should spring from the Mount of Venus, for the Mount marks a reservoir of energies which are utilized or given expression by the fingers in regard to relationships with other people – Venus being essentially the planet of harmony, relationships and so on. Mars in astrology associates directly with sexuality, and most strongly Martian personalities are of strong sexual appetites and energies, so we tend to see yet another connection between the traditional rulership of Mars and the thumb. However, the sexual life of the native is not studied in a horoscope merely from the placing of, or aspects to, the planet Mars, but must be assessed from a study of the combination between the Fire planets and the receptive Venus. It would seem to suggest, therefore, that the whole thumb is the index of precisely this kind of relationship in the personality and in the horoscope: cer-

tainly we shall see from the analysis on page 107 that the thumb is itself very much more an index of sexuality in its animal, physical sense than the finger of Mercury, which traditionally links with sex more in its communicative and spiritual sense. My own system, set out at page 98, endorses this view.

The top quarter of the hand to the right is active, but internal or subjective, and the area is dominated by the fingers of Apollo (dark red) and Mercury (yellow). In astrology, Apollo is more commonly called the Sun, and this is regarded by astrologers as the planet which reveals the conscious self-expression of the native. It is a most useful index, in terms of sign-placing, aspects, and house positions, of the artistic development of the personality, the degree and manner in which the native is able to give a material form to his emotional perceptions. The Sun indicates the type of person the native is: it is a mark of the underlying self, that curious invisible lens which transmits the wide variety of behaviour patterns and traits which we call personality or character. The finger of Apollo is studied by palmists mainly as an index of the creativity, the emotional vitality, and the sense of awareness of the subject. Clearly there is a link between the Sun of astrologers and the finger of Apollo, and it is not unreasonable to think of Apollo as representing the full expression of this quarter of the hand in terms of creative self-expression and emotional awareness. In fact, in the astropalmistic system which I have developed (see figures 153 to 157), the rulership of the Sun is transferred to the line under this finger, which is in traditional palmistry called the

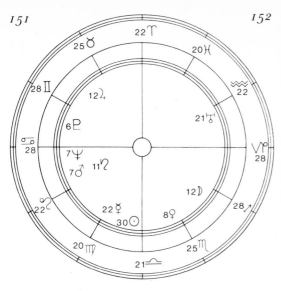

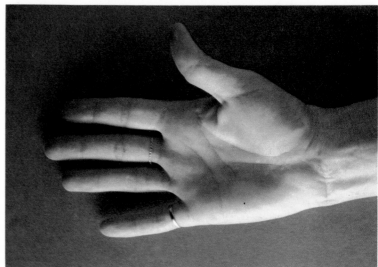

151. *Hand and horoscope. The low*
152. *set mount of Moon is more typical of a Water hand than of a Fire hand – in this case it is no doubt a result of the strong Neptune placing in square aspect with Venus in the fifth. This accounts for the ring on the finger of Mercury.*

153. *The hand with the colours of the ruling planets. See over.*

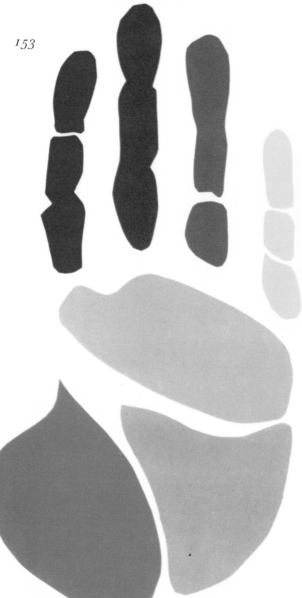

153

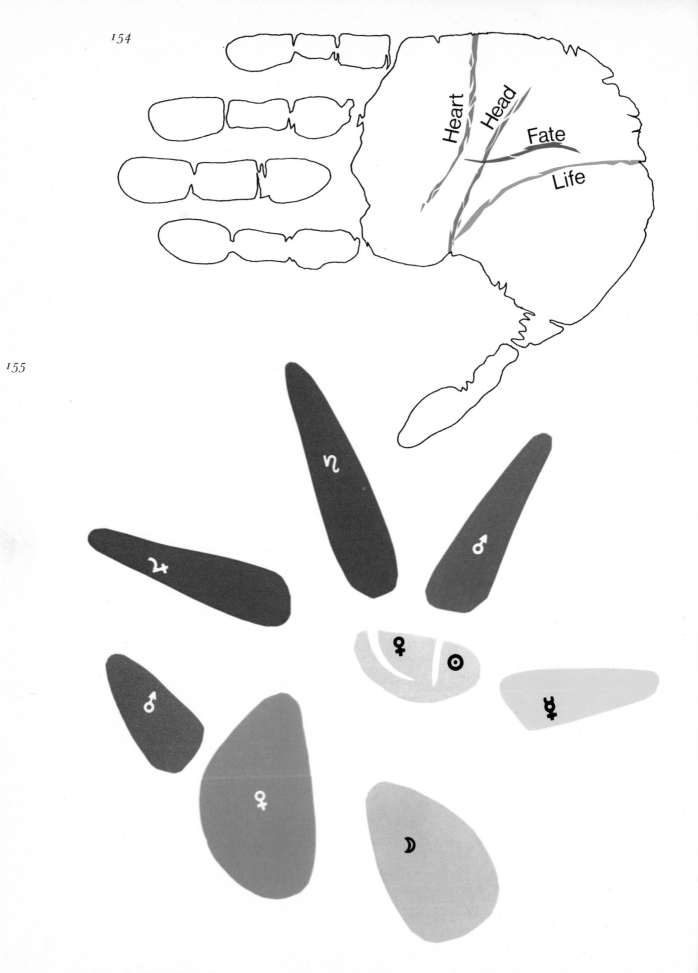

154. The four major lines, which Gemini, Leo, Sagittarius and Aquarius rule.

155. The eight major palm areas, ruled by the planets. The centre of the palm, occupied by the Girdle of Venus and the line of Apollo, is ruled by Libra, which contains within its glyph the image of the setting Sun.

156. When the information contained in figures 154 and 155 is put together, one begins too see that the hand is in fact a miniature zodiac.

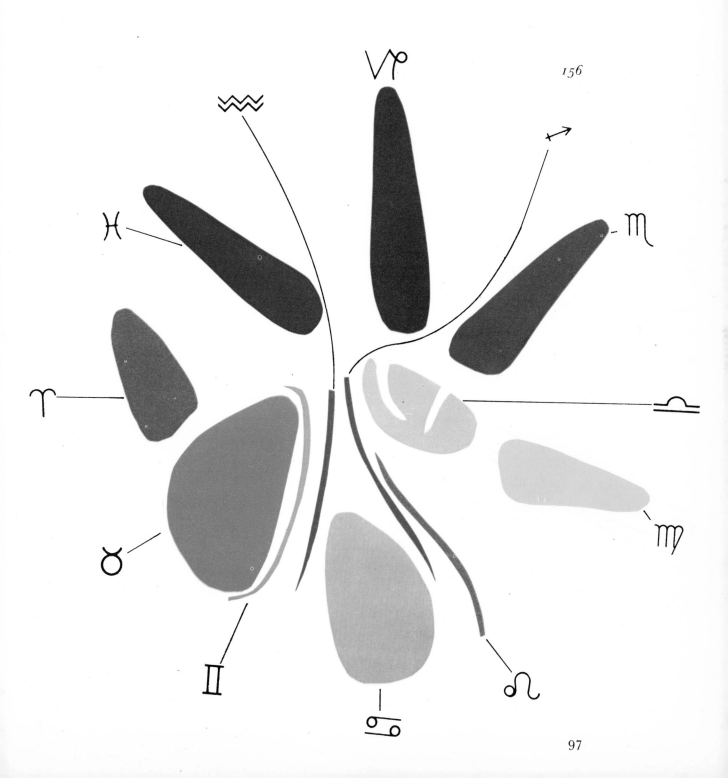

156

157. *A schematized study of the relationship which the hand holds to the zodiac.*

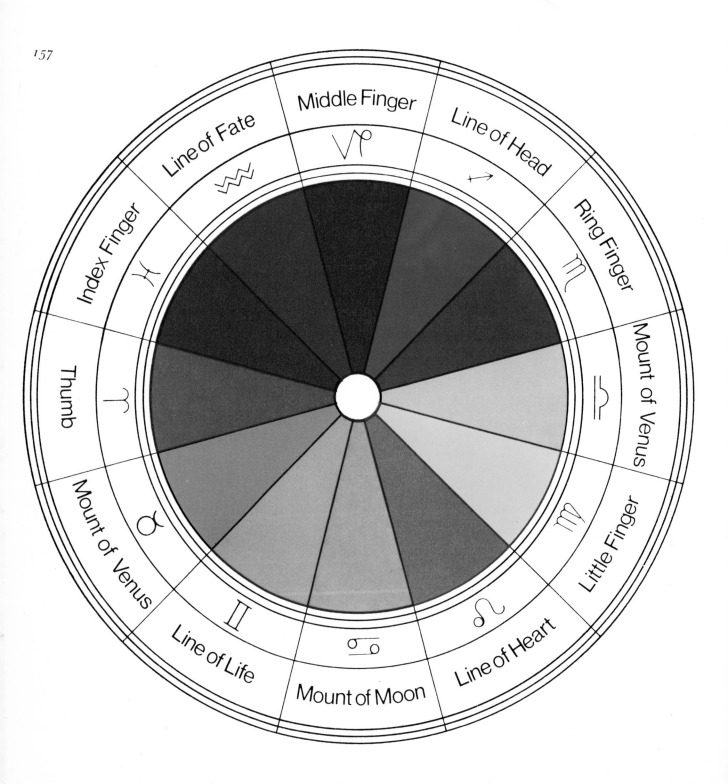

158. *From the schematized figure of 157 we may understand why a line of Apollo so frequently indicates creativity, for it is pouring solar energy into the finger ruled by the Mars of Scorpio. This is why a line of Apollo and a whorl on the ring finger is an almost certain sign of creativity in a personality.*

line of Apollo (figure 96), and Mars is given rulership over the ring finger. There is a needful logic in this change, for the outflowing energy of Mars, particularly in its association with the intense sign Scorpio, is more adapted to establishing relationships, through which the real creative ability of the subject is manifest. The intensity, the possessiveness, and the sense of inner regeneration which accompanies all satisfactory relationships between the sexes is more completely symbolized by a Scorpionic rulership than by Apollo. The rule of the important Sun is transferred not merely to the line of Apollo, which lies under the finger, and which is traditionally regarded as an index of the wish to be creative; the Sun is also given rule over the very important line of heart – not inappropriately, when one recalls that the Sun rules the human heart in astrology (figure 96).

In astrology Mercury is the planet involved with communication, and it is studied in a chart by astrologers in order to assess the mannerisms of the person, the way he will talk and use his hands or his body in order to communicate his thoughts. It is sometimes stated that Mercury rules the mentality, but this is true only insofar as it rules the *expression* of emotions and thoughts – it is Jupiter which has rule over the actual mind itself. Mercury is involved with memory and with intuitions, while Jupiter organizes these into thought patterns; hence Mercury rules the rapid externalization of that which is held in the subconscious reservoir. Mercury has been linked by palmists with both sex and money, and these two factors are at once the grass roots of most

159. *According to the occult
tradition there were ten signs of
the zodiac at one time. The
tenth sign was the Serpent.
After the Fall of Man the body
of the serpent was cut, to
symbolize the separation of
Adam from Eve. From the body
emerged the female Virgo and
the male Scorpio, who were*
separated by the 'concept of
relationships' which is Libra.

160. *The psychological truths
indicated in the myth of 159 is
often expressed through an
excessively long or badly broken
Girdle of Venus, which is
frequently accompanied by a
distorted finger of Mercury,
indicative of sexual difficulties.*

159

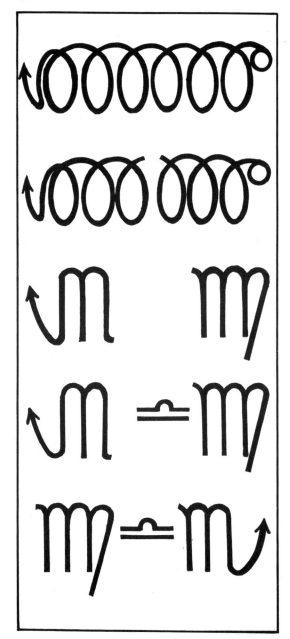

human communication and commerce, and are largely involved with emotional energies; it is not unreasonable, therefore, to think of Mercury as representing the full expression of this quarter of the hand in terms of sexuality and deep emotions involving intimate or close contact with others. We see then that the diagram of the hand represents two polarities or 'horns' upon which man hangs: on the left upper division (the externalization of the mind) is the finger of Jupiter, and on the right (the externalization of emotions) the finger of Mercury.

My own system of astropalmistry (figure 157), does not change the rulership of Mercury over the little finger, but amends the traditional interpretation to a certain extent by insisting that this is the Mercury of Virgo, and not the Mercury of Gemini. In this system, then, the quarter of the hand which links directly with emotions and sexuality actually consists of the male Scorpio (ring finger) and the female Virgo (the little finger), placed adjacent to each other. The first is outgoing, active and intense, the second withdrawn and rather concilliatory. All relationships are involved with balancing the two different outlooks of Scorpio and Virgo, with the eternal male and female, which according to the tradition were united before the Fall of Man in one zodiacal sign called Serpentarius. The glyphs for these two signs are vestigial remains of a severed serpent, the Serpentarius of the constellations (figure 159): the Virgo sign is the head, and the Scorpionic sign is the tail. This is perhaps why Virgo is so inclined to use the head for organizing and correcting

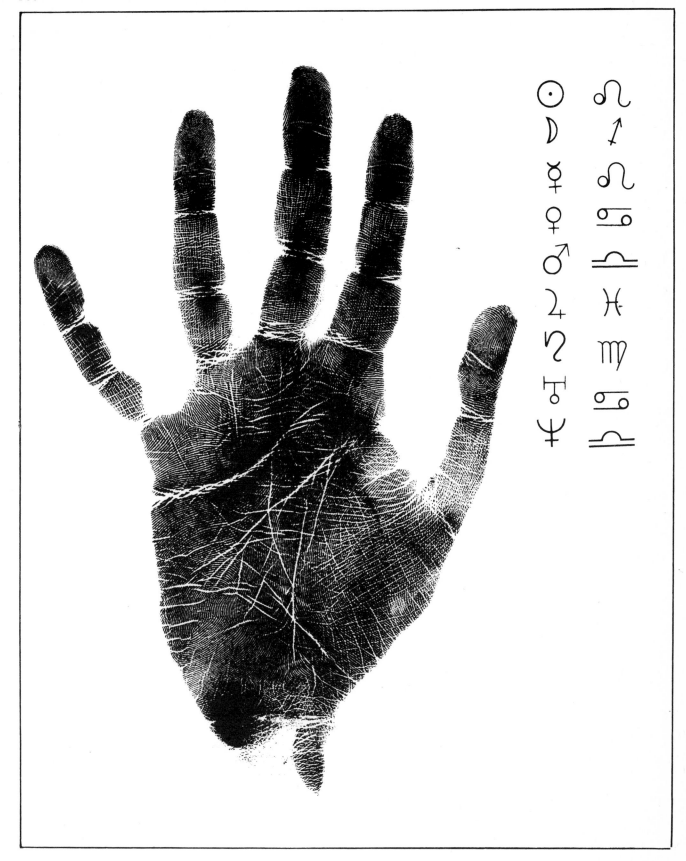

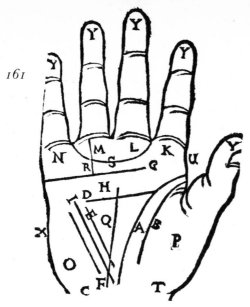

161

the world, and yet to be lost in attempting to relate emotional and sexual demands to her life (literally, she has no body), and why Scorpio is inclined to be blinded by intensity (he has no head, so to speak), and given to 'winding his coils around others' in a powerful and possessive embrace. The Serpentarius myth relates to the truth that all men and women are looking for their corresponding severed half, that they might find completion as human beings. Falling in love may be said to be the experience of such a temporary union and completion. However, we find always the 'equals' sign of Libra separating man from woman, and it would seem that the real domain of Libra must be understood, in the mystery of relationships which it represents, before total fusion with another may be possible. The teaching implies therefore that relationships must be worked at through the mastering of Libra, if they are to have any other significance than merely ego satisfaction. At all events, these characteristics of Virgo and Scorpio are to be observed in terms of the fingers of Mercury and Apollo. Meditation on the larger truths contained in this myth will enable one to see more completely the implications of this interesting quarter of the hand. In order to study the real creativity of the personality one has to balance the energies perceived in these two fingers, and to see how they relate.

The fingers of Apollo and Mercury represent the outgoing and withdrawing qualities of creativity and sexuality, in a tension which must be reconciled, but there are also two lines which do precisely the same thing, though in a slightly different way. These two lines are contained in that area of the hand traditionally called the Mounts (figure 161), which I have subdivided into three areas (figure 162), the central of which I regard as being ruled by Libra, the sign which separates and reconciles Virgo and Scorpio – the great 'equals' sign of the zodiac. This area of Libra (blue in figure 157) contains the line of Apollo, which is ruled by the Sun, and the Girdle, which is ruled by Venus. The significance of these lines will be discussed at the appropriate place, but we may note here that between them they represent different aspects of the male (Sun) and female (Venus) polarity. The emphasis of the first is on spirituality and creative giving, the other on materiality and sensuous enjoyment through receiving. This area of Libra in the palm is therefore an important one, for it demarcates the eternal Apollo-Venusian struggle, with all the polarities implied within this, such as energy and lethargy, male creativity and female sensuality, and so on. This polarity forms the basis of the drives which all those who wish for a relationship will have to master in their lives. The area which Libra rules is not a passive fount of relationships but an area which must be studied, worked at and controlled, for relationships to flower. Libra is easily reduced to passivity, but its true meaning may be found in an active and alert balancing of conflicts, tensions, likes and dislikes, ego drives and demands, in order to retain a creative relationship with another person.

It is evident that although the traditional nomenclature of palmistry may usefully be dissociated from the traditional nomenclature of astrology, the spirit of the one

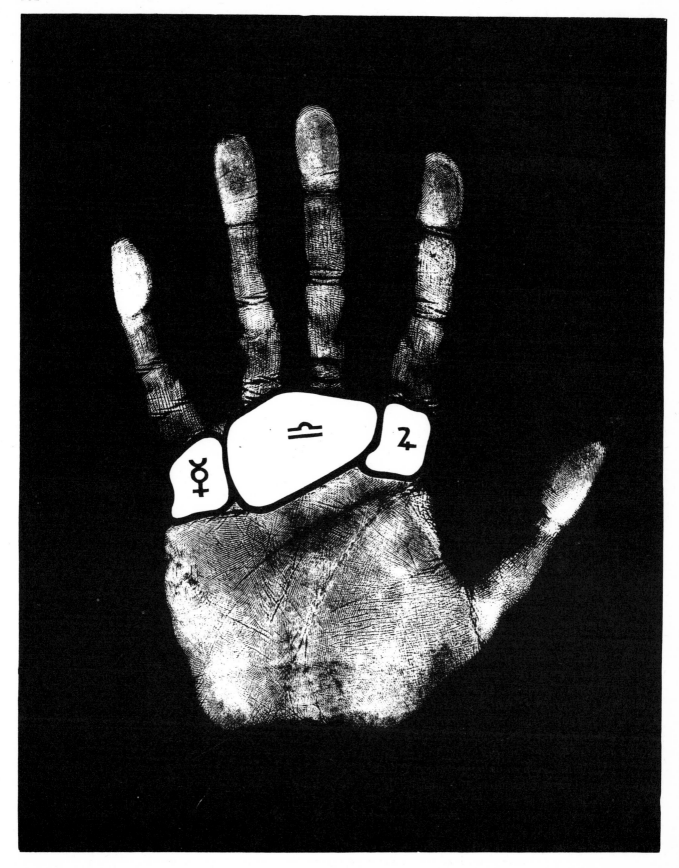

163 When a finger of Jupiter is
separated from the rest of the
hand by a papillary pattern,
then some conflict affecting
orientation to life must be
presumed in the personality.

164. When a finger of Jupiter is
disturbed by such a pattern as

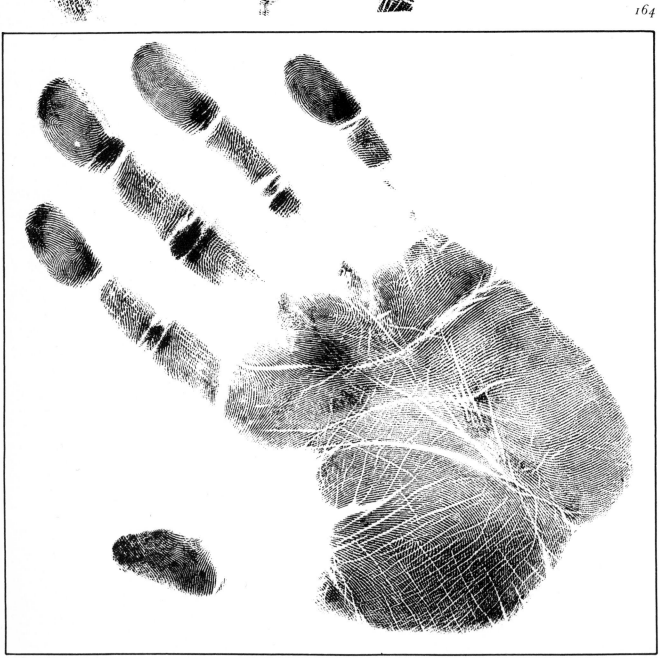

this one, in a hand which is otherwise not particularly creative, one may presume that the emergent whorl pattern will represent energies which drive the personality to seek for a creative outlook in life without the necessary artistic background.

165. *When the majority of planets are above the horizon, as in this horoscope, we may expect an extrovert personality.*

166. *A chart situation such as 165 often finds a parallel in a hand which is extrovert in that it contains many Fire whorl patterns.*

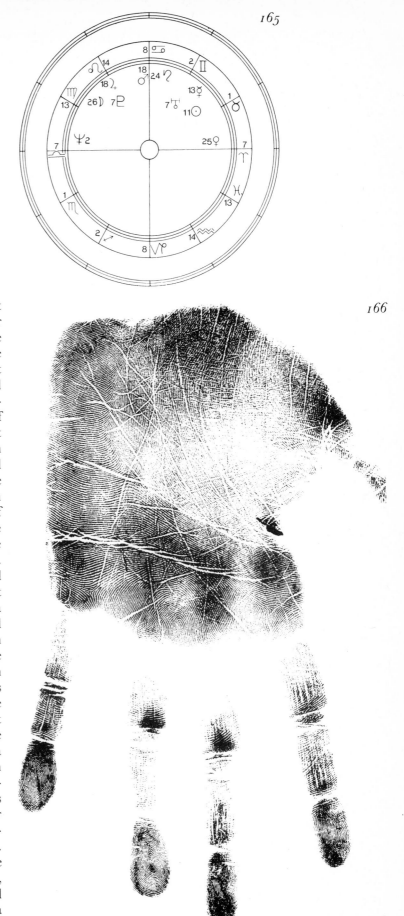

166

penetrates the spirit of the other. The planet Jupiter is not reflected directly in the finger of Jupiter, but the spirit of expansion, the ability to cope with the external world, the general feeling of optimism in the subject (all Jupiterian characteristics), may indeed be studied from the finger of Jupiter in relation to the hand as a whole. A finger of Jupiter which is not in conflict with the rest of the hand will suggest a personality which is orderly, optimistic, generous, loyal and capable of fitting easily, and without undue conflict, into the context of the society in which the subject is placed. A finger of Jupiter which does not harmonize with the rest of the hand to any extent, implies that the urge to expansion, the ability to integrate as a personality into the surrounding society, will not work harmoniously. This in itself may not necessarily mean that the person will be a failure in business or in life, but it would point to two possibilities which spring from either an excess or a deficiency in the Jupiterian nature. Either there will be an excess of optimism, a strong urge towards self-indulgence, and a reluctance to take the consequence of one's actions, or the subject may be pessimistic, timorous and quite unable to give energies freely. Jupiter is a Fire body, and therefore is involved with self-expression – in particular it is the self-assertive side of the nature which comes under its domain: a harmonious Jupiter suggests that the self-assertion of that subject is in accordance with the elemental type. Thus an essentially Fire hand with a Fire whorl on the finger of Jupiter (figure 166), will be of a warm nature, enthusiastic and inclined to be optimistic and self-assertive: a

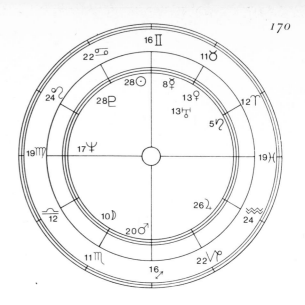

170

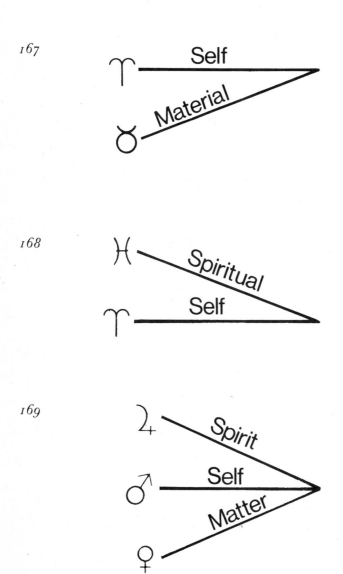

167

168

169

similar Fire hand with say, an Earth marking on the finger of Jupiter (figure 163), will tend to be of a lower quality of spirit, rather unsociable perhaps, and lacking in enthusiasm because the ego principle of Jupiter does not express itself through the mode essential to its character.

The other Fire planet is Mars, which is the planet directly representative of physical energy, sense of enterprise and endurance: it is involved almost entirely with the self, and with the wish to dominate rather than to live alongside. It therefore rules individuality and physical sex. When Mars is afflicted in a horoscope the sense of self is intensified and the type may be quarrelsome, selfish and irresponsible. The excess of Martian Fire results in brutality which puts others at hazard, whilst the excess of Jupiterian Fire results in unbounded self-confidence which puts the self at hazard. It is from the thumb that we may study these Martian impulses: if the quality of the thumb is markedly different from the quality of the rest of the hand, then we may assume that the type will be excessively Martian – restless, selfish, quarrelsome if not actually brutal, or we may assume a deficiency of Martian qualities, and the native will be timorous, fearful of projecting the self for fear of hurting others. A particularly strong thumb on a degenerate Earth hand, called by nineteenth-century palmists a 'primitive hand', was regarded as a sure sign of a violent nature. Some palmists of the blood-and-thunder type, called it the 'murderer's thumb'.

The Fire side of the personality, which is linked with self and the ability of self to

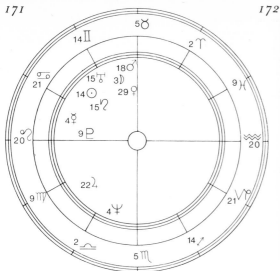

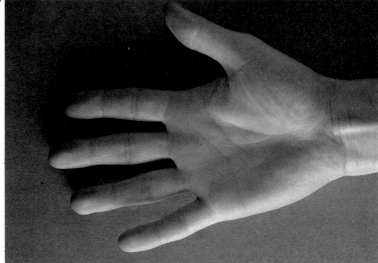

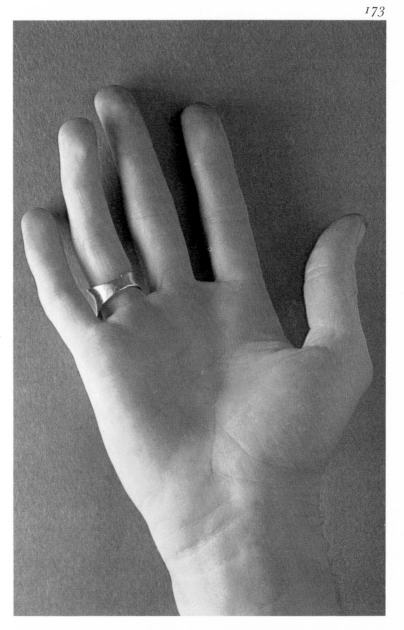

project into the world, is linked with the upper and outer part of the hand (figure 136), which includes the thumb and index finger. Just as the astrologer will consult the Fire planets – the Sun, Mars and Jupiter – in order to determine how the subject will relate to the world, so the palmist will study that quarter of the hand to see the relationship with the rest of the world. This is why a weak thumb or a short finger of Jupiter are regarded by palmists as a sign of an inability to deal with the world, sometimes even as signs of an inferiority complex. This quarter of the hand is clearly linked with the Fire aspect of the personality (see page 136).

The relationship between the hand and the horoscope may be more clearly grasped by studying something of the underlying theory, which unexpectedly unites the two. Astrologers are fond of saying that the second house of Taurus 'supports' the first house of Aries – that the manifestation of selfhood, which is symbolized in Aries, requires the material support of Taurus, which governs materiality, finance, food, and so on. This can be understood by considering the fact that a body is needed as a vehicle for spiritual growth, which is the purpose of life. Aries is ruled by Mars, Taurus by Venus (figure 169). Immediately above the first-house Aries we find the twelfth house cusp, ruled by Pisces. In ancient times, rulership of this sign was ascribed to Jupiter before the discovery of Neptune which is now acknowledged as the planet ruling the sensitive Pisces.

These two diagrams show that the self is symbolized by the drive of Mars which is the result of a tension set up between the pull

174

174. The Cross of Jupiter is supposed in the palmistic tradition to confer great spirituality. To a certain extent this tradition is explained by reference to the triad of palmistry, for it gives emphasis to the domain of Jupiter.

175. Hand and horoscope, both of

177. which manifest a strong polarity between Fire and Air, the Fire predominating.

175

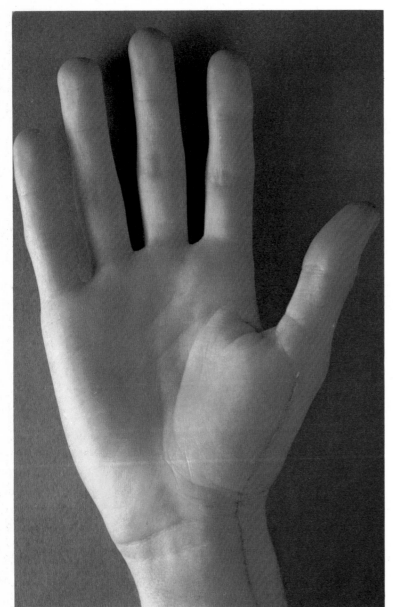

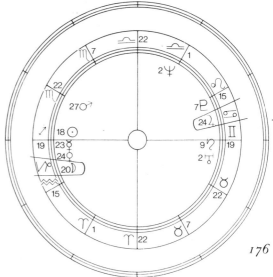

176

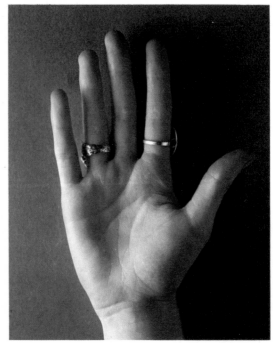

108

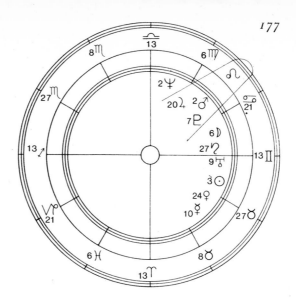

176. The wearing of rings is always highly significant. Emphasis in this hand is as it were forced towards an unnatural spirituality (Jupiter) and creativity (ring finger). The rings isolate the areas represented by these fingers. The tendency is noted in the horoscope above, which demonstrates a very strong force around the Ascendant, which emphasises selfhood, all weighed down by the opposition of Saturn and Uranus.

towards the spirit (the expansion of Jupiter) and the pull towards materiality (love of matter, by the attraction of Venus). Thus in simple astrological theory, the individuality of the Ascendant is given an expression (first house) in terms of the way it reacts to a pull upwards by Jupiter (twelfth house) and a pull downwards by Venus (second house). Everyone demonstrates this tension between spirit and matter, and the general quality of being of the personality may be determined from an examination of this triad of astrology.

Jupiter represents the expansive pull into the world of spirit, which is probably why it was linked with the twelfth house, the house governing mystical experiences and renunciation of the material world. The twelfth house comes under the most unworldly of the twelve signs, Pisces, which must descend into the physical world to find full expression, so the matter-loving and expansive Jupiter was an excellent ruler.

Venus represents the pull downwards into materiality; it stands for the love of the body, of food, of beautiful and sensuous experience, which is probably why it is linked with the Earthy Taurus, who loves above all things involvement with material, the sensuous life, and good food. The nature of Venus, however, is such that it can find complete expression of self only when lifted into the higher domain of the spirit, which is why Venus rules the arts and music. Thus we see that the world of spirit and the world of matter are striving towards each other.

Mars represents selfhood, the outgoing energy which results from the tension engendered by the pull up towards Jupiter and the pull down towards Venus. There is a

simple directness about Mars – unlike Jupiter and Venus, it is a planet of singleness of aim. As the ruler of Aries, Mars stands on the Ascendant, the most important single nodal point in the horoscope, which represents the self, that invisible entity which permeates the whole of an individual life.

The traditional associations of palmistry clearly link directly with this astrological theory. The simple triadic diagram of figure 169 may be directly superimposed over a hand print, and we find that the area of the Jupiterian twelfth house world of spirit (purple) covers the traditional finger of Jupiter, while the area of the Venusian second house (blue) covers the mount of Venus. Jutting out, perhaps rather awkwardly, between these two different forces is the area of the thumb itself (red), that important indicator of what the nineteenth-century astrologers called will, and which most modern palmists call determination or sense of selfhood; the thumb is traditionally ruled by Mars.

It is significant that the important triad of astrology should find a parallel in the triad of palmistry. Just as the thumb itself is rooted in the ball of the thumb, so is the self of Aries rooted in the material world of Taurus. The gap between the Mars of the thumb and the Jupiterian spirit of the finger of Jupiter finds a curious traditional link in the so-called 'cross of Jupiter' (figure 174), the presence of which is supposed to indicate a close tie with or propensity to mystical experiences. This curious marking, sometimes called the 'mystic cross' or the 'Seal of Solomon', indicates that the native is rooted more in the spirit than in the material. At all

178. A strong triad of palmistry militates against the disruption which the simian line — the line running across the palmar surface — would otherwise engender in life.

179. Certain of the diagrams from older textbooks show the line of Apollo sweeping up in one strong line from the Mount of Moon: such an idea would agree with the teachings contained in the present system,

events, it is clear that the Ascendant of the horoscope receives much of its force from the tensions between the two very different houses which enclose it, and a study of these houses, the signs upon them and the planets within them, is invaluable in forming some idea of the basic *self* of the native. Just as it is wrong to consider the Ascendant in isolation, for it is a result of a tension between forces, so it is wrong to think of the thumb in isolation, for it too is a result of two forces. The thumb's actual physical ability to grip things (literally, to take hold of material for some purpose) is determined by its relationship with the finger of Jupiter: the thumb alone can grip nothing, put nothing to use; the finger of Jupiter alone can do nothing other than indicate direction. Thus, the important triad of palmistry may also be used for forming some idea of the basic self of the native. This is why a weak thumb, or an ungenerous Mount of Venus, or a short or otherwise deficient finger of Jupiter, is always an indication of a weak personality. A strong triad of palmistry (as in figures 178 and 183) can in itself indicate sufficient drive to overcome many difficulties which other parts of a hand might suggest as harbouring obstacles to growth.

It would seem that both astrology and palmistry are based on the idea that there is an invisible self, which requires materiality and spirituality as food for growth. The expansion of Jupiter, and the attachment to body or materiality of Venus, support the growing man: the growth is symbolized by the planets in astrology, by the relevant finger and Mounts in palmistry, but the idea of the growth of self is only symbolized. Jupiter

does not deal exclusively with spirit, nor does Venus deal exclusively with matter. When the self is expansive, lifted upwards towards the spiritual realm of Jupiter, then it loses much of its materiality, and contact with the physical world becomes more ethereal, more unworldly. The self may occupy itself with those intermediaries of spirit which seek a spiritual expression through the material, rather than seek mere nourishment from the material. In such cases, an expansive spiritual life drives the native towards music or the arts.

It is important to understand that it is not merely Venus which attracts to the arts – it is the relationship between the triad. Venus will attract the self down into the mire of materiality, and if Jupiter is not strong enough to operate within the triad as an expansive force, then certainly the native will be involved with a sensuous, Earthy life, symbolized by Taurus. Should Jupiter be strong, then the self will wish to use Venus' rather than be used by it, and the end product is usually involved with artistic expression, the most ethereal of which is music. Music represents the most intimate contact with the spiritual world which human beings are permitted to experience under normal earthly conditions. The triad of astrology will always find a correlation in the triad of palmistry, and indeed (as we shall see) they together form the most important relationship for evaluating personality traits in a simple way.

The triads would appear to proclaim that the purpose of life is to achieve spiritual growth by balancing the world of spirit and the world of matter. Certainly the triads of

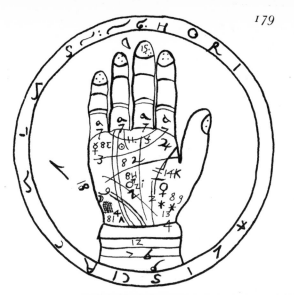

suggesting a contact between the subconscious domain of Moon, and the conscious domain of the fingers.

180. The hand print of the artist Leighton, made by "Cheiro".

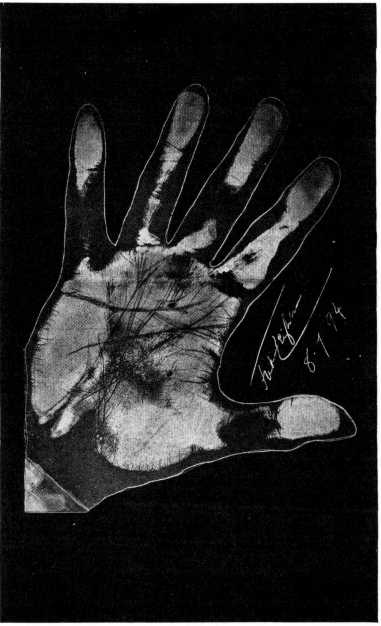

astrology and palmistry form an indispensible index of how this growth is being nurtured by the individual. One may see why the Ascendant is so important in astrology, and why certain Hindus should use merely the thumb for personality reading and prognostication. It will be noted that at no point is it suggested that there is a direct link between the planet Mars in an individual horoscope and the thumb, which is ruled by that planet; or that there is a direct link between the planet Jupiter in an individual horoscope and the finger of Jupiter. The point is that the self of the palm will be the same as the self of the horoscope, that the expansive and spiritual qualities of the native as manifest in the horoscope will be the same as those manifest in the hand.

The traditional rulership of the Sun over the finger of Apollo leads to interesting speculations. The Sun is the Fire planet *par excellence,* and we would expect to find its rule connected with that part of the hand which is outer and upper within the Fire quarter. However the Sun, unlike Jupiter or Mars, does not seek to dominate others: if anything it seeks more to exhibit itself, to radiate its energies freely, and often to the advantage of others. The astrologers will look at the Sun in a chart to determine in what way the native will seek to exhibit his personality and his energies to find out how he is creative and capable of expressing the self. This is clearly the domain of the line of Heart, which is ruled by the Sun (page 38). The Sun in astrology relates to the purpose of the native's life, as well as to his feelings. We find, therefore, when relating palmistry to astrology, that the traditional palmistic

181. The hand of a guitarist. The whorl pattern and the strong line of Apollo are typical of the creative type.

182. The hand of an entertainer. The line of Apollo is constructed from a variety of individual lines, suggesting great versatility.

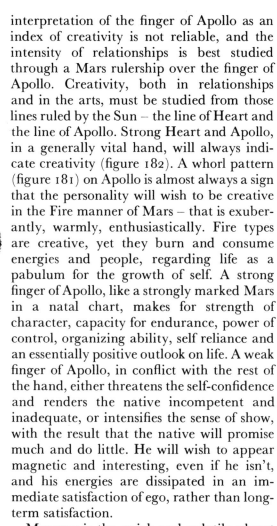

182

interpretation of the finger of Apollo as an index of creativity is not reliable, and the intensity of relationships is best studied through a Mars rulership over the finger of Apollo. Creativity, both in relationships and in the arts, must be studied from those lines ruled by the Sun – the line of Heart and the line of Apollo. Strong Heart and Apollo, in a generally vital hand, will always indicate creativity (figure 182). A whorl pattern (figure 181) on Apollo is almost always a sign that the personality will wish to be creative in the Fire manner of Mars – that is exuberantly, warmly, enthusiastically. Fire types are creative, yet they burn and consume energies and people, regarding life as a pabulum for the growth of self. A strong finger of Apollo, like a strongly marked Mars in a natal chart, makes for strength of character, capacity for endurance, power of control, organizing ability, self reliance and an essentially positive outlook on life. A weak finger of Apollo, in conflict with the rest of the hand, either threatens the self-confidence and renders the native incompetent and inadequate, or intensifies the sense of show, with the result that the native will promise much and do little. He will wish to appear magnetic and interesting, even if he isn't, and his energies are dissipated in an immediate satisfaction of ego, rather than long-term satisfaction.

Mercury is the quick and volatile planet of communication and intuition. A well-integrated Mercury in a chart indicates a person who is good at communication and usually of a fine mentality. A badly-placed Mercury often indicates an excessive urge towards communication, a strong need for

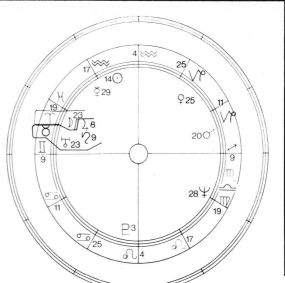

183. *Left hand and horoscope of a potter and teacher. The right hand will be found at figure 307, an analysis at figure 268.*

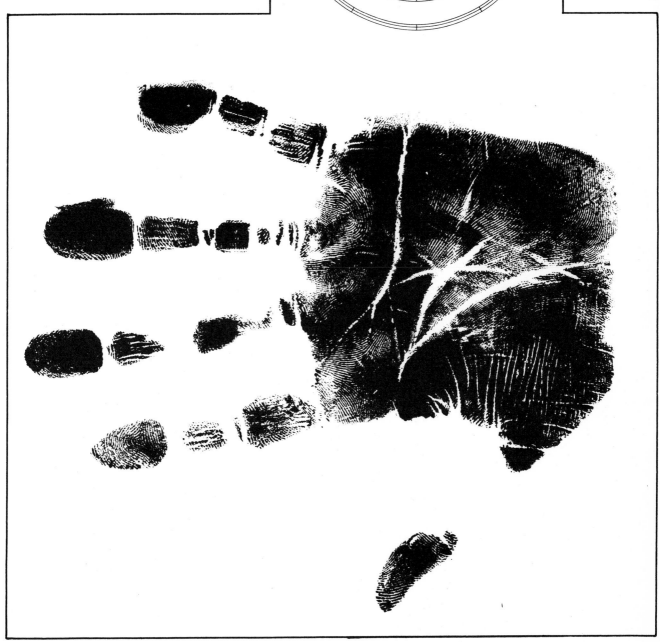

184. *Whilst rings may* appear *to be*
185. *worn for conscious reasons, or for social purposes, they do in fact represent deep subconscious urges in terms of the finger upon which they are placed (see figure 99). The actual form, size and quality of the ring is involved with the expression of deeply rooted emotions; for example a ring on Mercury is always connected with sexual problems.*

184

185

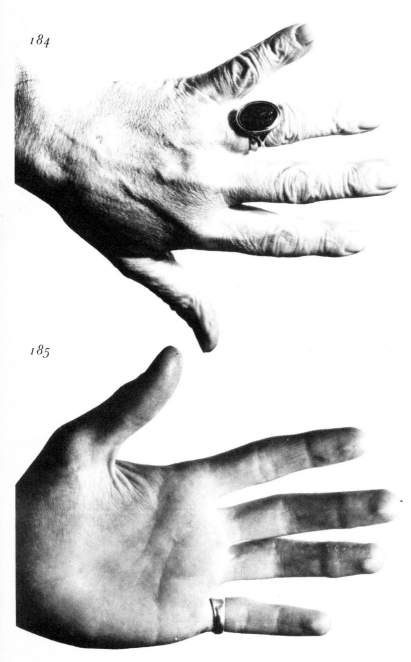

an audience, and an inadequate sense of responsibility, so that the native may be given to exaggeration or to lying. Such a Mercury will take freely from others, the 'communication' being a one way business. In palmistry a Mercury that is not well-integrated into the hand points similarly to a weakness in the ability to communicate – mental dishonesty, or the deceit of the confidence-trickster. A tendency to steal ideas or to act irresponsibly or coldly towards others is always indicated in a palm which shows a badly-integrated Mercury.

This may be understood when the Mercury of the finger is considered in relation to the sign Virgo, which Mercury rules. Virgo is essentially the sign of discrimination, and for this reason it sometimes gives the impression of being merely critical or faddy – however, it is really intellectual, and being relatively retiring it tends not to express its opinions strongly. Virgo has a very good memory and a clear mentality, which is why the finger of Mercury is generally considered as an index of memory powers. Virgo tends to use the head, the intellect, at the expense of the emotions – it is reluctant to throw itself physically into relationships, whereas the opposite sign Scorpio, which rules the ring finger, is only too ready to do so. The type often prefers ideals to realities – for this reason it is fond of literature and the arts, which once more brings us back to the traditional palmistic interpretation of Mercury, for it was in the past supposed to be an index of 'love and literature and arts', which is, of course, more the domain of Venus and the Sun. When the Mercury of Virgo is under pressure, then there tends to be an even

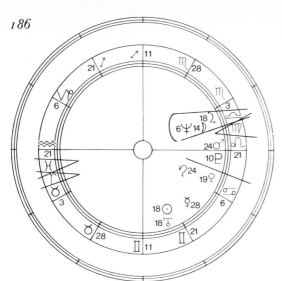

186. *Related hand and horoscope.*

187. *The strong Air quality of the horoscope is particularly noticeable, for there is a trine between the Ascendant, Sun and Uranus and Jupiter, with three other planets in Air signs. The hand is of the Air form, though the heavy and broken Girdle of Venus is not usually so evident: this finds a parallel in the square aspect thrown on to the Libran Jupiter by Venus and Saturn, which will excite the emotional life.*

187

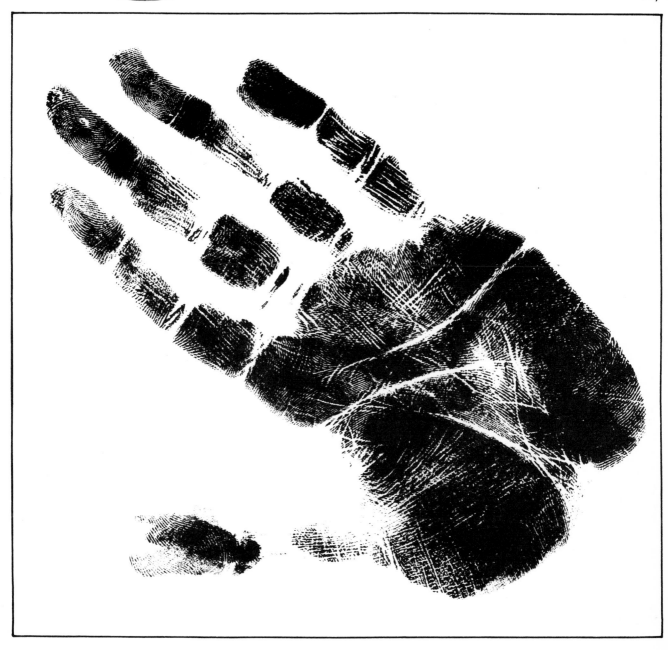

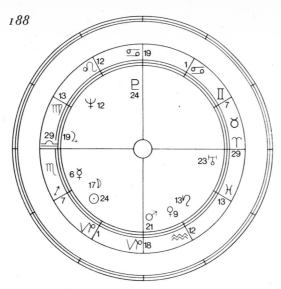

188. *Related hand and horoscope.*
190. *The hand is basically of the
Air type, though with the Fire
lines we might expect from the
horoscope. The two oppositions
between Jupiter and Uranus
and Pluto and Mars form a
cross, so that the figure
consists of square aspects close
to the angles. This is always*

more marked withdrawal of emotional response to life, and the personality becomes
cold and rather calculating, even downright
materialistic, reminding us that Virgo is an
Earth sign (see page 73). These characteristics are envinced in the case of a deficient
finger of Mercury.

Both the finger of Mercury and the finger
of Apollo are specifically linked with the way
in which the subject deals with other people,
as would be expected from the part of the
hand which relates to the inner personal side
of the nature. This quarter of the hand is
clearly linked with the Air aspect of the personality, with communication: Mars as the
ruler of the ring finger represents the outer
drive towards people, Mercury the inner
control, the restraining factor, which is
necessary for the fruition of relationships – it
is significant that the sign Libra, in which the
drive of the Sun and Venus reconciles the
force of Scorpio and Virgo, is itself an Air
sign.

Standing sentinel between Fire and Air,
between that part of the hand which deals
with self-assertion, and that part of the hand
which deals with the ability to relate to
others, is that strange finger of Saturn, sometimes called by palmists the finger of balance,
sometimes the finger of Fate. In astrology
Saturn is the planet of limitations, and in
Ptolemaic astrology it was the outermost
planet in the solar system, marking the outer
limit of universal form, which found its
correspondence in the human skeleton,
marking and supporting the form of material
man. The rule of Saturn is not exclusively
concerned with outer limits and restrictions,
but also with inner limitations, which means

that on a physical level one may study the
planet in a horoscope, by sign and aspect, in
order to determine the underlying fears and
inadequacies of the subject. Saturn marks
that which is lacking in a personality, as well
as the ability of the native to create a balance
from the conflicting drives and urges within
the personality: his ability to impose form on
his inner drives. When strongly placed in a
horoscope, it limits the personality, makes
for a conservative attitude and renders the
native both cautious and circumscribed.

Saturn rules Capricorn, with which this
finger is associated, and Capricorn is pre-
eminently the sign of control. It wishes for
precise self-control as well as for control over
others: this is why it is regarded as such an
ambitious sign, and perhaps why it has an
unfortunate reputation in the zodiac, for
most people prefer to go their own way, and
do not seek to be controlled by others –
especially by the dry and rather slow Capricornian nature. The attitude of most people
to bureaucracy is reflective of this truth, for
all bureaucracy is ruled by Capricorn. The
planet Saturn, as well as the finger of Saturn,
have a rather gloomy association which
colours our understanding of the roles which
this planet and finger play in our lives.
Saturn is certainly the yoke, but it is a yoke
which cannot be thrown off; it may be
removed only with effort and with patience.
This is perhaps why the finger has been so
often called the 'finger of Fate'. We have
such a misguided image of self, of human
nature, that we object to the idea of fate, of
higher forces controlling us. We reject the
concept, even when we subscribe to the idea
of fate in its *karmic* sense, in the sense that we

significant of difficulties in life
which the spirit must struggle
to overcome.

189. The finger of Apollo shows
what may be regarded as a
'budding' whorl. This
indicates a strong wish for
creative expression, though it is
one which does not manifest
so easily as the pure whorl.

190

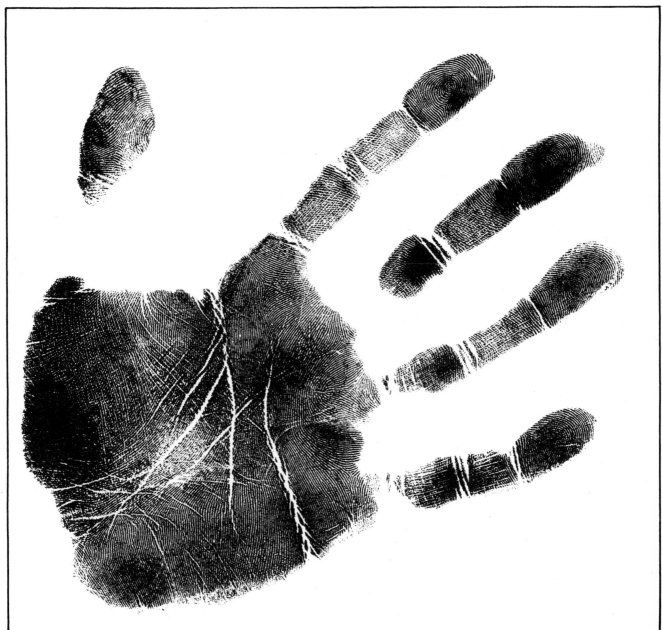

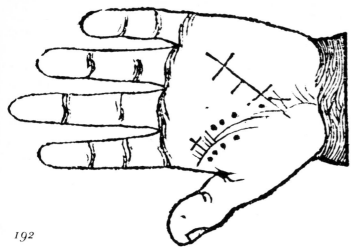

If you find a croſſe in this ſoꝛt about the ʋpper coꝛner, pꝛocedinge oute of the line of life, and on the nether ſide, thꝛee ſmal lines, and on thupper.ſide two, as you may ſe by this figure, it ſigniſieth a libidinouſe and an ʋnſhamfaſt woman. But if the thꝛe lines be found in the ne-ther ende of the line of lyfe towarde the

192

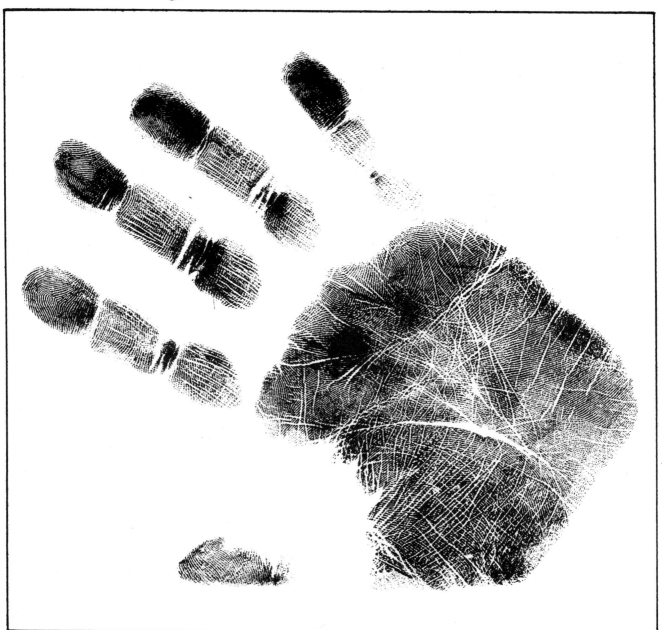

192. *Such ideas as the one expressed here have greatly influenced the concepts of popular palmistry. The hand below (figure 192) does contain such 'small lines' as the one Indagine discusses, but there is no trace of a libidinous nature about the female concerned. Such a nature would have been detected in the plain of Libra, rather than in the Life line.*

193. *Saturn. In popular astrology the most evil of forces, but in spiritual astrology the reservoir of order and memory, highly beneficent to mankind.*

193

De Saturno domino genituræ.

must pay, either in this life or in some future life, for all our mistakes. We are, in fact, objecting merely to the idea of justice, for which we scream when we ourselves are subject to injustice, but which we reject when we ourselves are the perpetrators of injustice. Capricorn, and the finger of Saturn, should be seen as ruling fate in this sense, and in this light it becomes an extremely important finger: we sense this when we look at the hand, for the other fingers gather in to it, and it marks the highest point in the hand, just as the M.C. (ruled by Saturn) marks the highest point in the ecliptic. Our life drives revolve around Saturn, around the planet of justice, and it is only the *self* of the Martian thumb which stands apart from Saturn, seeking to assert itself. There is a deep significance to be realized from such considerations of the structure of the hand, and in this case we may say that human alienation (the thumb) is due to a misunderstanding of the nature of Man and cosmic justice. If we understand this aright we would see that justice is a necessity, for crime can be at best merely a temporary expedient.

In palmistry Saturn is studied to assess the general 'balance' of the native and it is significant that the finger should stand between the two areas of expression, for Saturn itself marks limitations and boundaries. When badly placed it deepens the sense of limitation of self, making the native despondent, heavy and slow. Saturn demands effort, and an emphasised finger of Saturn suggests that the native will have a strong sense of duty and self-control, demanding effort not only from himself, but also from other people: in a word, he will have an inherent sense of

justice. It is characteristic of gloomy Saturn that such effort will be made without joy: everything about Saturn is heavy. A weak finger of Saturn will lessen the sense of responsibility so that the personality may be feckless, and unable to balance or concert the externalized energies to any purpose. Saturn normally requires a purpose for everything, however long-term that purpose may be, and a weak finger of Saturn implies either an entire lack of purpose, or a personality which is satisfied with a series of short term aims. There is no structure satisfactory to the life of such a personality: Saturn stands alone and for his Earthy nature, aloof from the four elements which circle the hand. It is typical of Saturn to stand apart, mediating or separating, in order to lend structure and coherence to form.

The outer and lower part of the hand is dominated by the Mount of Venus which we have to a certain extent examined. In astrology Venus is a planet of harmony, the planet one examines in order to tell how well, and with what types of people, the native will get on. The highest expression to which Venusian energies can give external expression is through love. Love of this kind is softer, and altogether more idealistic, than the selfish love of Mars, and we may presume that Venusian love has an element of unselfishness about it which is foreign to the sexual love of Mars. Mars can pioneer and organize, it demands and will rarely create, but Venus will give, and often enjoys creating. Mars prefers to stand alone, Venus prefers to work with another or with others – from this we may see why the

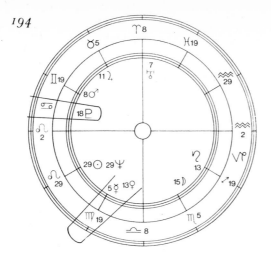

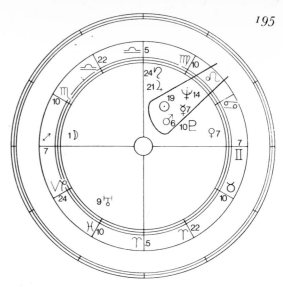

thumb, rooted in Venus and expressing itself through Mars, stands apart from the hand, and yet is so strong an index of power, and why the quality of the thumb marks the quality of being. We may see also, from this part of the hand, why sexual energies and love energies are so frequently intermixed in human affairs. What begins as love often finishes up as sex, though the energies rarely work in the other direction, so that it is virtually impossible for a relationship beginning with sex to end up as love: energies tend to run outwards, from the palm, through the fingers: this is why love (Venus) manifests itself most completely through sex (Mars). The self of Mars is concerned exclusively with projecting self, while the self of Venus is concerned with the opposite person and with co-operation. A strong Venus in a chart makes the native refined, fond of the arts and tends to make for general harmony of being; a badly placed Venus tends to look to others for support, and makes the native lazy or evasive. In palmistry there can be no doubt that the fount of Venusian energies may be found in the large root of the thumb, the Mount of Venus, which is the reservoir of energies for expression of the self, either in its refined sense of artistic creation or enjoyment through the sexual act. Clearly, this part of the hand is linked with the Earth element in the human being.

The lower and inner part of the hand is, according to the tradition, largely occupied by the Mount of Moon, and since it links specifically with the subconscious of Man, it is in itself more the domain of the sensitive and Watery Moon, as well as linking with

Neptune, a planet which was presumably unknown to the ancients who drew up the planetary associations in palmistry. When Neptune is emphasised in a chart (particularly when it is on an angle – figure 201) it sensitizes the personality and opens it to deep creativity, especially in the field of music and poetry. When it is emphasised, yet under pressure, the native will be sensitive yet lacking in creative purpose, which is why so often nowadays such a placing results in a personality who takes drugs or excessive alcohol. It is a very deceptive and insidious force, for its influence is to open the native to experience and desires for experiences, which he is not capable of integrating into his normal life. The danger of drug-taking is a very real one, for it opens the consciousness up to experiences which it is not capable of integrating into life experiences. Few human human beings are sufficiently developed to take drugs without the possibility of extensively damaging the spirit, and thereby piling up an enormous *karmic* debt. Such considerations as these may be studied in the Mount of Moon. The palmist assesses the underlying sensitivity of the native from this part of the hand, and is able to determine the degree to which the sensitivity is utilized and integrated into the life of the native, as well as the degree to which it remains separate from normal life, and is therefore potentially dangerous. A long, low-set Mount of Moon (figure 202) is always an indication of a high power of imagination, just as a line of Head which sinks into the Mount (figure 200) is indicative of an over-fertile imagination, which sometimes finds expression in lying or exaggeration. Whether this force is used in

194. *The horoscope of a modern musical genius. Note the proximity of Uranus to the M.C.*

195. *The Moon on the Ascendant is extremely powerful, in terms of the sign it occupies – in this case the subject will be strongly Sagittarian.*

196. *The hand of an Indian deity.*

197. *Frequently such hands are stylized both in form and linear structure, to indicate their non-human qualities. In the case illustrated we see an interesting division which hints at the one arrived at when the four elements of astrology are traced in the hands (see figure 136).*

197

some creative endeavour, or whether it disrupts the life of the native, must be determined from the hand as a whole. One may see how the tradition in palmistry, which links this area with imagination and sensitivity, is in accord with the elemental division of the hand. Lines running into or across the Mount of Moon must be regarded as tapping the strong forces of imagination. Whether such direct contact with subconscious reservoirs is used creatively or auto-destructively must be determined mainly from a study of the area of Libra. This part of the hand is linked with the Water element in the human personality (see page 86).

The division of the hand into four quarters, with the mediating central line of Saturn, finds a curious parallel in the hand markings commonly drawn of the hands of Buddhas and Indian gods (figure 197). Perhaps these markings carefully avoid the actual linear structure of normal human hands precisely because these are the hands of gods who are not themselves subject to the workings of fate. This strange idea, that the pattern adopted should so fundamentally reflect the fourfold division, links with astrological theory through hinting at the four angles. Applying the system of the four elements to these symbolic palms, along the same lines as diagram 136, it is seen that the topmost outer links with Fire, the topmost inner with Air, the lower inner with Water, and the lower outer with Earth. Unlike the areas on the human hand, these divisions create areas which are approximately equal, and this is in itself significant. According to the occult tradition, before the Fall of Man

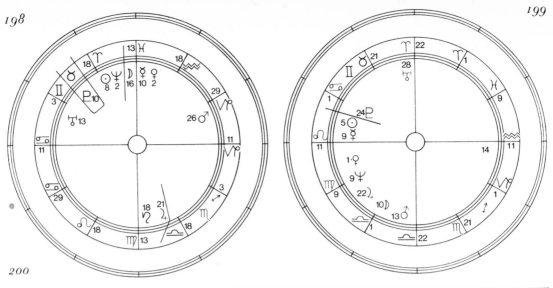

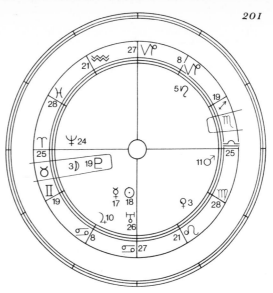

198– Of the three horoscopes and two
202. *hand prints on this page only*
one print corresponds to one
horoscope. The reader should by
now have sufficient knowledge
of astropalmistry to determine
which set corresponds. The
answer will be found on
page 168, where the hand and
horoscope are discussed.

The answer will be found on page 168

202

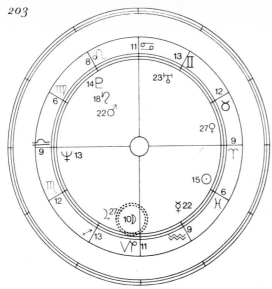

203. *A Moon isolated in Capricorn. The figure is discussed below.*
204. *A strong Fire hand, with the*
206. *typical Air posture of open fingers. The powerful trine aspect between Sun, as seen in this chart, is often manifest through a strong line of Saturn, expressive of self-confidence and a sense of purpose.*
205. *The fingerprints taken from the hand below, showing the influence of Air.*

there was neither sickness nor unhappiness, because the four elements in Man were perfectly balanced. Since the Fall, no one save the gods has had a harmonious relationship of elements within his structure, with the result that every person has a predisposition towards a particular illness or vice – and everyone is off-balance, so to speak. It could be that the Indian linear technique hints that the structure of the hand itself may be the index of the particular harmony in all sublunary creatures!

The basic mistake most palmists or astrologers have made in the past, in attempting to relate the form or structure of the hand with astrology, is when they have assumed that the traditional associations linked with the parts of the hand find a strict correspondence in the natal chart. They have assumed for example, that the associations of Jupiter with the index finger (figure 203) would link directly with the planet Jupiter in the natal chart, in terms of its sign or house placing, or the aspects to it: they have assumed that Jupiter in the natal chart would be reflected in the finger of Jupiter. This is evidently not so: for example, one may find Jupiter in a Fire sign (as seen in chart 205), well aspected from a planet in another Fire sign, and yet the finger of Jupiter of the native may have a papillary ridge pattern which in no way reflects a Fire tendency (as in figure 192). The fact is that the relationships between the hand and the natal chart is not of a strict linear kind but more of a qualitative kind. For example, with particular reference to the index finger, one may find that this finger may itself evince characteristics which do not link in any clear

way with the rest of the hand, and one may take this itself as indicating that Jupiter, the power of expansion in the personality (see page 110), is in some way alienated in the native, and this alienation will be evident in the natal chart. For example, the hand at figure 192 is obviously of a Fire form but with a Water line structure – one is therefore surprised to find that the finger of Jupiter is clearly of an Earth quality. We must consider this area of the temperament, which rules expansion and the ability to deal with the world (the finger of Jupiter), to be inadequately expressed: it must somehow block the Fire/Air energies, and prevent their free expression. This would imply that the native will have difficulties in asserting her personality in life, because the underlying energies of Fire, rising in an Air nature, will obviously not be able to express themselves naturally in the outer world through the Earth element. The corresponding chart (figure 203) bears this assumption out, for the Ascendant is Libra, there is a planet in each of the Air signs and there is also a planet in each of the Fire signs, thus reflecting the basic Air/Fire polarity of the hand itself. Significantly, we note that the Moon, expressive of personality, stands alone in Capricorn, which is a placing traditionally linked with a cold, cautious, suspicious personality, which we would in no way associate with a Fire/Air personality. This Moon placing accounts for the fact that the finger of Jupiter, which is an index of how the person relates to the world – the finger of ambition – is distinguished from the rest of the hand.

This chart is particularly interesting for it

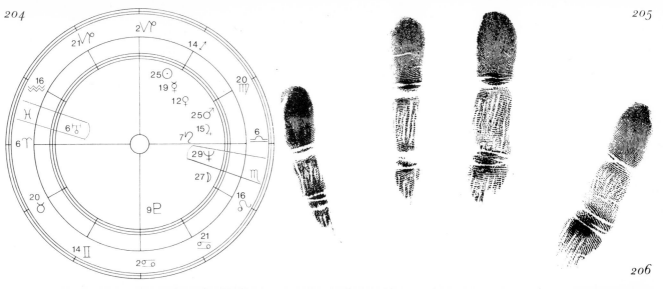

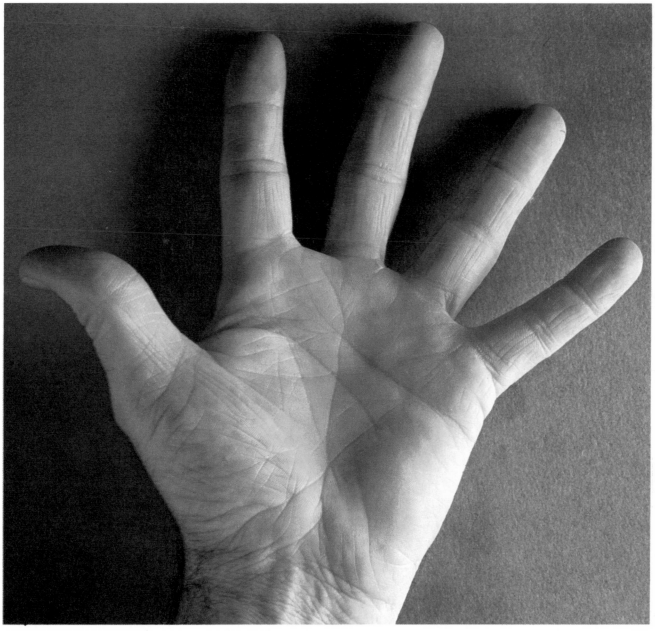

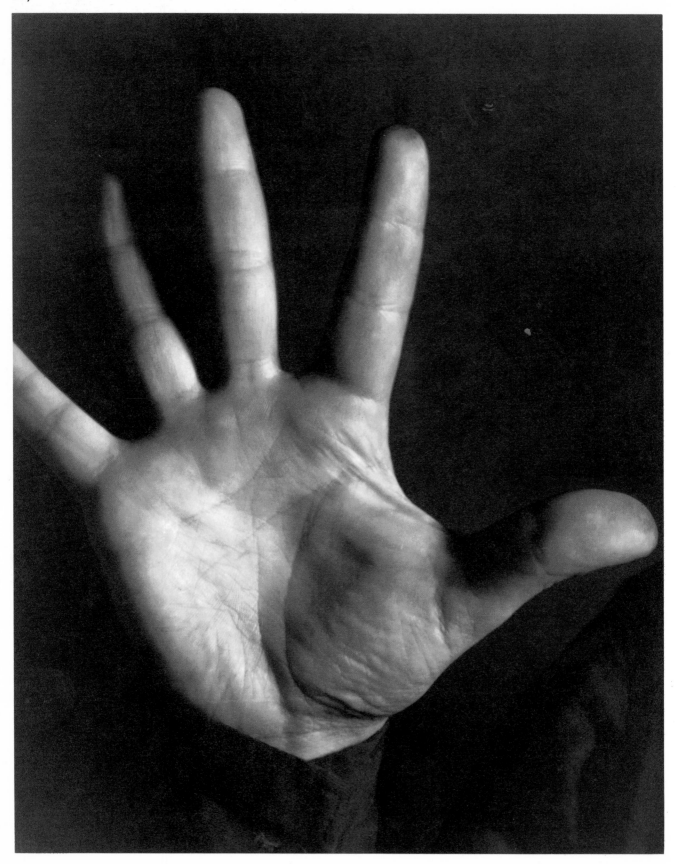

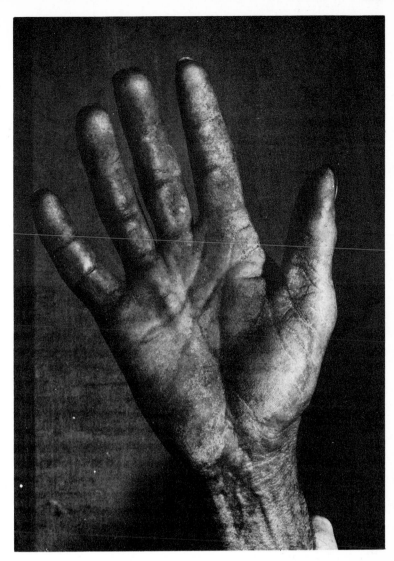

207. The hand and horoscope of an
209. Italian university professor,
      discussed in the text at page
208. The hand of an Italian
      peasant, discussed in the text at
      page 163.

demonstrates precisely the absence of a linear connection between the planet Jupiter and the finger Jupiter, for in the natal chart Jupiter is in a Fire sign, and is very well fortified by an exact trine with the beneficent Venus. This leads one to expect that the power of expansion will be expressed harmoniously, in an ardent (Fire) manner, in such a way as to benefit the social standing and disposition of the native, making her genial, friendly, attractive and popular, particularly in regard to relationships. The placing and fortunate aspect, when viewed alongside the Capricornian Moon, would suggest that the native will get on well and harmoniously with others (through the domain of the finger of Mercury, in fact), but she will have difficulties in expressing herself in ordinary life, will feel inadequate, and will be constantly frustrated in her ambitions. This is because her hopes, wishes and drives are of the Fire/Air polarity, but she will manifest them (save to intimates) through a discordant Earth. A classical reading of the conflict would be, 'feels good with other people, but cannot cope alone'. Here then we have an excellent support for the contention that the chart and the horoscope do correspond when related to subject, and even a simple analysis shows a strict relationship between chart and hand, but the relationship must be expressed in terms of energy flows, blockages or outlets, and not in terms of a strict traditional cross-correspondence between planets and palm-area associations. The diagram at figure 218, and not the traditional associations of planets with parts of the hand, must form the mediator between the palm and horoscope.

209

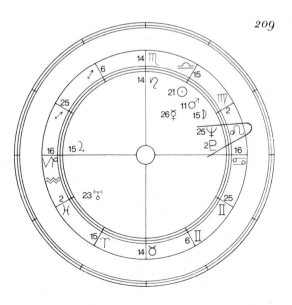

210. *The arch pattern, which has no triangular formation to join it to the finger base.*

211. *Arch patterns on all fingers are indicative of strong Earth qualities in the personality.*

The Finger Patterns

210

211

Each of the finger patterns is distinctly different, even on fingers on the same hand. It is possible to say that there are as many finger patterns as there are people and fingers, but there are in fact only three basic types of pattern. These are the arch, the whorl and the loop.*

The simplest pattern formation is called the arch, and this is distinguished by a series of almost parallel lines running across the finger, rising in a gentle swelling at the centre which eventually merges with the structure of the finger and itself (figure 210). This is the most elementary of the formations and, although it relates specifically to the Earth nature, from an astrological point of view it is best to think of it as denoting fixity (see page 189), for it suggests a rigidity and a rather coarse physical energy in association with the finger upon which it is found. It is significant, in view of what was said about the triad of palmistry, that the arch itself, while not commonly found, appears most frequently on the finger of Jupiter, where it is always indicative of a strong materialistic strain in the personality, suggesting that the native will enjoy good food, and strong physical involvements at the expense of the spirit. If one thinks of astrological fixity in terms of its personalized expression one sees that it is indicative of stubbornness and a certain emotional slowness. Just as the fixed Earth of the Taurean Bull is not easily goaded into action, but once pushed beyond endurance will become rebellious and even violent, so is fixity slow to gather momentum, but once driven to action becomes ruthless and terrible: the fixity will slowly, under certain circumstances, change its nature to

*See glossary, p. 182.

*212. The whorl pattern, balanced on
two triangular formations
which join it to the finger base.*

*213. Whorl patterns on all fingers
are indicative of strong Fire
qualities in the personality.
The type is usually creative.*

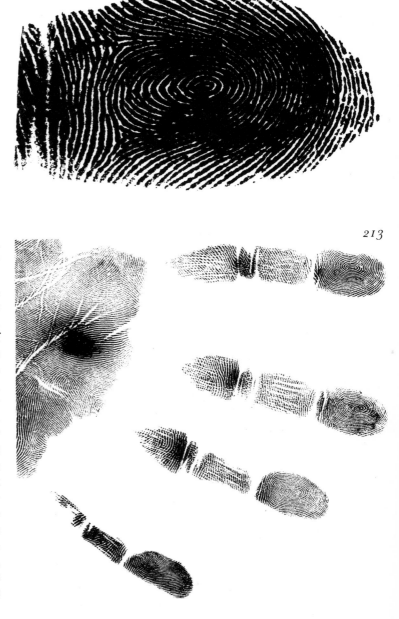

212

213

cardinality in which it resembles volcanic action. It is helpful to picture the arch as representing a volcano holding down the pent up furies of magmatic forces which are best left in the earth. The arch is repressive as a force. The astrological associations with Earth, with fixity and with their characteristics, as set out on pages 187 and 189, must be considered afresh if the arch is to be correctly understood.

The most complex pattern is called the whorl, and this is distinguished by a series of concentric circles or ellipses which fill the entire finger end, and are supported at the base of the first phalange by two triadii (see figure 346). The arch pattern is rooted in the base of the phalange, while the whorl gives the appearance of being almost free from the base, as if it were a free force revolving in its own dynamic energy, forming a cosmic spiral of its own. This is a reasonable image when one considers that this pattern is a sign of cardinality, which is descriptive of 'pure movement' (page 186). It is pictured as an arrow pointing upwards, cardinality putting emphasis on the active, purposive and restless. It is best to think of it as a tendency to dominate others and the external world in terms of the associations with the finger upon which it is found. The arch inclines to violence through its restraining fixity; the whorl inclines to crime of a non-violent type through its impetuousness and restlessness, for it projects the personality into situations where restraint would be more satisfactory for survival. In a hand which shows no particular indication of criminality, the appearance of whorls on all of the fingers and even on the thumb itself is

214

*214. The loop pattern, which has
one triangular formation to join
it to the finger base.*
*215. Loop patterns on all fingers are
indicative of a strong Air
quality in the personality.*
216. This is a difficult hand to
*217. evaluate on first analysis, as it
is clearly strongly Air in form,
though the purity of this form is
marred by the raised area*

215

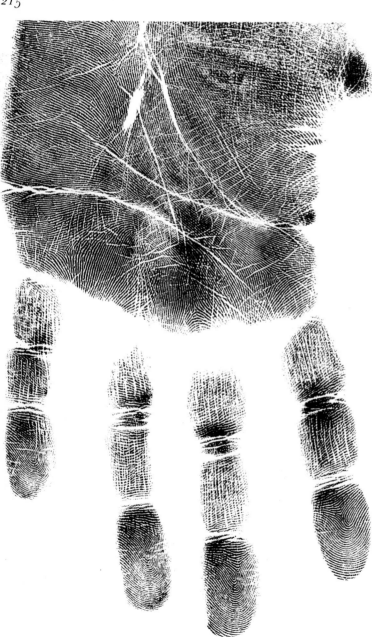

usually a sign of creativity as well as of great restlessness. Considering astrological cardinality in this context one sees that it is indicative of a restless and highly complex nature, and the relevant finger may be thought of as highly personalized and particularly sensitive in the area it rules. The individualism expressed by the whorl pattern tends to render the native sensitive to his own needs, though surprisingly insensitive to the needs of others: if the arch may be called repressive, then the whorl may be called selfish.

The third formation is called the loop and this is by far the most common of finger patterns, being distinguished by a series of parallel loop lines which rear over a single triadus (figure 346), the general contour of the loop filling the phalange completely. It is normal for palmists to distinguish radial loops from ulnar loops, but for the purpose of our present enquiry this is not necessary. The loop represents the quality of mutability (see page 34). The keywords given for the loop are 'clear spirited, cool and reflective in judgement, cool and restrained in expression', all words applicable to a force which is a product of fixity and cardinality. The first impression that one gets from a hand with many loops on the fingers is a sense of balance and right timing. Enthusiasms are slow to develop and are rarely clung to tenaciously. The loop falls between the two extremes of fixity and cardinality and is coloured largely by the reconciling quality of Air. Mutability puts the emphasis on thought and is flexible, unreliable and changeable. It is not surprising that one most frequently finds it on Air hands.

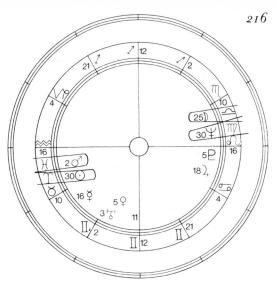

beneath the fingers of Jupiter and Saturn. Also, the lines are strongly Fire. The basic Air form, and the Air finger patterns, are reflected in the Aquarian Ascendant and in the distribution of planets in Gemini and Libra, whilst the Fire lines are reflected through Sun, Pluto and M.C.

217

*Schema of zodiacal
distribution throughout the
hand.*

218

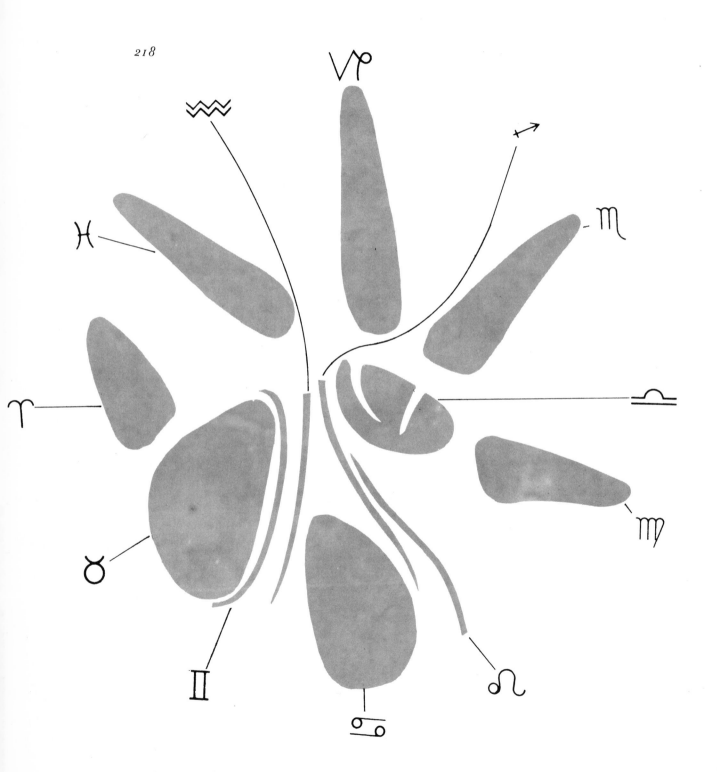

The Lines

Ideally there is a distinct relationship between the form of the hand and the palmar markings; for example, it is reasonable to expect that a hand with a long palm and short fingers, being a Fire hand, should have lines of a Fire quality. The four palm prints at figures 102, 106, 114 and 124 set out palms representative of the four elements. This does not mean that all Fire hands have Fire lines, and indeed, the conflict between the structure of the hand and the palmar surface is itself often of considerable value in attempting to ascertain the basic conflicts in the personality. Just as one might say that a basic conflict or harmony in personality may be studied by comparing the Ascendant with the Sun placing, so may a similar discord or harmony be ascertained from a simple comparison between the form of the hand and its linear markings.

The most important characteristic of line markings is the overall quality, the general feeling of the palm as a whole, for this sets the general quality of the person's relationship to life, the degree to which he acts upon life or is acted upon by life. The individual lines represent distinct drives and energies, and it is advisable to think of the lines as conductors of energies from one part of the hand to another.

There have been many attempts in the past to link the palmar zones, the fingers and the lines with the signs of the zodiac or the planets, ranging from the absurd and useless methods of Belot (figure 8) to the relatively simple methods of Muchery (figure 67). My own experience has shown that the only valid relationship between the zodiac and the hand formation may be presented along the lines of the diagram at figure 157, which sets out the relationships between the palmar zones, the lines and the fingers, showing the correspondence between these three elements and throwing light on their natures in terms of the zodiacal associations.

The purpose of the diagram is to enable us to see how the hand may be reduced to a series of zones (figure 155) and lines (figure 154) which link directly with the traditional zodiac (figure 157). The step-by-step reduction of a palm (figure 156) to its zodiacal constituents is set out at figure 218. The lines of Life and Fate are situated in the passive half of the hand, while the lines of Heart and Head are in the active part (figure 136). It is significant that the first two are governed by Air signs and the latter two by Fire signs, and these are on opposite sides of the zodiac. The so-called 'modern' planets have been excluded from the figures – this is mainly because palmistry has never been sufficiently 'modernized' to account convincingly for these modern planets in relation to the hand, and also because the traditional rulers must be used if one wishes to establish a valid connection between traditional palmistry and traditional astrology. Thus the ancient tradition is followed, giving Mars rulership over Scorpio, Saturn rulership over Aquarius, and Jupiter rulership over Pisces (figure 218). With these rulerships we find that the hand is indeed a small model of the zodiac, which is itself an image of Man.

The diagram casts aside almost all the traditional systems which attempt to correlate astrology and palmistry, yet it presents a simple relationship between the hand form and the zodiac which is very practical: the

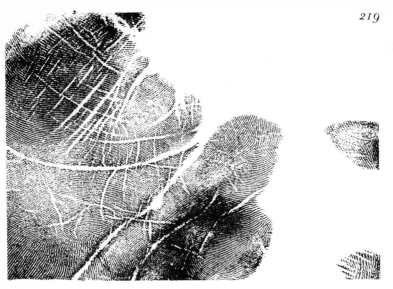

219. *The Life line starting below the line of Head, but not separated from it. This is a healthy commencement, as it creates a balance between Venus and Jupiter in terms of the triad of palmistry.*

220. *A graphic explanation as to why Mercury, as ruler of Gemini, should separate the two eminences of Venus and Moon.*

220

diagram is in fact a useful 'philosophical machine' by which one may apply one's knowledge of astrology to the understanding of palmistry, or one's understanding of palmistry to astrology, in order to revitalize either or both.

The rulership of Mars over the thumb, and of Jupiter over the Mount of Venus, have already been discussed (page 78). Mars embodies the power to dominate and to lead, and is represented by the Arietan thumb. Venus embodies the power of attachments and love, in this case to the materiality of the Taurean world, and is represented by the traditional Mount of Venus. The Mount adjacent to this has always been traditionally called the Mount of Moon, and of course the Moon has sole rule over the sensitive Cancer which, in its position at the very bottom of the zodiacal plan, is clearly the domain of the subconscious, of what palmists insisted upon calling the world of imagination. Separating the Mount of Venus from the Mount of Moon (figure 220) we find the Life line which is governed by the dual sign Gemini. The glyph for Gemini is supposed by some to represent two columns, one for materiality, the other for spirituality, symbolizing the Geminian caught between matter and spirit. Insofar as everyone is a spirit living in a body, everyone partakes of the Geminian dilemma; perhaps this is why the ancients said that the dilemma* had horns, for Mercury (which rules the life force of Gemini) certainly does appear to have horns.

In the zodiac Gemini separates the sensuous Venus from the sensitivity of Cancer, and it performs the same function in the

*Literally a *lemma* is 'something taken for granted'; a dilemma is two things which are taken for granted – in our example, the two worlds of the spirit and the material, which everyone must choose between. There must be a loss, for one needs the body as well as the spirit to conduct life with dignity. This is the predicament of Gemini, and of the line it rules.

221. A line of Life which commences above the line of Head must be regarded as reaching out for the Jupiterian energies of the spiritualized Pisces. For this reason the type tends to be ambitious – usually in a material sense, since energies are being pulled down towards Gemini.

hand. The Geminian Life line encloses the Mount of Venus (with all the implications considered at page 109) and yet at the same time links this materialistic Venus, this fount of energy, with the subconscious represented by the sensitive Moon and Cancer. All life energies, as represented by the Life line, spring from a meeting between an attraction towards life in its material phase (Taurus) and the subconscious attraction to the inner world (Cancer). The quality of the Life line may be considered, in theoretical terms at least, as representing the relationship in the native between the outer and inner worlds. By definition he belongs to both, and if he indulges in one at the expense of the other, then he loses his balance as a human being. It is essentially to this quality of balance that the line of Life refers. The line is an extremely useful index of the considerations noted in connection with the triad of the hand on page 106. The line may be looked at on two levels: first in relation to the traditional palmistic interpretations of the line, then in relation to the zodiacal associations set out in figure 218.

It is often said that the length of the line of Life gives an indication of the qualities of the subject's physical energies. In some books on 'popular' palmistry it is even claimed that the length of the line is an indication of the length of life, which is rabid nonsense. In fact the line reveals the conflict between the Venusian energy of Taurus on the one side, and the sensitive lunar energy of Cancer on the other; in this sense it may be considered as linking with the physical energy of the subject. A long line of Life, broad and stable in appearance, is representative of a healthy

relationship between the attraction to the physical and the attraction to the inner world. This is why in traditional palmistry a chained line of Life, or one which is weak in any way, is always regarded as a sign either of physical debility or of vacillation, and of an inability to either come to decisions or put decisions into effect – this is the result of a lack of balance between the inner and the outer worlds, suggesting that the subject confuses the things of spirit with the things of matter, and is consequently at a loss in dealing with the world. One outcome of this is a general impression of inertia, which would of course lead to the idea that the subject is lacking in physical energy.

When the line of Life starts fairly high on the hand (as in figure 221) then it is clearly tapping at source the expansive energy of Jupiter. This naturally means that there is a strong ambitious drive, in that the native wishes his successes and achievements in life to be observed: he is constantly performing to some audience imaginary or real. There is sometimes a line, running down the Mount of Jupiter and into the beginning of the Life line (figure 225), called by some modern palmists the 'line of ambition'. This affords the same interpretation, for it is an adjunct to the Life line, connecting the expansive Jupiter to the lively and changeable Mercury of the Geminian Life line. How the ambitions will manifest themselves, whether spiritually or materially, and how far the subject is successful in achieving his ambitions, must be determined from a study of the quality of the Geminian line of Life, and the relative strength of the two zones it separates.

Sometimes the Head line is inserted into

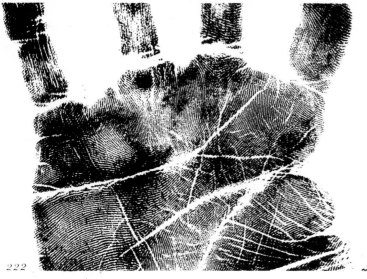

222

222. *A chained commencement for line of Life mingles the Fire nature of Sagittarius with the Geminian life force, usually giving rise to exuberance. It also gives a strong intellect.*

223. *A wide separation between the insertion of the line of Life and Head tends to weaken the intellect. In the example here the forces behind the emotional life are very strong however.*

223

the origin of the Life line, which in astrological terms means that the Fire ambition of Sagittarius (figure 222) is mingled with the Geminian life force. This tends to emphasise the intellectuality as well as the instability of the type, for both Sagittarius and Gemini require constant change, variety and excitement to recharge their energies and ambitions. When the line of Life terminates on the Mount of Moon there is a predisposition for the Geminian energies to fritter themselves away in unreal fantasies, unrelated to the basic materiality and practicality of the Taurean Mount of Venus. The dual Gemini in the astrological tradition has a strong materialistic strain (represented in palmistry by the Mount of Venus) and a strong spiritual strain (represented in palmistry by the Mount of Moon). Any imbalance in Gemini is therefore particularly noticeable. A thoroughly materialistic Geminian is a nasty piece of work, since he has all the resources of a fine intellect and splendid energies associated with a Mercury ruler, and yet none of the sense of responsibility and restraint which an awareness of spiritual values brings. This dichotomy, which is inherent in the life of everyone, may be studied in the Life line which is governed by Gemini. It is perhaps no accident that the symbol for Mercury, which rules over the dual Gemini, is composed of the sign for Venus, topped with a half circle which symbolizes the Moon in a position to carry spiritual energies (figure 220).

Between the Mount of Moon and the finger of Mercury, which in the association chart (figure 218) is ruled by Virgo, is the insertion of the line of Heart. In traditional

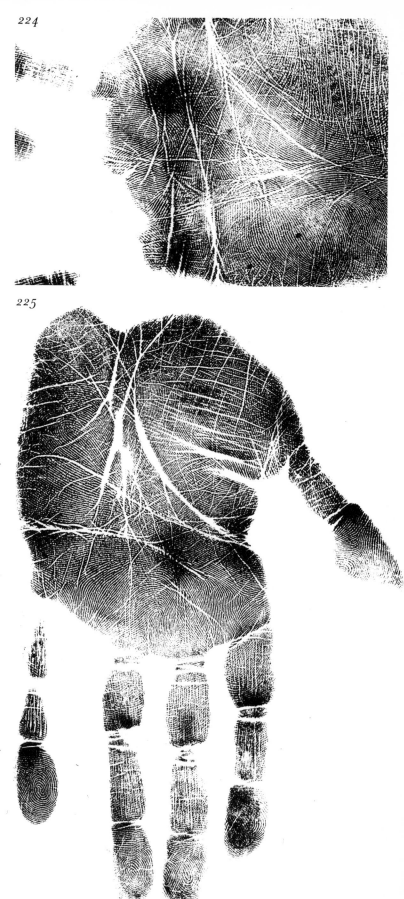

224. *In such a case of a close tie between Head and Life, in which an extremely strong Girdle, as well as a rather cold line of Heart are involved, one must presume that the emotions have virtual control over the intellect.*

225. *A well-balanced insertion of Head and Life, with a steady curve to the path of the line of Head indicate an excellent mentality. This is the hand of a woman author.*

225

palmistry this line is used for assessing the emotional calibre of the personality, and a study of its formation is made in order to understand his attitude towards sex and creativity. It is therefore a valid correspondence which links this line directly with the creative sign Leo and by association with the fifth house (page 25). It is significant that the the line runs across virtually the entire hand, thus separating the subconscious domain from the conscious, for it is in the act of creation and in the act of sexuality that the relationship between the subconscious and conscious is most clearly evident, in which the division between what is visible and what is invisible becomes of great importance. Creativity, and a creative attitude to life, is possible only when there is a harmony of working between the subconscious and conscious, for the conscious world gives material form to the potential energies in the subconscious. The line of Heart stands as a kind of sentinel between these two domains, and its course, structure, and termination determine the degree of creativity in its largest sense. In the diagram, below the line of Heart lies the domain of the Moon, the reservoir of subconscious forces, and immediately above the line is the finger of Mercury, ruled by Virgo, in which order and structure predominate (page 34). The diagram therefore reflects something of the nature of the creative act, for the creative activity is a matter of giving form and external structure to undifferentiated subconscious drives.

Sex energies are obviously linked with artistic creativity, and find their most healthy manifestations when the line is

226

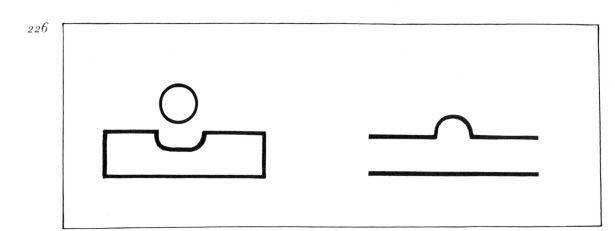

227

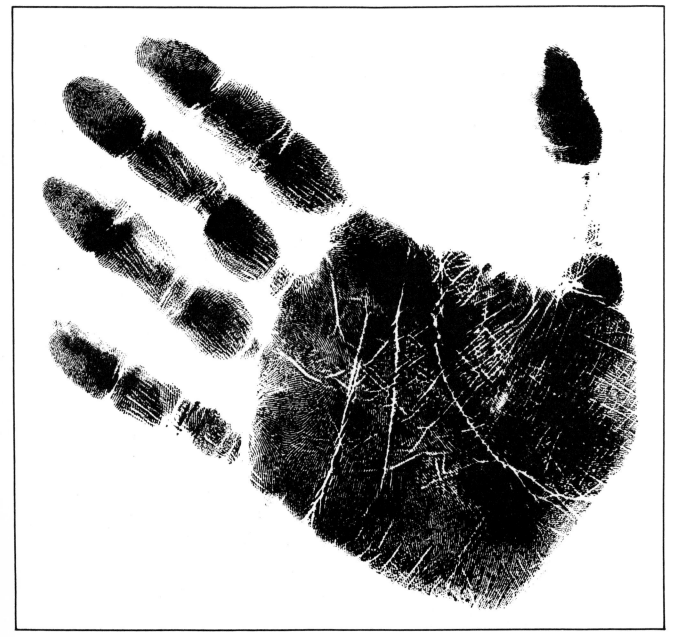

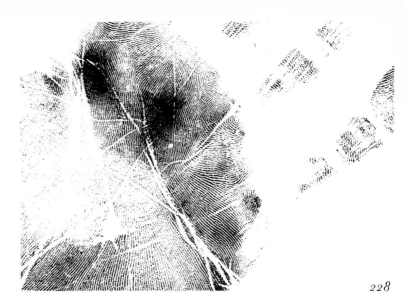

226. *The evolution of the sigil for Libra from the Egyptian image of the Sun setting into the Earth. The solar link, and the association with Venus (which rules the body – see figure 16) points to the validity of a Libran rule over Apollo and the Girdle.*

227. *An incipient Simian line, in the hair line which joins Heart and Head.*

228. *The Heart line reaches right across the hand, but it is the descending line joining Head and Heart which constitutes the Simian proper.*

228

steady and unchained, sweeping across the hand from below Mercury to terminate in a gentle curve on or around the Mount of Jupiter. Should the line sweep downwards and terminate on the Head line or on the line of Life, then the energies are being deflected: such a termination is usually found in a personality with a strong sense of insecurity. The curve upwards, towards the area of Jupiter, is a healthy sign, indicative of a wish to give emotional expression to self, of a wish to be warmly creative and to receive love, as one might expect of a line which links the domain of the Sun with the domain of Jupiter. It is significant of the nature of sex, which this line controls, that in sweeping across the hand it touches upon the mounts of all the main externalized planets, suggesting that the sexual energy permeates everything in human life. If the line does not curve upwards but runs straight across the hand, then this is indicative of a strong independence, since there is not the same Jupiterian contact, the same striving outwards to meet and make contact with other people. The other extreme, when the line of Heart sinks down at its termination to touch the line of Head or Life, indicates a distinct insecurity springing from an inability to relate to people in a harmonious way. It is important to distinguish such an example (figure 227) from the Simian line which is of an altogether different order (see page 147). In terms of the 'philosophical machine' at figure 169, we see that these three points of termination which indicate expansive relationships, independence and coldness may be understood in terms of the planetary nature of the area of termination. The termi-

nation on the Mount of Jupiter, which is also on Pisces, indicates a sensitive response to others (Water) and a wish to be expansive (Jupiter). A termination which links with the first house Mars indicates an Arietan wish to be independent, to stand alone yet powerful, as the thumb itself stands. A termination deeper down on the line of Life (figure 228) indicates an association with Gemini which is notorious in giving the impression of being cold and indifferent in emotional matters.

In between the finger of Mercury (the index of sexuality, work and attitude to money) and the neighbouring finger of Apollo (which in our system is ruled by the Mars of Scorpio, the sign which deals with passionate involvements and the deeper side of life), we find the area ruled by Libra (figure 162). The function of Libra is to reconcile the female (Virgo) and the male (Scorpio) principles, which is why the glyph for Libra looks a bit like an equals mark. In astropalmistry this Libran area marks out a similar conflict, or duality which requires reconciliation. On this area are two important common lines, one linked with creativity (traditionally called the line of Apollo) and the other linked with sexual relationship (traditionally called the Girdle of Venus). The two lines of the glyph for Libra (♎) may be seen as representative of these two palmar lines, for the glyph originated from an Egyptian drawing of the sun setting over the earth (figure   ): thus the solar energy of Apollo (the Sun) is related to the elements of the Earth itself (Venus). The two lines may usefully be studied separately, but it is important to recall that

229

229. A well-balanced Girdle and Apollo.

230. An extremely violent Girdle, which throws the subject emotionally off-balance.

231. A strong Girdle, though significant of a high-pitch emotional life, may often support an artistic temperament.

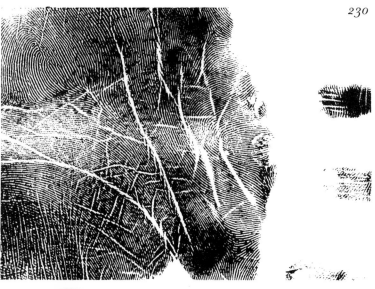

230

231

the equals sign of Libra requires that the two lines be integrated for a complete understanding of their combined influence in the domain of relationships.

The line of Apollo runs upwards, directly under the finger of Apollo (figure 233) and if strongly marked is taken in traditional palmistry as indicative of a creative urge, though not always of a creative ability. Any person with a strong line of Apollo would wish to be creative, usually in one of the more obvious art forms such as painting, literature or music. This line, which is vertical when the fingers are held skywards, may symbolize the creative upsurge of the spirit wishing to find correspondence in the spiritual spheres above. The line clearly corresponds to the solar disk in the original Libran glyph. It is interesting to observe the incredible length of the line of Apollo on the Fire hand of the great Victorian painter Sir Frederick Leighton, as it was preserved by Cheiro (figure 180): this line runs in a long sweep alongside the whole length of the Mount of Moon, suggesting a splendid reservoir of solar energies.

The Girdle of Venus, when clearly marked, starts between the finger of Jupiter and the finger of Saturn and usually terminates before it reaches the ascending line of Apollo (figure 229). Whilst the line of Apollo relates to spirituality, the Girdle of Venus relates to the material aspect of the creative urge, to the physical side of sex for example, which is why the traditional form of palmistry claims that a strong or long Girdle of Venus indicates great sensuality. To understand the hand in its Libran aspect, which is to understand the force of this equals sign

140

232. *A well-balanced Girdle and Apollo in the hand of an artist.*
233. *The hand of a well-known singer. Note the rich Girdle and Apollo.*

233

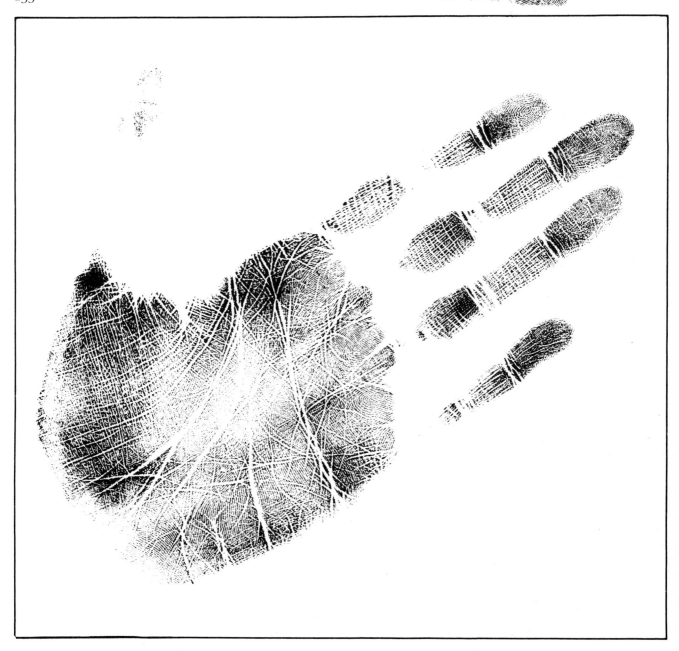

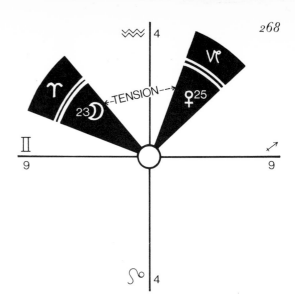

268

269

linking Virgo and Scorpio, we must attempt to balance the two lines of Apollo and Venus. If they are both strongly marked, if neither is deformed and provided they do not cross, then we can assume a healthy balance between the spiritual side of creativity and the material side. With specific regard to sex, we may assume that a hand with a Girdle and a line of Apollo, such as at figure 231, shows a strong wish to be creative and involved spiritually, balanced with a healthy physical appetite for the opposite sex. Absent, weak, vacillating or short lines in this Libran area will point to a deficiency in the field of relationships which Libra governs, and which between them Apollo and Venus represent. It is best if the lines do not cross, for the intersection of spirit and matter which is a human condition is really the subject of the entire hand. When they do cross, or when the line of Apollo has many horizontal subsidiary lines, or when Venus has many vertical subsidiary lines, then it is an indication that the energy represented by the line which is being dissected is not finding satisfactory fulfilment. For example, subsidiary vertical lines on the Girdle of Venus (plate 303) indicate that the physical side of life is being marred by an insufficient spiritual quality.

The line of Head is that line which runs below the Heart line in a normal hand (figure 96), linking in a gentle curve the materialism of the Life line with the domain of imagination, as represented by the Mount of Moon. In its direction, energy and function this line is directly linked with the Jupiterian sign Sagittarius, the symbol for which is an arrow carrying the cross of

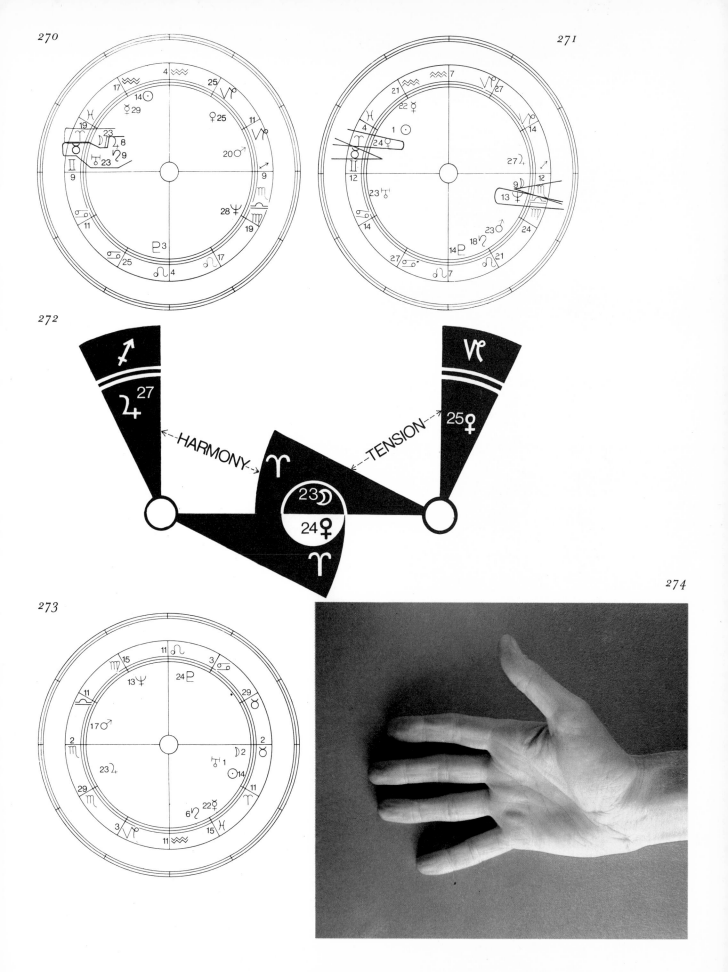

270

271

272

HARMONY

TENSION

273

274

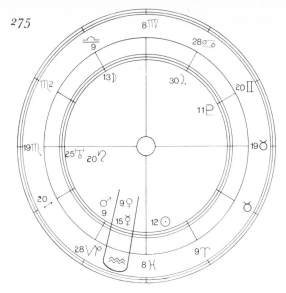

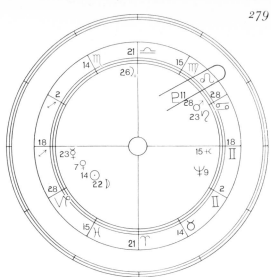

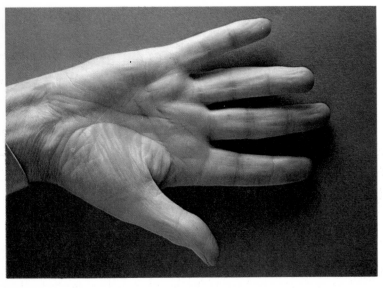

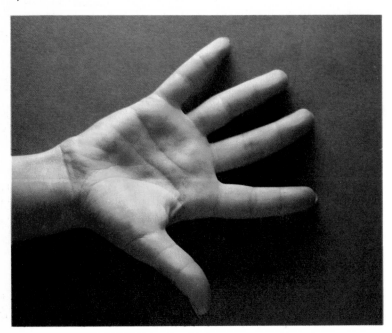

materiality (figure 21), and indicating the aspirational side of Man striving upwards into the spiritual world of ideas. To understand the real force of this important line of Head, in either its theoretical or practical aspects, it is necessary to examine the nature of Man from a slightly different standpoint than usual, for the significance of this line was determined at a point in human development when the mental nature of Man was understood in a more meaningful way than it is today. The normal modern concept of Man fails to realize the extent to which Man stands between the world visible and a world invisible. Because of this it fails also to realize the extent to which Man is himself a transforming unit for energies: with his perceptions, which stand at an intermediate point between the world of material phenomena and the world of the spiritual, he unconsciously transforms the vibrations received from the phenomenal world into a more refined quality of vibrations, which we call ideas. Man is constantly forming ideas about the world: he is transforming the material world into ideas, and because of this he is involved with a very curious alchemy by which the matter of the world is being refined into the spiritual.* Ideas are free of matter, even though they have their origin in material form.

The course of the Head line links the practicality of Gemini, in its conflict between Earth and Spirit (see page 134), with the upper part of the imaginative domain of the Moon. The insertion of the line itself reveals the tendency to refine the world material by injecting it with imagination. This is why palmists regard a Head line which curves

*The ancient occult tradition maintains that all ideas in the spiritual world, which have been derived from the material world, are preserved for ever. Thus there exists a record of all aspirations and all relationships which have occurred in the world of mortals. This record may be consulted by high-quality mediums.

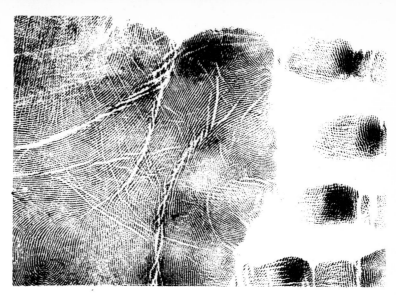

275. *Hand and horoscope of an*
276. *architect, showing a strong*
Water quality. See figure 77
in which Earth qualities are
discussed.
278. *Hand of a female University*
279. *lecturer. Note the excellent*
Head line.
280. *Such a Head line is*
representative of a highly
imaginative outlook.

downwards, either in a single plunge (figure 280) or in a fork (figure 282), to terminate on the Mount of Moon, as a sign that the understanding and mentality are coloured with too much imagination, which may manifest in lying, an inability to see clearly and report events accurately, because of the confused emotional state of the subject. Ideally, the line of Head should rest on top of the Mount of Moon, as in figure 207, which is the hand of an Italian professor. If the Head line penetrates the Mount of Moon, then it is tapping the undifferentiated energies which manifest as dreams and imagination, and a strange, imaginative view of reality must be expected. Such a termination may result in someone who is 'lost in dreams', but if the other signs in the hand indicate considerable executive power, then such a view of reality may be utilized, and given form, through one of the arts – especially through literature. The low termination of Head in figure 282 is fairly typical of the creative writer or painter. The quality of the Head line, in terms of its intensity or chaining, will determine the flow of mental effort. It is for this reason that a chained line of Head is regarded by palmists as indication of poor concentration: each chain in the line symbolizes a damming up of the mental process, a weakening of the ability to transform matter and phenomena into abstract ideas.

The line of Saturn is the one which normally runs up through the centre of the hand, thus enforcing the separation of the hand into the active and passive division which we noted on page 90. The line certainly is the most variable of the main lines, and is

merely vestigial in about one in five hands. In most cases the line terminates at the intersection with the Head line or with the Heart line (figure 280), but in some cases it persists through the Mount area, and terminates under the finger of Saturn.

We have seen that the finger of Saturn is in fact ruled by Capricorn, and so it is important to understand that the line of Saturn is activated by quite a different quality of Saturn – that which rules Aquarius. Obviously, the Saturn which has rule over the heavy Earth of Capricorn is not the same in scope, feeling or application as the Saturn which has rule over the rebellious, original and Airy Aquarius. In the traditional forms of astrology Saturn did rule this Air sign, and though the modern rulership of Uranus is obviously more apposite, one still discovers certain of the Saturnine traits manifest in Aquarius. Traditional palmistry has always maintained that Saturn had rule over this finger, but it rarely specified which aspect of Saturn was intended, and the line has been variously interpreted as relating to destiny, fate, inner balance and so on. Modern opinion is fairly united in the idea that it is related to the adaptability of the subject, as one might expect of a line which runs upwards to the 'sentinel' finger of the hand. The two Saturn influences of line and finger appear to separate the hand into the active and passive areas, and the channel of the line may thus be regarded as being involved with acting as a mediator between the two: it may therefore be seen as an index of the subject's inner sense of freedom in relation to his life. In one sense the presence of this line in some strength may indicate

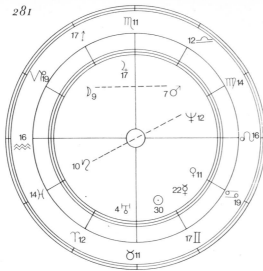

281. *Hand and horoscope of a*
282. *female author and journalist.*
The chart presents an excellent example of how oppositions and squares may drive towards material success, which will manifest in a line of Fate.

a reasonable adaptability: in another sense it may show a developed sense of self-love, which permits of a harmonious relationship with the world. It is essential that a person should learn to love himself in the right way before he can hope to be in a position to love others and the world at large: it is in relation to this sort of self-love, which in a sense marks a certain freedom from the ego of Mars (figure 146), that the line must be studied.

A weak line of Fate, or one which is badly broken (figure 158) implies a marked sense of insufficiency in these terms, as though the ego of Mars is strangling the subject and preventing a harmonious development with world demands. Sometimes such a psychological block will manifest in acquisitiveness and the subject may build forces in the world material in order to compensate for his spiritual lack – however, what is significant in his life is the lack of freedom. A strong line of Fate implies a creative and warm relationship to selfhood, which will permit the subject to relate in a warm and unselfish manner to the external world, and in particular to other human beings. It is significant that a strong line of Fate is found in the hands of those motivated by the humanitarian ideals of brotherhood and universal peace which are so much associated with the Aquarian ideal, but which are unfortunately so little understood by those who talk about this ideal.

The line could well be re-named the line of Freedom, for the connotation which this evokes would counteract all the dark forebodings associated with the ancient nomenclature which calls up the gloomy Saturn,

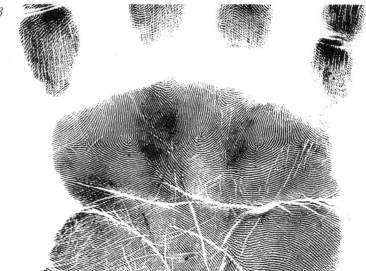

283. *Simian line in the hand of a manual worker.*
284. *Often the Simian lines are*
285. *conducive towards artistic expression, as though the tension within the psyche must be released into the material. Two hands of artists.*

lord of fate and destiny. In spite of what the majority of popular books on palmistry report, this line does not form an index of how the subject will fare in life, nor is it an index of what course the life of the subject will take, in the sense of indicating the milestones of fate – most authors of this kind of book do not have the slightest notion of what fate is. Since the well-developed line is an indication of a strong sense of self-love, and since a well-placed sense of self-love lends a harmony to the inner world, then on the principle that 'like attracts like', the life of the individual will generally tend to be more harmonious than in the case of a hand with a weakly displayed line of Fate. The harmony which springs from well-adjusted self-love will retain its nature under many circumstances which would prove disastrous for men of a lesser calibre, or a lesser attuned adaptability. Happiness is in the soul, not in the external world, though in an ordinary human being the one interpenetrates the other: a strong soul may impress harmony upon the most distressing of material conditions, whilst a different quality of soul will be able to digest the experiences which spring from distressing material conditions, and thereafter discover an inner harmony. Such considerations as these may be studied in the line of Saturn – it is significant that the length, insertion, point of termination, course and quality of this line are the most variable of all major lines: so is the life course of men!

The Simian line is one which runs right across the hand, as in the particularly marked example at figure 285. This strange line had a very unfortunate reputation in

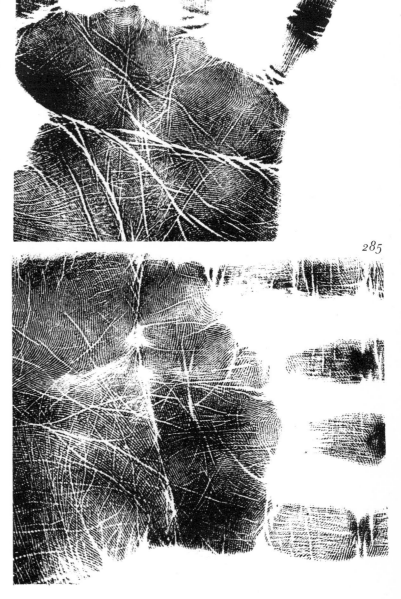

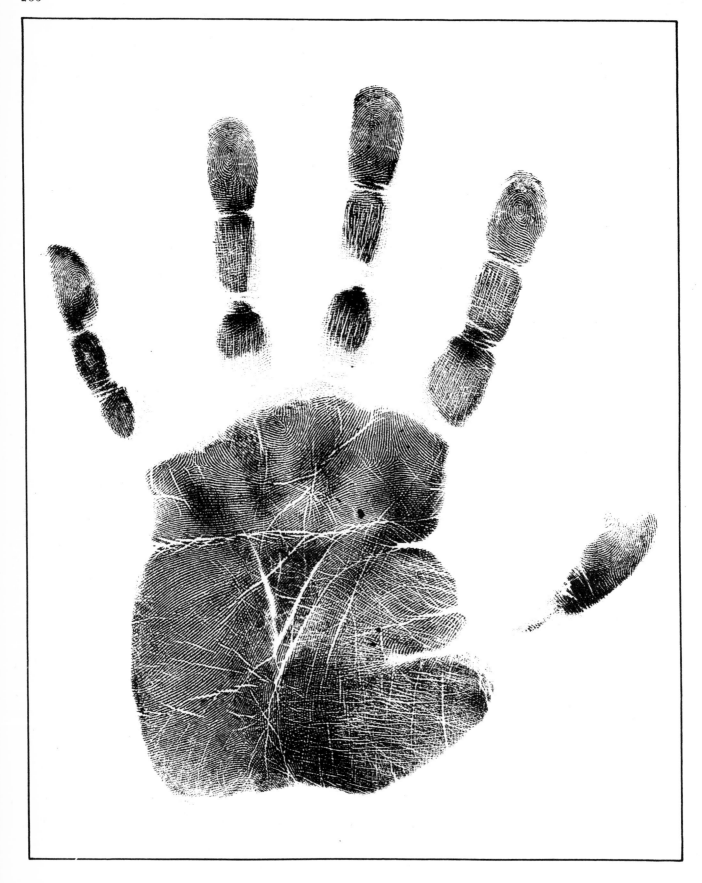

286. *A strong Simian line in which the component Head and Heart still remain behind in vestigial form.*

287. *Such traditional material as this accounts for the unfortunate associations linked with the Simian line. The line is interpreted as an indication that the type will be a murderer and thoroughly evil. Such interpretations survived even into twentieth-century palmistry, though the evidence suggests creativity as well as destructiveness.*

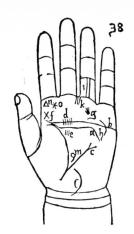

A *Naturalis inclinata verſus menſalem, ſignificat hominem iniquum, & iuuenem moriturum.*
B *Naturalis ſcindēs vitalem, & menſalis ipſi in principio vnita, homicidiarium notat, & aſtutum in malum.*
C *Linea hepatis bifurcata in fine, mortem violentam minatur, et hoc ab vno capite, quantum ab alio.*
D *Multæ lineæ ſecantes menſalem in oppoſito medij, damnum notant in ſubſtantijs.*
E *Lineæ tranſuerſales in angulo ſupremo, nō ſcindentes tamen, notant hominem pœnitere ſuæ prodigalitatis, & eò magis quò angulus fuerit diſiunctus.*
F *Lineæ interſecatæ ſupra montem indicis, notant perſecutiones ab eccleſiaſticis.*

earlier centuries, and was referred to by even such serious palmists as Benham as the 'murderer's line', while it is still generally believed in medical circles that the line is an atavistic sign. In certain types of hands the line is *sometimes* an indication of a violent or unbalanced nature, but it is not itself always representative of misfortune: indeed, the Simian is found in the hands of some of the most evolved people. The fact is there are different types of Simian lines, and the significance of these depends upon the nature of the hand upon which they are found. Before we examine these different types however, we should consider the astrological significance of the Simian line which enables us to understand something of the ancient reputation as well as something of its importance in the study of personality.

The Simian line in its most marked phase may be considered as the total merging of the line of Head with the line of Heart. In astrological terms this means the two Fire elements of Sagittarius and Leo mingling their energies (figure 157). In this sense the Simian line is itself a sign of excessive Fire in the hand. Fire in excess and out of control is extremely dangerous and thoroughly destructive. The Fire of Sagittarius tends in any case towards prodigality, the Fire of Leo tends towards excessive ostentation or selfishness – the Simian line represents the full force of these two intensifications, obviously calling out for conscious control on the part of the personality. It is extremely important in the assessment of any hand which contains the Simian line to determine whether the excessive Fire represented is under control or not. It is only when this excessive

Fire is out of control that the criminality and violence associated with the Simian line will find expression. My observation is that although the Simian line in primitive hands occurs frequently among criminals and the mentally disturbed, the same line is also very common in the hands of highly developed people, especially in deeply religious people who are themselves far removed from the world of crime and violence. We must assume from this that the line itself indicates excessive Fire which will under natural circumstances tend to degenerate, but, when consciously controlled or utilized, will evolve. The occult teaching upon which palmistry and astrology is based insists that it is natural for things to degenerate – special attention and effort, even suffering, is required to enable organisms to evolve: it is against all nature that man must strive if he is to refine his inner world. This applies to all material manifestations, from individual lives to whole civilizations. The Simian line, when seen in its true perspective, is a sign of the need for inner struggle towards spiritual evolution, which will be deeply felt and clearly manifest in the life of the native. The Simian line corresponds most closely to the cross of astrological aspects: the palm at figure 313, for example, has a fairly strong Simian tendency, reflected in the chart through a Moon square Saturn.

In the light of these considerations it may be understood why psychologists, who tend to take their examples from case histories exclusively connected with marked emotional problems, tend to see the line as an indication of either abnormality or atavism. The term itself reflects this unfortunate attitude. It

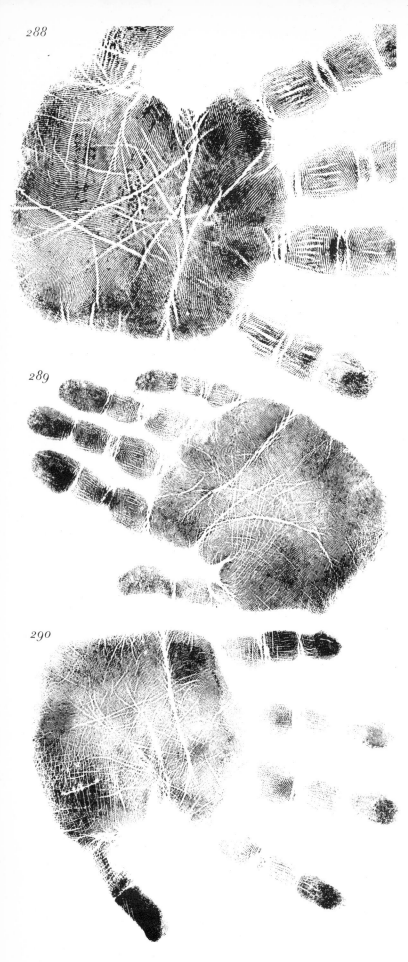

288

289

290

288. The Simian line in children
289. often give parents an
290. unnecessary cause for concern,
mainly due to the unfortunate
tradition associated with the
line. Its appearance would
suggest that the child should be
guided towards a healthy
creativity, in which emotional
and intellectual energies are
directed towards expression
through the manipulation of
matter. In simple terms we may
see the excessive Fire of the
Simian as requiring the
support of Earth practicality.

must be stressed that the line will be found in the hands of geniuses, as well as in the hands of idiots and maladjusts, for it is pre-eminently a sign of tension.

The examples of prints at figures 283 to 285 are themselves representative of the inevitable Fire conflict as the two different planes of human experience meet and interact.

It is my impression that the Simian higher energies are destructive only when their outflow is impeded or repressed, a state which may be seen from other factors in the hand or chart.

The excessive Fire of the Simian line appears to do less 'damage' in a Fire hand than in any of the other hand forms: presumably this is because the Fire personality will be able to integrate the Fire into his system, and will automatically provide the right kinds of outlets for its expression. A Simian line in an Earth hand tends to create rebellious, violent or even criminal tendencies, as though it were parching the hand dry with excessive heat. Sometimes, however, there is the strange contradiction of a strong Simian line in an Earth hand, with an artistic personality: in such a case the art forms are usually derived from the direct manipulation of materials, as in sculpture or pottery. It is clearly important to relate the element of Fire suggested by the Simian line to the various elemental interactions of the hand as a whole. This last statement in a sense summarizes the art of astropalmistry, for it is essentially the art of relating parts in such a way as to unite them into a harmony which expresses the whole of Man.

Practical Examples of Charts and Hands

It will be evident from what has been said so far that the relationship between astrology and palmistry has in fact never really escaped the serious limitations imposed upon it by the late mediaeval tendency towards strict symbol interpretations. According to this method of interpretation, one part of the hand is linked irrevocably with one astrological symbol, and any distinctive line on the hand or fingers is accorded a definite and quite fixed interpretation.

A fair example of this astropalmistry will be found in the plate at figure 8, which is from a seventeenth-century book by the French palmist Belot. The fingers are each accorded the traditional rulerships of Jupiter, Saturn, Apollo and Mercury, whilst the thumb is under the rulership of Venus. Belot takes the rulership further and ascribes each of the phalanges to one of the zodiacal signs: thus, Jupiter has the top phalange ruled by Aries, the middle phalange by Taurus and the lower phalange by Gemini. Needless to say, there is no explanation of what these rulerships imply. They appear to be on the same level as the line readings on this diagram, which are of a strictly symbolic kind and quite useless. For example, under Venus, on the top phalange of the thumb, we find two lines, the bottom one ending in a circle which is supposed to mean 'loss of chastity', whilst the grid structure under the finger of Mercury is supposed to indicate heresy. This is the palmistry of the 'fixed-symbols' kind, hiding beneath that all too common front put up by so-called occultists – meaningless complexity! The finger of Jupiter is no more connected with Aries, Taurus and Gemini than it is in fact connected directly with the planet Jupiter itself.

To understand the relationship between a hand and a horoscope, to grasp the relationship between palmistry and astrology, it is vital not to be misled because the two systems appear to have in common a number of symbols, nor must one allow oneself to be confused by the symbols: this form of 'palmistry' must be rejected, though to judge from the majority of modern books on the subject, it is far from being merely mediaeval.

The attempt to link astrology with palmistry must not be hindered by the traditional associations. On the other hand, this does not mean a complete rejection of the spirit which gave rise to these associations. The spirit behind astrology is very much the spirit behind palmistry, and once the confusion concerning symbols and rulerships has been cleared up, it is possible to see the similarity between the two spirits.

An examination of one or two hands in relation to horoscopes will help to drive home some of the more important teachings concerning the relationships between astrology and palmistry.

The two hands at figures 208 and 207 could hardly be more different. The first is hard, primitive in structure and feeling, weak in the all-important 'triad', and of a Fire structure with Earth lines. This is the hand of an Italian labourer (see page 164), the horoscope for whose birth is shown at figure 294. The second hand is resilient, lively in structure and feeling, vital in the 'triad', and of an Air structure with Fire lines (see horoscope at figure 209). This is the hand of

℥

14 ♑

15 ☽

♏

♃ 15

♑

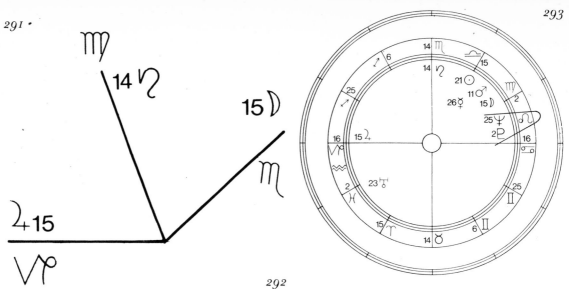

♓ ♀14

18 ☽

16 ♑

♊

an Italian university professor, the horoscope for whose birth is shown at figure 293.

The major contrasts in the charts are also found contrasting in the palms. In the case of the professor's hand, the two planets which rule different aspects of the mind (Jupiter which rules the expansive mentality, and Saturn which rules deeper thought) .are placed on the important angles of the Ascendant and the M.C., with Jupiter in an exact trine with the Moon. There could hardly be a better augury for intellectual brilliance. The general Air form of the hand, with its typical 'rounded' square palm, and long intelligent fingers, widely stretched out, has its parallel in the presence of the Sun, Mercury and Mars, the active planets, in the Air of Libra on the ninth house, which governs deeper studies, philosophy and universities. The Fire nature of the lines themselves (figure 207) is reflected in the placing of Venus, Neptune and Pluto in Fire signs. The brilliant mentality, suggested by the harmonious trine between the Ascending Jupiter and Moon, with the mediator Saturn sextile to both (figure 291) suggests an attitude to life which is linked to practical matters (Jupiter and the Moon are in Earth signs, refreshed by Saturn in a Water sign), and which permeates the entire life of the native. This significant binding of an Earth nature to an Air nature, as studied in this trine and sextile, may be seen reflected in the way the strong line of Fate cuts the hand into two areas. The finger patterns on the Jupiter/ Saturn half of the hand are of an Earth nature (simple arches), while the finger patterns on the Apollo/Mercury half of the hand are of an Air nature (simple loops).

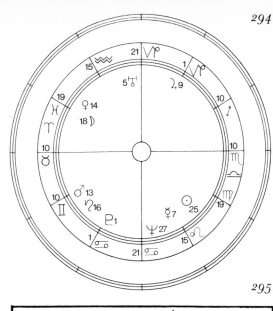

294

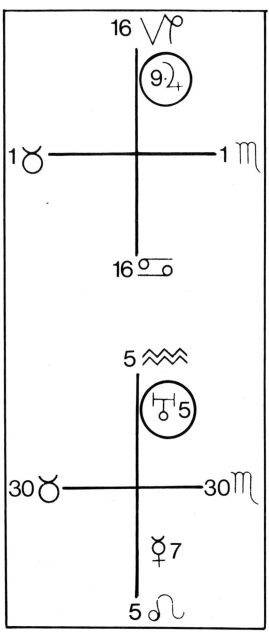

295

These are again reflected in the simple groupings of planets in Earth and Air signs. The line of Fate is strong in both the chart and the hand because of its good relationship with Jupiter and the Moon (sextiles), and also because it is the ruler of the Ascending sign, and by virtue of being on the M.C. will have contributed much to carrying the native high in his chosen career, though with considerable demands of effort and application, which always attend Saturnine forces. The line of Heart is strongly chained, and to a certain extent of a different quality to the other lines – this may be understood as reflecting the square which the Ascending Jupiter throws on to the Sun, creating difficulties of emotional adjustment.

We may contrast this print and horoscope with those at figure 208 and 209, which show the hand and chart of an Italian labourer. The brilliant mentality of the professor was reflected in the planets of intellect being magnified through two of the angles: in the present case, there is no real proximity* to an angle – the nearest planet being Neptune to the I.C. It is true to say that one of the most common signs of greatness is the presence of a strong planet or planets on the angles. The general strength, especially strength of the 'triad', which was noted in the hand of the professor, was mainly a result of a harmoniously integrated Jupiter. Because of the angular placing, and because of the sextiles from both Jupiter and the Moon, it could be said that the prominent Saturn (reflected in the prominent line of Fate) would require much effort and work, but would grant in return a high position, and respect, as a result of its being on the

*See page 165 – this horoscope has been rectified.

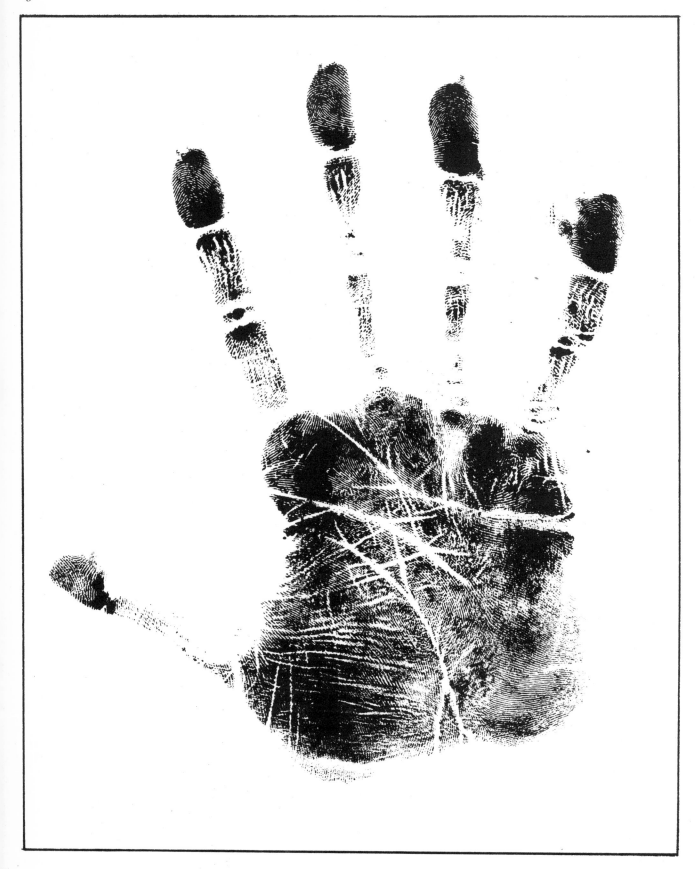

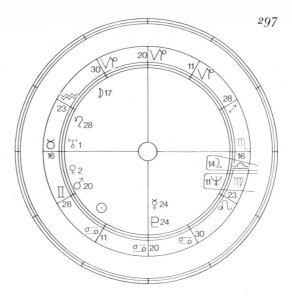

296. Hand and horoscope
297. discussed below.

M.C., and thus acting as a fulcrum for the rest of the chart. The Saturn of our labourer shows no such good fortune. It is placed in the second house, implying that money will have to be worked for: the conjunction with Mars implies that it will have to be worked for under difficult conditions, and with much physical energy. In this case we see that Saturn is also squared by the Moon and by Venus, which implies considerable difficulties throughout life, and very little opportunity for general expansion of the personality though considerable potential for the refining of the spirit. The Moon-Saturn square is generally regarded as one of the most difficult which can be brought to bear on a human being, and it is indeed a severe test of the inner quality and calibre of the person during a lifetime. The Earth quality of the lines reflect the Earth of the Taurean Ascendant, the Capricornian M.C. and the Jupiter in Capricorn, whilst the unexpected warmth of the upwards sweep of the line of Heart into Jupiter is reflected in the presence of the Sun in the fifth house (see page 22). A study and comparison of these two hands will help greatly towards the understanding of the relationship between horoscopes and hands, for they represent the two extremes of personalities – the one forceful, vital and intelligent, and the other weak, weighed down with inner conflict, and of no particular intellectual merit.

The hand at figure 296 is a fairly uncommon one: it is of a clear Air structure, with long fingers and a strong square palm, yet even from the print one can sense the hard Earth quality of skin, whilst the Earth quality of the lines is quite evident. It is the hand of the manager of a building firm. The horoscope (figure 297) itself naturally reflects the Air/Earth polarity in a very distinctive manner: the Ascendant is Taurus, with its ruler Venus in the Air of Gemini. The M.C. is Earth, and both Neptune and Uranus are in Earth signs – otherwise, the weight of planetary placings is in Air, with the Moon, Venus, Mars, Jupiter and Saturn evenly distributed through the three Air signs. The Simian line is fairly strong, and this may be taken on one level as reflecting the exact conjunction of Mercury with Pluto, which will introduce a high degree of originality into the life. In fact the Simian line marks excess of Fire, as has already been discussed, and therefore is always indicative of a tension in terms of the hand form itself. The tension between Air and Earth is always a curious one, for Air and Earth do not mix, and therefore the tendency for these is to separate when a tension between them is established. Thus, from the Simian line in a hand of this nature, one would expect a wide separation in the two major directions indicated by the hand – we would expect one part of the life to be dedicated to the Earth principles – construction, building, working with raw materials, and so on, as is ideally expressed in the building trade; while another part of life will be dedicated to the communicative principle of Air. This truth is established when we observe that the native is a keen practising musician, and runs his own dance band. One sees in both sides of this interesting personality the interaction of the Earth/Air principles, with the emphasis in each case reversed: in the building phase of Taurus, he introduces the

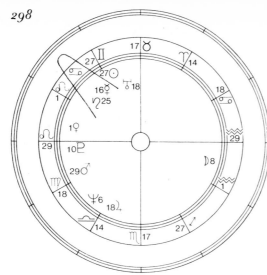

298

298. *Hand and horoscope, both of a*
299. *strong Air and Fire nature, as*
discussed on page 157.
300. *Analysis of the balance between*
Air and Fire in the horoscope
and hand below.

299

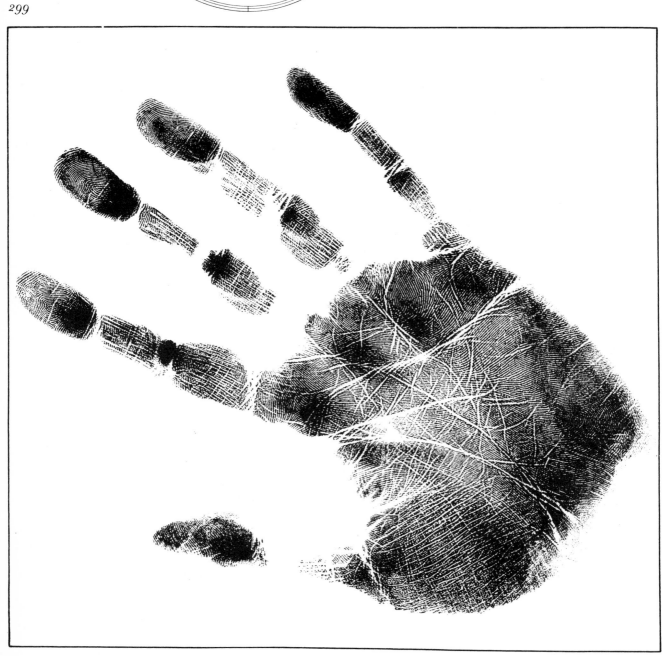

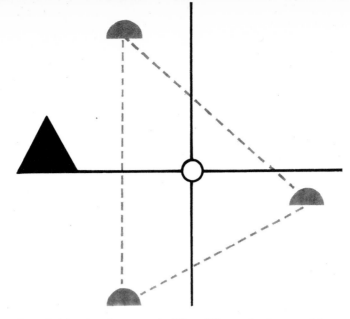

organizational impulse of Air; in the communicating phase of Venus, Moon and Jupiter in Air signs, he introduces the rhythmic needs of Taurus, which is a sign traditionally involved with music and sound generally.

Not all hand-analyses are quite so straightforward as the preceding examples have suggested, for the elements sometimes combine in such a way as to make it difficult for a beginner to assess the basic tensions and harmonies in the hand, thus rendering any comparison with the horoscope unproductive. It will be clear to anyone beginning the study of palmistry that the hand at figure 299 presents something of a problem, for it has indications of being of the Air nature, yet the palm is rather long. The hand is not narrow or effeminate looking in structure, and this fact effectively eliminates the possibility of its being a Water type. It is clearly a hand of a composite type. A preliminary diagnosis would suggest strong Air characteristics from the form of the hand and from the three loops (note the radial loop on the finger of Jupiter). From the structure of the lines on the hand, and from the whorl on the finger of Apollo, one would expect strong Fire tendencies. Examination of the chart immediately confirms the suspicions, for five planets are in Air signs and three are found in the single Fire sign. Leo on the Ascendant embraces Venus, Mars and Pluto: the ruler, the Sun in Gemini, as is Uranus, while the Moon is on the Descendant Aquarius. Jupiter and Neptune are in Libra.

The chart, like the hand, suggests a strong division in the personality between Air and Fire. The palmist would note the whorl on the Mount of Moon, as well as the creative urge from the whorl on Apollo which, in this instance, would reinforce the Fire side of the nature. The Water elements in the hand are accounted for by the presence of Mercury and Saturn in Cancer (which is ruled by the Moon). The emphasis on Apollo as a Fire element finds its astrological equivalent in Mars being so close to the Ascendant, for planets on or near angles always intensify the working of that planet in terms of the sign it occupies. The complexity of the chart may be simply assessed in the terms of the fixity of Fire working in fair harmony with the trine relationships of the planets in the three Air signs (figure 298). Quite apart from this, however, the chart shows a distinct correspondence between the Air structure of the hand, for the Sun ruler is in Gemini on the eleventh house, which is of course the house natural to Aquarius. The hand structure taken in relationship to the Fire line structure is echoed in the diagrammatic 'analysis' at figure 300. The finger of Apollo in itself points to one of the major factors in the horoscope which underlies the harmony of the Fire/Air polarity. Any lack of harmony in the personality will presumably spring from the conflict (square) created by Mercury and Saturn in afflicting Jupiter in an Air sign – it is interesting that the line of Saturn and the line of Mercury are quite scattered and undefined, usually an indication of an affliction to Mercury. Palmists might assume, from this scattered line of Mercury, that the creative urges indicated by the whorl on the finger of Apollo will in this case not be given a satisfactory outlet, and

301. *Hand and horoscope of an*
303. *office secretary. Note how in*
both hands there is a rather
indistinct line of Saturn
emerging from the Mount of
Moon. This is generally a sign
of emotional insecurity, a
tension involving Saturn, as is
manifest in the opposition
between Saturn and Mars in
the horoscope.

302. *The hand of a mechanic. Even*
a relatively short line of Fate,
when it emerges from the
Venusian half of the hand, will
give a high degree of confidence.

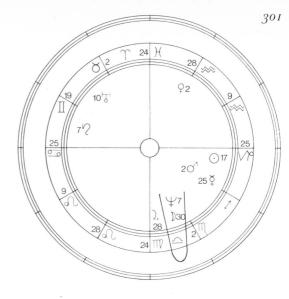

302

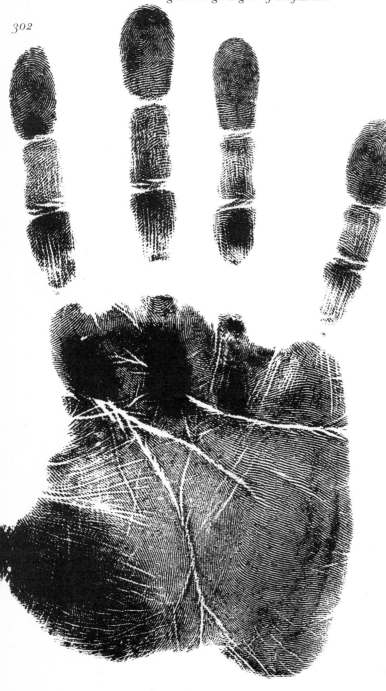

consequently there will be an underlying
sense of frustration in the life of the native.
This is indeed the fact of the case, for in spite
of all the rich potential indicated the native
herself is in no way creative, but rather the
lively, well-balanced, attractive female one
would expect from the Air and Fire polarities. The radial loop is in itself an interesting
factor in the hand and one would therefore
expect to find some indication in the
horoscope which would reflect this curious
Air marking: and of course Jupiter is in
weak trine harmony with the ruler Sun,
Mercury is in strong square aspect with
Jupiter, and Saturn also weakly squares this
planet. Astrologers would expect this conflict
to manifest in a rather curious way in regard
to the intellect, for all three planets involved
in the square are connected with different
levels of the mentality – Mercury with the
expression of intuitive thought, Jupiter with
the intellectual nature, and Saturn with the
restrictive quality in thinking. The astrological conclusion might be that the basic
Fire/Air polarity of the chart, which would
work naturally to free self-expression, would
not be supported by a strong intellectual or
mental system. This view is echoed in the
hand. It is this restrictive weight on the
mentality which is confirmed on the finger of
Jupiter, for just as the square weighs down
the Air/Fire polarity (figure 300), so the
papillary loop pattern points to some curious
manifestation of an Air nature which dis-
turbs the creative expansive expression of
the personality into life: the promise of Fire
and Air is not fulfilled in life. The very many
so-called chance lines on the Mount of Venus
are a common indication that a Venus is in

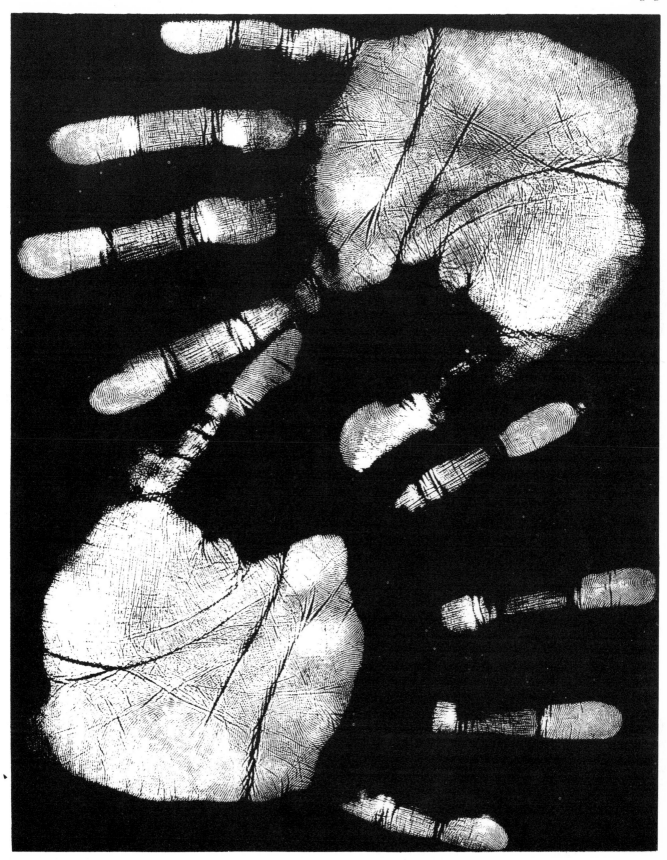

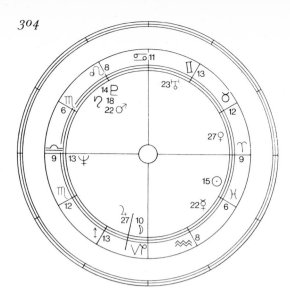

304

304. An interesting horoscope which is basically of an Air distribution, though with an underlying Fire trine. Moon is isolated in Capricorn.

305. The hand for the horoscope at figure 304. The interpenetrating triangles show the balance of Air and Fire. One observes the isolation of the fingers of Jupiter and Saturn, as manifest in the chart, in the Moon placing.

a Fire sign. It should be noted once more, from a general analysis of the hand in relation to the chart, that the hand itself points to those factors in the chart which are of the most obvious importance in the life of the subject. A practising astrologer would perhaps have little difficulty in seeing the major personality traits from the horoscope; he would immediately grasp the importance of the harmonious relationship of the Air placings, see the dual polarity of the three Air signs as emphasised by the second group of planets around the Ascendant Leo, and note the underlying conflict involved with Saturn and Mercury in Cancer. The beginner in astrology, however, might not be able to assess the chart quite so quickly and would therefore have recourse to the study of the palm, which will prove invaluable in helping him to see the major pattern implied in the horoscope, and interpret it accordingly.

Yet another hand is worth looking at in this connection, if only because it is quite clearly of an Air form yet with strong Fire lines. In this case, however, the two fingers (Jupiter and Saturn) have Earth papillary formations, while Mercury and Apollo have Air papillary formations. The horoscope for this person is at figure 304. There is strong Air quality in the chart, for the Ascendant is Libra and the sensitive planet Neptune is almost on the Ascendant: Mercury is in Aquarius and Uranus is in Gemini, so once more there is a trine, though of course the nature of the planets involved will make it a less harmonious aspect than in the previous example. The strong Fire nature is seen in the placing of Mars, Saturn and

Pluto in Leo, Jupiter in Sagittarius and Venus in Aries – Venus being exactly trine Jupiter. The polarity suggested by this particular Fire and Air relationship is of a different quality from the one discussed in figure 299, for the trine suggests a much more expansive, influential effect on the life since it interpenetrates the trine of the Air planets, and is not isolated in one place, as in figure 298. The diagram of interpenetrating triangles at figure 305 summarizes this. Any conflict in the personality will arise from the two very strong placings of the Sun and Moon one of which is in a Water sign, the other in an Earth sign. The Moon governs the personality – the way in which the person manifests the various energies contained within him – and therefore it relates to the fingers which govern the external, objective side of the personality – Jupiter and Saturn. The papillary patterns on the finger ridges are themselves of an Earth nature, and of course it is in the Earthy sign Capricorn that we find the Moon. It is clear from this that the personality will not manifest as freely as the Air and Fire natures would themselves suggest – in other words, the expansive, creative qualities suggested by Fire and Air combined will be blocked by the placing of the Moon in Capricorn, suggesting a personality somewhat weighed down in spite of the underlying richness of energy supply, and in spite of the vibrant personality envisaged in the Fire and Air. This quality, this unexpected trait in the personality which is symbolized by the Moon placing on the cusp of the I.C., is reflected in the unexpected Earth structure of the fingers of Jupiter and Saturn.

The hand at figure 307 is strongly Earth

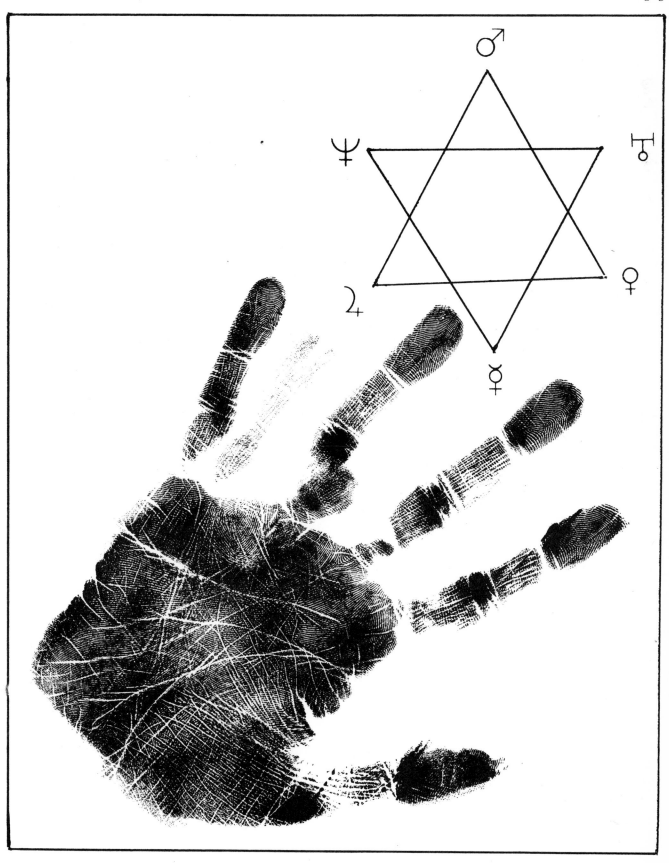

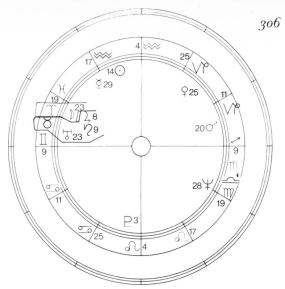

306. Horoscope and hand of the
307. creative potter and teacher,
whose chart was examined in
figures 268 and 272, alongside
the hand and chart of his wife,
whose chart is reproduced once
more at 308. The proximity
of Moon and Venus is fairly
typical of the basis for a good
relationship.

307

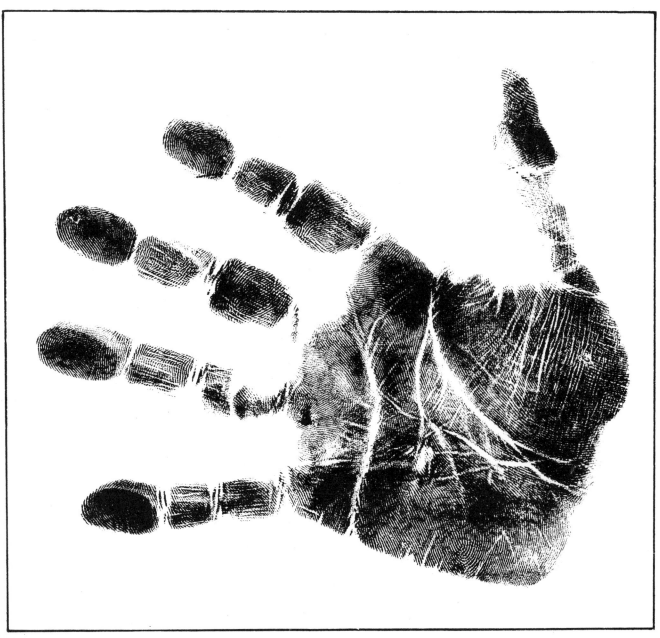

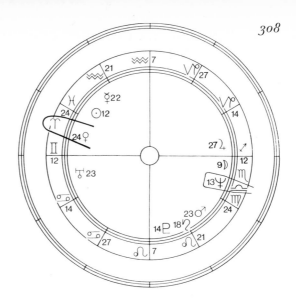

*308. Horoscope of the wife of the
male subject opposite.*

in structure. It is heavy, rather coarse, and possesses very few lines. The palm is square, the fingers short and rather thick. As the corresponding horoscope figure shows, the subject has in fact five planets in Earth signs: Venus, Jupiter, Saturn, Neptune and Uranus. It would be reasonable to expect these major Earth influences to have arisen from the three planets in Taurus. The presence of the Simian line, always indicative of great pressure in the personality, whatever the type, is of course reflected in the chart. We would expect there to be some conflict which strikes at the Earth nature, and the interaction of elements being what they are (page 32), we would expect this conflict to arise from some Fire source. In fact, the Venus in Capricorn is directly afflicted by a strong square from the Moon in the Fire sign Aries. A square from the Moon always manifests itself strongly in the life of the native, for the Moon is the most important planetary influence over personality. A conflict and tension between personality (Moon) and the love impulse (Venus) must therefore be expected in this native (figure 306). On a constructive level he will be impelled towards some expression involved with rhythm, or with some physical art form (he is a creative potter, and also a teacher of this craft). On a less constructive level he will tend to be attracted to romantic situations which, in the long run, are productive of tensions. He is in fact married to the young lady whose horoscope is shown at figure 306. It will be observed that her own Venus is almost exactly on his Moon, in 24° Aries. In a comparison of these two charts, it will be seen how the man is attempting to reconcile

his own tension by taking as his *anima* a woman who will in some ways resolve the conflict established in his own life between the square of Moon and Venus; he is, so to speak, appropriating a Venus of his own (figure 272). This is perhaps an unromantic way to describe what must have been experienced by the native as falling in love, a meeting of two souls, but astrology, even more than ordinary psychology, recognizes the extent to which falling in love is subconsciously involved with attempting to strengthen certain weaknesses, or in attempting to appropriate deficient qualities. Comparison between charts is not the object here, but it is most interesting to note that the wife's Moon occupies the same degree and sign of the seventh house as the male chart. This correspondence in itself usually offers the possibility of a love match, and indeed is often a sign of marriage. The female chart shows five planets and the seventh house in Fire signs. It is inevitable that the male should experience through his Moon placing in Fire a tremendous liberation of his own personality in the presence of this female. There is a distinct possibility that this fact in itself will ultimately disturb the more restricted Earth placing which predominated in his own chart.

A particularly valuable application of palmistry to astrology is found when a chart is to be cast for a subject whose date of birth is given, but the actual time of birth is not known.

Figure 309 is the hand of an Italian peasant, who was born at Fiesole, on 18 August, 1913. At noon on that day the planets occupied the positions indicated at figure 310 – the house

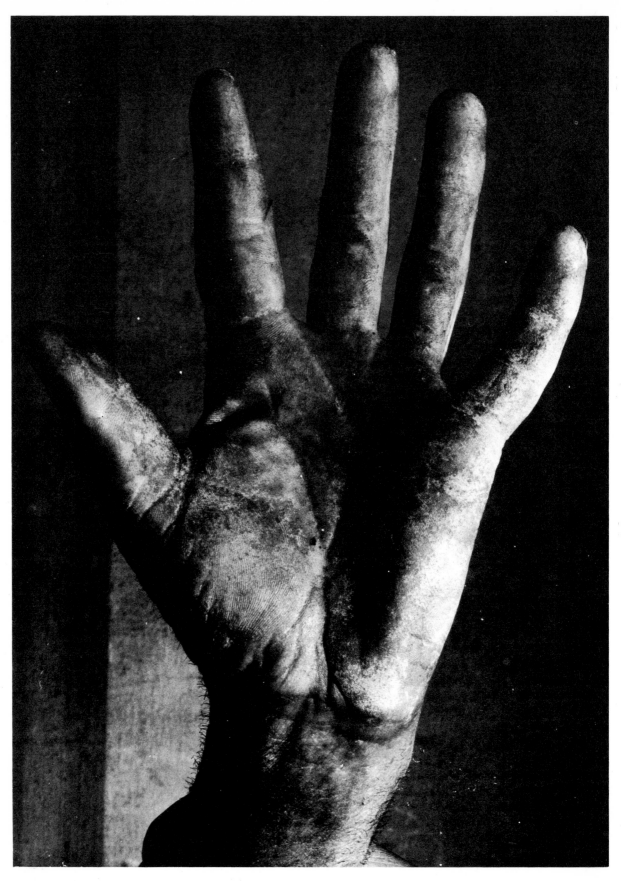

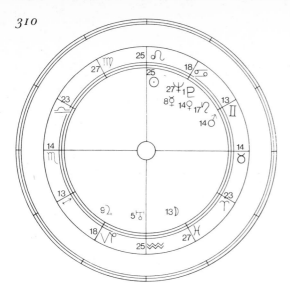

309. *Hand of the Italian peasant
discussed below.*

310. *Figure cast for noon on the day
of birth. This is a suitable
time to cast a chart for an
unknown time of birth, as a
basis for rectification – which
is attempting to find the
moment of birth by relating
known character or events in
life to a chart, a kind of
reversal of ordinary astrology.*

divisions being irrelevant. This is a particularly primitive hand, but of a Fire form with extremely simple Earth lines. The Mount of Moon is low-set and marked with a strong whorl, the thumb and finger of Jupiter being pointed and extremely weak. Perhaps the first thing to observe is that with such strong Earth lines one might well expect to find a strong Earth force in the horoscope, yet the only planet in an Earth sign is Jupiter, which is in Capricorn. The Fire shape of the hand is echoed in the noon chart through the placing of the Sun and Mercury in Leo. The emphasis on Water (the Moon, Venus, Neptune and Pluto being in Water signs) manifests itself in the low-set Mount of Moon, in the general weakness of the hand as a whole (especially in the weak thumb), and in the loop patterns on the fingers. Most Earth hands are extremely robust and impress one with their general feeling of vitality – this one impresses one with the idea of weakness, which is reflected in the Water of the horoscope. Returning to a consideration of the Earth quality of the lines, it is seen that only Jupiter is in an Earth sign, and thus it would not be unreasonable to expect an Earth sign to be on the Ascendant, in order to account for the particularly strong Earth lines. There is a choice of Taurus, Virgo and Capricorn in this direction, but before trying these in a chart, it is a good idea to study them in the hand. Taurus is connected with the Mount of Venus, which is well-formed and fleshy in a hand not over-corpulent in itself. The finger of Mercury, which is connected with Virgo, is short in the lower phalange (typical of a regressive hand), as well as bowed in shape.

The finger of Saturn, which is connected with Capricorn, is not noticeably long or well formed. It may be assumed from these considerations, therefore, that the native must have had a Taurean Ascendant at birth, implying that he was born late at night. The two diagrams at figure 295 show the angles for the place of birth (Fiesole), for 1° Taurus ascending, and 30° Taurus ascending. Should the Italian have been born with 1° Taurus rising, then Jupiter (in 9° Capricorn) would have been fairly near the M.C., which would be unlikely in the figure of someone who has not risen to prominence in life, as Jupiter near the M.C. would normally imply, and in the case of a person who has had to work hard physically to gain a livelihood. With the extreme of 30° Taurus ascending, he would have had the disruptive Uranus on the M.C., and Mercury on the I.C., implying that the elements of both would have been pulled into the fore in his life and personality, and suggesting a nature too rebellious, abrupt and versatile for the life of a peasant farmer. In order to find an intermediate point between these extremes of Taurus, an intermediate point which prevents any planet being given an undue emphasis by being on an angle, we have to find an I.C. somewhere between 16° Cancer (Ascendant of 1° Taurus) and 27° Cancer, in which Neptune is placed. If we take an I.C. of 21° Cancer, this will give us, for the latitude in question, an Ascendant of 10° Taurus, and a horoscope as set out at figure 294.

This horoscope has been checked against details and dates of the native's life and has been shown to be reasonably accurate.

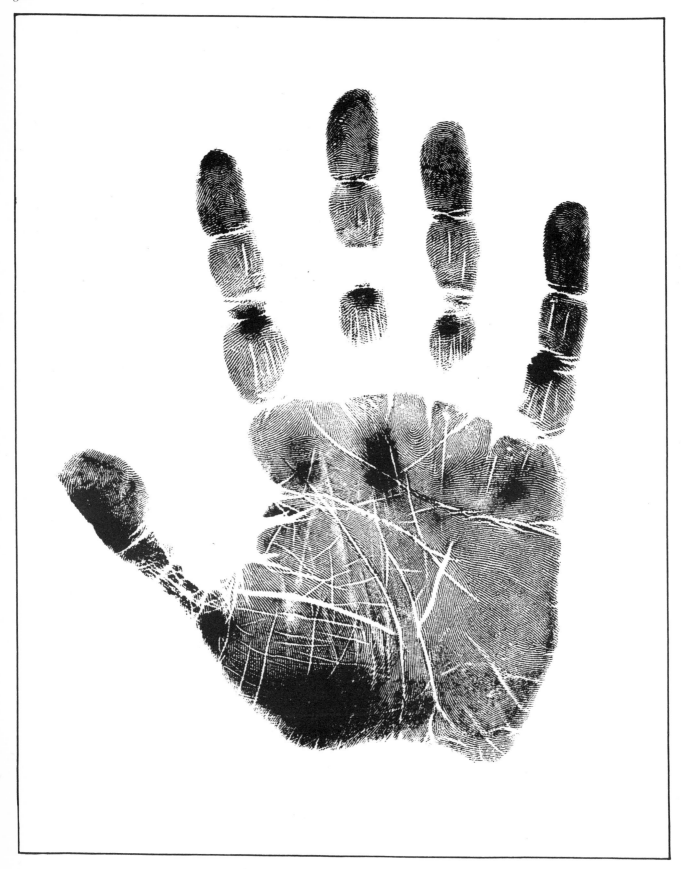

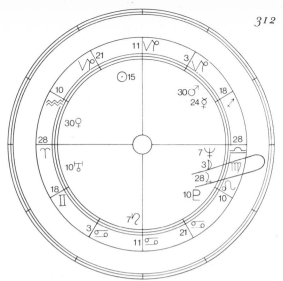

311. This single horoscope is related
312. to only one hand on these two
313. pages. By now the reader
      should be able to tell without
      difficulty which hand it is. The
      hand and horoscope are
      discussed on page 172.

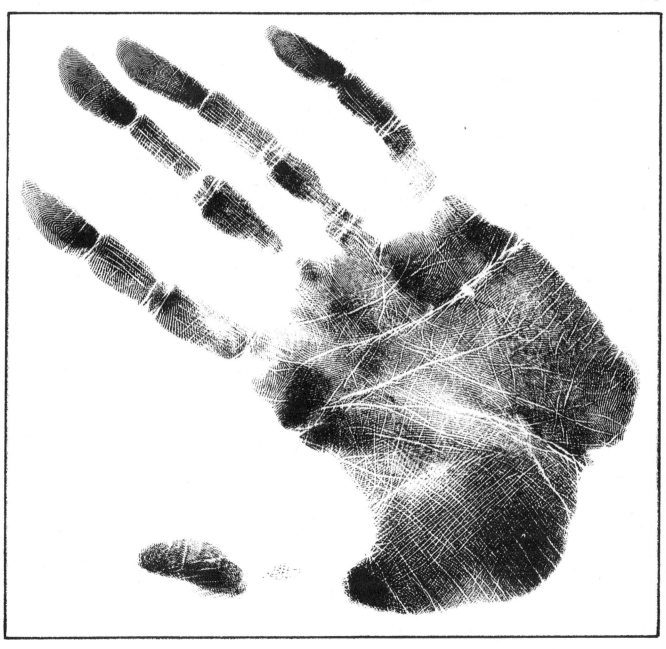

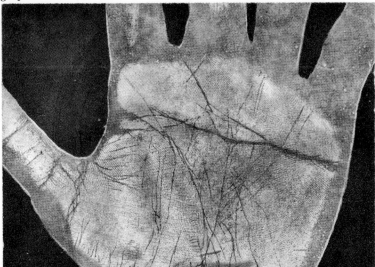

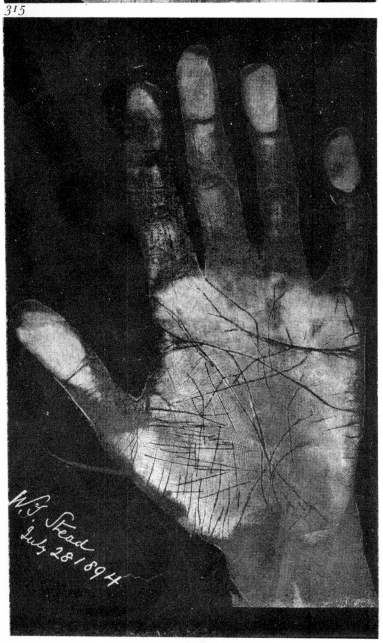

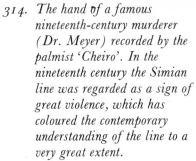

314. *The hand of a famous nineteenth-century murderer (Dr. Meyer) recorded by the palmist 'Cheiro'. In the nineteenth century the Simian line was regarded as a sign of great violence, which has coloured the contemporary understanding of the line to a very great extent.*

315. *The hand of the journalist and reformer W. T. Stead, recorded by 'Cheiro'. The excellent line of Head, the*

After a consideration of the more complex applications of this system of astropalmistry, it may be as well as for us to examine a number of hands in connexion with horoscopes, in order to study the relationship between the two in a more simple way. It must be emphasised, however, that experience and understanding may be gleaned only from dealing with charts and hands of people from one's own immediate circle and social level. Good astrology may never be learned purely from books: conscientious practice is required.

The hand print at figure 317 is of the Fire type, though with all fingers exhibiting Air loops. The horoscope is of a strong Fire quality, with a Leo Ascendant, and with both Sun and Mercury in this sign. Uranus is on the midheaven Aries. The underlying Air nature is expressed through the Moon and Mars in the fourth house Libra, and through Saturn in Aquarius. This hand and horoscope make an interesting comparison with those at figures 320 and 321, in which the dualities are equally strongly represented – basically we have an Air formation with extremely strong Earth characteristics in terms of line-markings, and the low-set mount of Venus. The planets and nodal points are strongly orientated towards this conflict between Earth and Air, for there is a Capricornian Ascendant, and the ruler, Moon, Jupiter and Uranus are in the Earth of Taurus, whilst Sun, Mercury and Neptune are grouped together in the Air of Gemini. This very simple level of chart-handprint comparison is invaluable as a guide to the beginner who is anxious to discover which strong line of Ambition (the line of Life reaching up to Jupiter), and the powerful line of Apollo are notable. The strong and curious line of Mercury, which rises from the mount of Venus, may be connected with his concern for psychic affairs, as he ran a spiritualist newspaper.

316. Hand and horoscope discussed
317. below.

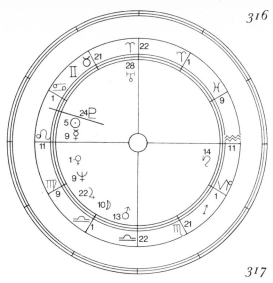

316

317

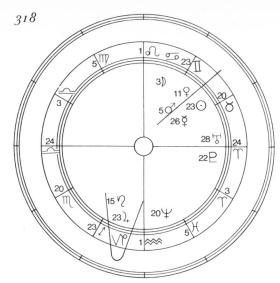

318. The hand and horoscope of
319. Sir Arthur Sullivan, the
      composer, discussed below.

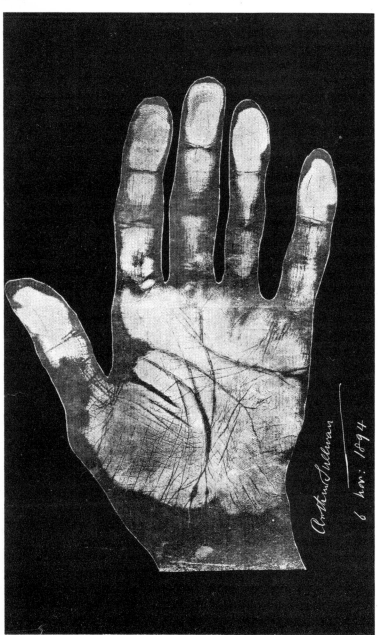

parts of the zodiac are being activated in particular nativities.

For example, a glance at the horoscope at figure 318 might suggest to the beginner that the proximity of Uranus and Pluto to the seventh house cusp might well indicate a rather strange person, and because of the Aries influence, one of a Fire disposition. Certainly this is the chart of a strange and forceful personality; it is cast for the birth of Sir Arthur Sullivan, the composer of the famous comic operas. However, the hand is obviously of an Air formation (that is, if one ignores the lines drawn around the print) and this a mature astrologer would have anticipated from the Airy quality of the horoscope – Libra ascending, Aquarius on the fourth house, with Neptune in this sign, and both Venus and Mars in Gemini. The Moon in Cancer is always a sign of a great imaginative facility, and this is confirmed in the chart by the descent of the Head line into the Mount of Moon. Unfortunately, the print is not of a sufficiently good quality to determine the nature of the finger patterns: from the horoscope one would expect them to be mainly arched to show the strong Earth influence.

The hand at figure 324 is clearly of the Air formation, and the corresponding horoscope (figure 323) contains no fewer than seven planets in Air signs; Sun, Mercury, Mars and Jupiter in Gemini, Saturn and Neptune in Libra, and Moon in Aquarius. The linear, papillary and finger patterns are of the Air quality, though the numerous striations on the Mount of Venus appear to set off this area of the hand from the other parts – this may be astrologically explained by the

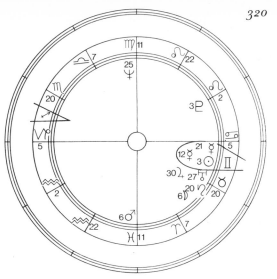

320 *A strong Earth hand, with*

321. *Air loops, expressive of the marked duality of grouping in the horoscope.*

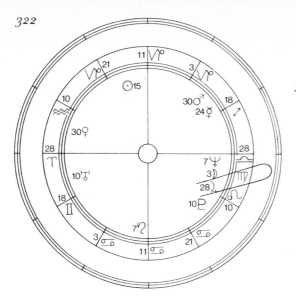

322. *Horoscope for the hand
reproduced in figure 313,
discussed below.*

presence of Venus in Aries, which is in opposition to the conjunct Saturn and Neptune. Such a figure will imply difficulties in the love-life, in the sense that the impetuous Venusian placing will be frequently frustrated (Saturn) by rather strange, nebulous or intangible (Neptune) occurrences. This personality trait will be much in evidence in the life of the native because of the conjunction of Mars with Mercury, which will add a high degree of force and sexuality to communications. The latter characteristic will express itself in a harmonious manner (especially towards women), as a result of the Moon as well as Saturn and Neptune being trine to this configuration, making for a general ease of expression. The native is a student of economics, as one might expect with so much of the intellectuality of Air seeking an external expression through a Capricornian tenth house.

Another horoscope with an Arietan Ascendant and Capricorn on the tenth house may be seen in figure 322. This is the chart of a male student of philosophy, whose hand print is reproduced at figure 313. Here once more there is an Air form, though the papillary patterns and life structure are altogether more complex than in the previous example. The general Air formation of the hand is reflected in the horoscope through the presence of Venus, Uranus, Moon and Neptune in Air signs. Jupiter is exactly squared by Mercury, and weakly squared by Mars in Sagittarius, indicating that out-going energies will be in some way restricted, and channelled through an Earth element (Virgo). The Earth element is not given great emphasis in the hand or the

chart, in spite of the Sun being placed in Capricorn. One sees this parallel in the chart through the arch papillary formation on the finger of Jupiter, which is thus separated from the other fingers which all have Air loops. It is mainly the conflict engendered by the square between Neptune and Saturn which accounts for the nervous and sensitive distribution of the lines; the chief markings are mainly of the Fire nature, as one might expect from the three planets in Fire signs, but they are set against a background of short, nervous and very 'watery' hair lines. The long, though broken, Girdle of Venus on this hand finds an interesting correlation with the chart, in terms of the theory set out on page 139, through the exact semi-square between the Sun and Venus.

I remember that when I was introduced to this young man, he asked me what sign I guessed him to be, some time before I did his horoscope. Now, although astrology is by no means a guessing game I am quite used to answering this type of question, as indeed are most astrologers. The problem is that it is quite possible to 'guess' the dominant sign from the appearance, but this of course is not always the Sun sign. Yet it is the Sun which most people take to be *their* sign, as a result of the pernicious form of 'astrology' which is purveyed through newspapers. Because of this one has to attempt to be really clever when playing such 'guessing games' and one has to assess not only the dominant sign, but also the actual Sun sign. This is difficult in some cases, of course, but as one's sensitivity to the signs and to the nature of astrology is increased, the ability

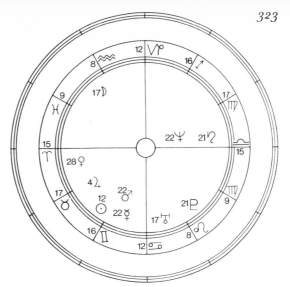

323. *A hand and horoscope of the*
324. *Air type, discussed on page 171.*
Observe how the strong line of
Mercury finds a parallel in the
chart through the conjunction of
Mars with Mercury exactly
trine Saturn and Neptune, in
Air signs.

324

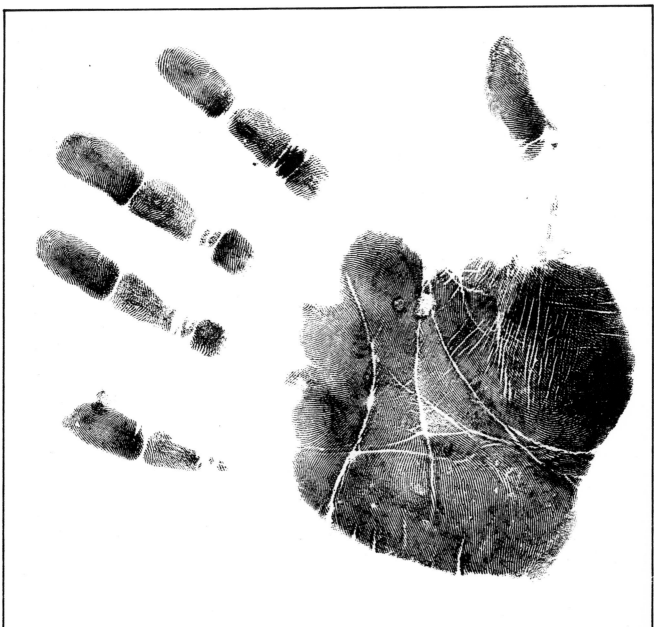

325

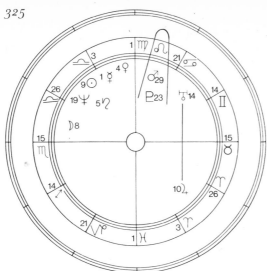

325. *Hand and horoscope discussed*
326. *below. Note how the aspects to Jupiter, the ruler of the Sagittarian line of Head, account for the broken quality of this line. Both the chart and the hand point to a need to integrate the expansive mental forces of Jupiter into the personality.*

327. *Pisces is placed at the M.C. in this fifteenth-century zodiac to show that Christ is in full glory in the skies. This sign rules the first two thousand years of Christianity, the Age of Pisces.*

326

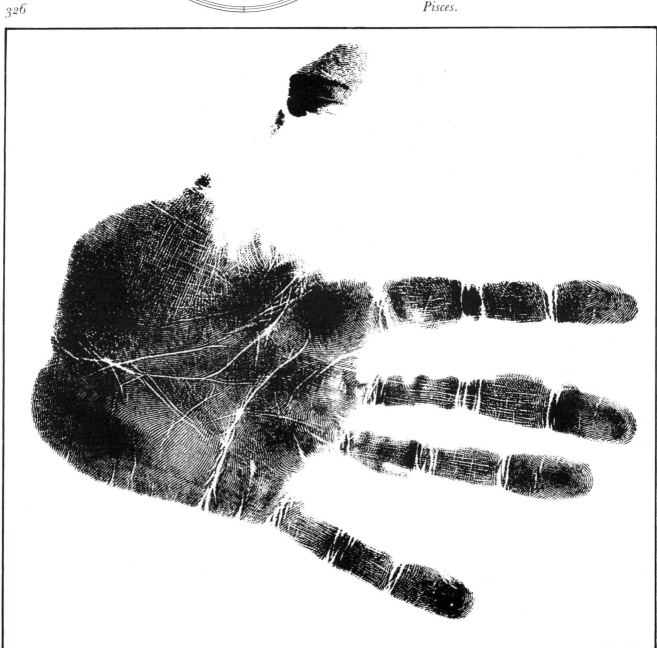

to do such things begins to grow. After a while it is possible to assess not only the dominant sign (which is usually the Ascendant, or a satellitium), but also the Sun and Moon placing. Of course, as one talks to the subject and studies their thinking processes, behaviour, movements, and so on, then it becomes relatively easy to draw up a list of sign placings, but the really skilled astrologer should be able to give the dominant sign, and at least one other placing, merely from a first impression of the person.

However, to return to the case in hand: I guessed, quite correctly, that his Sun was in Capricorn – not particularly difficult, when one considers its placing in the tenth house! I also said that he must have a strong force of an Air sign around him, probably in Libra, from the way in which he expressed himself, in a curiously gentle manner, especially noticeable for one with Sun in Capricorn. I knew that neither Venus nor Mercury could be in the gentle Libra when Sun was in Capricorn, for Venus can never be more than 48 degrees from the Sun, and Mercury never more than 28 degrees from the Sun, when measured geocentrically; and so I guessed that the planet in question might be Jupiter – though it proved in fact to be the Moon in Libra. I knew, of course, that Neptune would be in Libra, as this is a placing common to the whole group of people born about that time. The case, not particularly unusual in itself, is recorded here, because it shows how much of practical value may be learned about astrology through following such lines of thought with individuals who are prepared to have their horoscopes cast *after* one has recorded im-

pressions of the probable astrological background to their various personality and behaviour patterns.

The hand print of a female hand at figure 326 also evinces a basic Air form, as we might expect from a horoscope which has Sun, Mercury, Saturn and Neptune in the Air sign Libra.

The pattern on the finger of Jupiter is of the arch formation, and is thus isolated from the other fingers, which show the loop formation. This separation of the Jupiterian impulse, representative in psychological terms of a feeling of insecurity, of an inability to deal effectively with the external world, is paralleled in the chart in the placing of Jupiter, and the aspect to it.

Jupiter is the only planet under the Ascendant-Descendant axis, which is to say the only planet 'under the earth' at the moment of birth and in relation to the place of birth. This fact would itself tend to isolate the Jupiterian impulse from the other planetary impulses, but there is another factor which serves to emphasise the isolation and tension of Jupiter in the personality: Jupiter is subject to very strong and unfortunate aspects. The most obvious is the direct opposition from the Sun, which would alone stimulate Jupiter, perhaps even lend it considerable force – opposition is generally regarded as productive of tension, but when 'beneficent' planets such as Jupiter and the Sun are involved the aspect may result in creative drives which appear to be beneficial to the well-being of the native, though never so convincingly as with a trine between such planets. In the case before us, however, the balance established by the pull between Sun

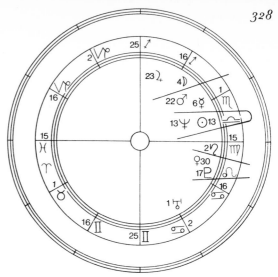

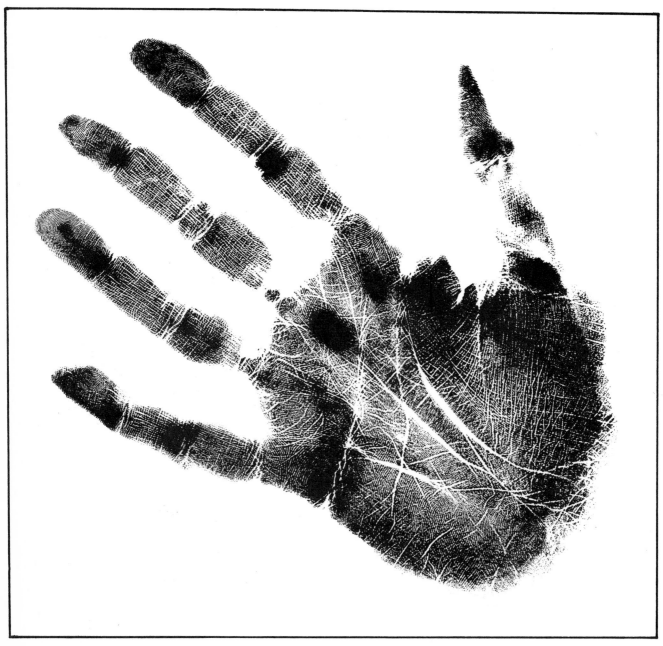

328. *A hand and horoscope basically*
329. *of the Fire type. The very
broken Girdle, along with the
strong ascent of the Heart line into
Jupiter, afford an interesting
key to the nature of this subject,
discussed on page 178.*

328

329

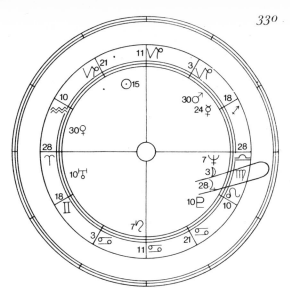

330. The hand and horoscope of the
331. boyfriend of the girl studied in
328 and 329. One observes that
it is the girl's Jupiter in
Sagittarius which attracts the
male Mercury, only one degree
away. The effect of such a
planetary relationship is for the
Mercury to be made expansive
by the other's Jupiter, and for
the Jupiter to be made more
inclined towards talk and
communication by the Mercury.

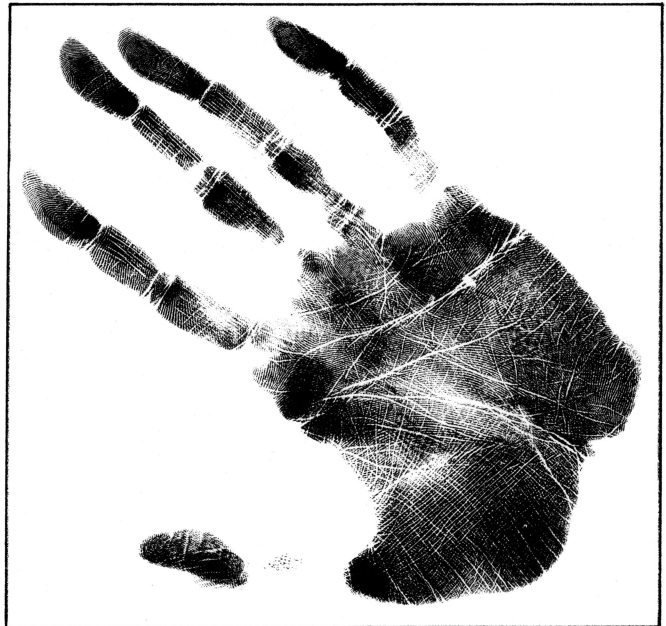

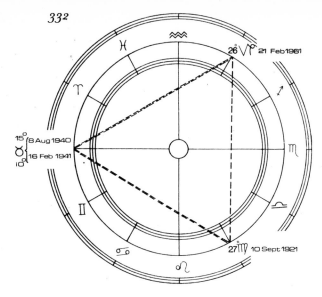

332

332. The 'Golden Triangle' of the
Ancients; a recurring
conjunction between Jupiter and
Saturn which draws a triangle
against the zodiacal belt. Such
conjunctions are held to be of
considerable importance to the
spiritual development of
mankind. Each of the other
planets draws significant
patterns against the skies by
recurring conjunctions with the
Sun. See page 180.

and Jupiter is greatly disturbed by the square between the disruptive Uranus and Jupiter. Such a tension requires a life pattern in which the energies may be disposed towards some creative end: the native is indeed an artist, studying three dimensional form.

A Scorpionic Ascendant, and the Moon in Scorpio, remind me that I originally met the subject because she wanted bibliographical advice in connexion with a thesis she was writing on superstitions: Scorpio is always interested in such things! The ruling planet, Pluto, is conjunct Mars, implying that she would feel compelled to be actively creative (Mars) in respect of strange and penetrating studies (Pluto), but behind this is the Moon in Scorpio which is notorious for its attractions to occult fields of study, as well as to the merely strange.

The print of the female hand at figure 329 is of the Fire form, with the multitude of chance lines behind the usual main lines, which suggest that conflict within the native will be between the two strongly opposed elements of Fire and Water. The chart gives strong nodal points in both these elements – the Ascendant is Pisces, with Uranus in Cancer and both Mars and Mercury in Scorpio. The M.C. is Sagittarius, with both Moon and Jupiter in this sign, and with Venus and Pluto in Leo.

What is particularly evident about the hand is the richly broken mass of lines which compose the Girdle of Venus, as well as the strong Heart line which runs right up to the base phalange of the finger of Jupiter. Clearly, strong and exuberant energies are at play both in an emotional and sexual

sense – perhaps to be expected from the placing of Uranus on the fifth house. In many cases a strong Girdle of Venus is involved with aspects between Sun and Venus, and this chart is no exception for these two planets are in semi-square to each other; this is the only strong aspect which may be formed between them, save for conjunction. One suspects that the solar force is particularly sensitized in this chart because of the exact conjunction with the planet Neptune: there will be an insidiously strong Water quality about the native's dealing with other people as a result of this aspect. When this is linked with the semi-square to Venus, one may see how unexpected difficulties will arise because of the tension between self (Sun) and love for others (Venus).

Inner tension is reinforced by the strong square between Saturn, which is near the house of relationships, and the Moon. Such a placing as this is generally regarded by astrologers as one of the most 'difficult' of aspects for the personality to deal with, for it represents a kind of crisis in the life pattern: issues are 'black and white', but no easier to resolve. For various technical reasons, to do with progressions, the Moon square Saturn aspect permeates the entire life of the native. Whether it is regarded as a welcome opportunity for a struggle towards greater spirituality, or whether it is regarded as a back-breaking cross which spoils the life of the native, will clearly depend upon the subjective opinion of the native herself. Both attitudes are possible at different points in life, but certainly the force of the aspect calls for a great deal of effort, and when the

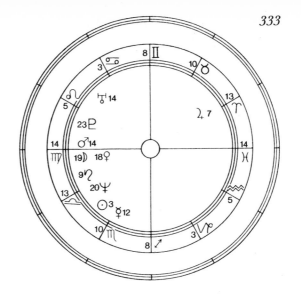

333. *Horoscope and hand of a*
334. *female Earth type, discussed*
   below.

psychological traits are not struggled with, unpleasant material conditions inexorably manifest themselves. The aspect carries with it a strong sense of fate, and an inability to accept responsibilities either for actions or for truth in the generally accepted sense of the word. A struggle with such a characteristic may be very rewarding spiritually.

The native must feel herself to be caught in a strong tension of relationships as a result of the frustration (Saturn) of personality (Moon), and the complicated web of frustrations and deceits which arise from the sensitive aspect between Sun and Neptune. The native cannot have an 'ordinary' view of life, because of these two aspects. This is indicated in the hand mainly in the complex weavings of the Girdle of Venus, but the strong imaginative drive may be studied in the descent of the Head line well into the Mount of Moon as well as in the marked loop formation which dominates this striated area. Energies such as these must either be directed into some creative activity, in which imagination is impressed upon material form; otherwise it will run riot within itself, sensitize the imagination, and make the understanding of truth as seen by others, more and more difficult. When used creatively, the energies will carry the native towards a greater grasp of inner truth, but when allowed to run out of control, without direction, these same energies will carry the native towards a greater alienation from truth and from others.

The hand at figure 334 is clearly of the female Earth type, with the typical rounded square palm and short fingers. The lines are of a Watery nature, though clearly marked, and are set against a background of fine, Watery, hair lines. As the print itself suggests from the loss of detail, the hand was unexpectedly soft considering its basic Earth form, and this again reinforces the idea of a strong Water connexion. The corresponding horoscope supports the interpretation of a strong pull between Earth and Water, for the Ascendant is Virgo, and gathered around this important point are the planets Mars, Venus and Moon, all conjunct with the Ascendant. The three Water signs are represented through the Sun and Mercury in Scorpio, the Descendant on Pisces, and Uranus in Cancer. We observe that the finger of Jupiter is shorter than usual, and find this reflected in the chart through the strong opposition between Saturn and Jupiter, which in terms of astrological tradition will incline the native towards a melancholic outlook on life, and introduce a restless element into the nature. This particular comparison between hand and horoscope indicates just how careful one has to be when assessing the relative strengths of aspects, for if one were to concentrate purely on the Saturn-Jupiter aspect, at the expense of the strong conjunction of three planets around the Ascendant, then one might be tempted to draw a picture of a rather melancholic type, which would not accord with the true personality of this native. Certainly, the basic Earth nature, as well as the opposition between Jupiter and Saturn, will leave a substratum of melancholia (moments of depression, as the modern terminology has it), but with activity (Mars) and love (Venus) augmenting the Moon characteristics in such an important

place, we may expect a very lively personality, with a strong emotional reaction to life. This latter reading is supported by the strong line of Heart, which reaches well into the finger of Jupiter.

Aspects between Jupiter and Saturn do indeed relate to the mental and spiritual spheres, as do the fingers. Conjunction between these two planets occurs only once every 20 years or so, creating a periodicity which has great importance to the inner life of Man. In a 60 year period they draw an equilateral triangle against the zodiac. This fact was well known to the Ancients, who referred to it as the Golden Triangle, and held it to represent the spiritually stimulating force of the Trinity working upon mankind. Perhaps it does not overstretch the ancient teaching concerned with the relationship between the microcosm of man and the macrocosm of the heavens, when one seeks for the manifestation of Jupiter-Saturn relationships in the mental plane of the fingers, rather than in the physical plane of the palm.

From the few analyses above it will be seen that a real evaluation of the hand in terms of the horoscope, or of the horoscope in terms of the hand, depends upon a thorough knowledge of the living zodiac as it is found in the human hand. It is only through practice and the cultivation of a sensitive intuition that the real study of astropalmistry may be conducted. One must remember that astropalmistry may be a powerful force both for good and evil, and for this reason the student should attempt to develop alongside his practical knowledge and intuitive faculty a sense of responsibility towards both the art form and his subjects.

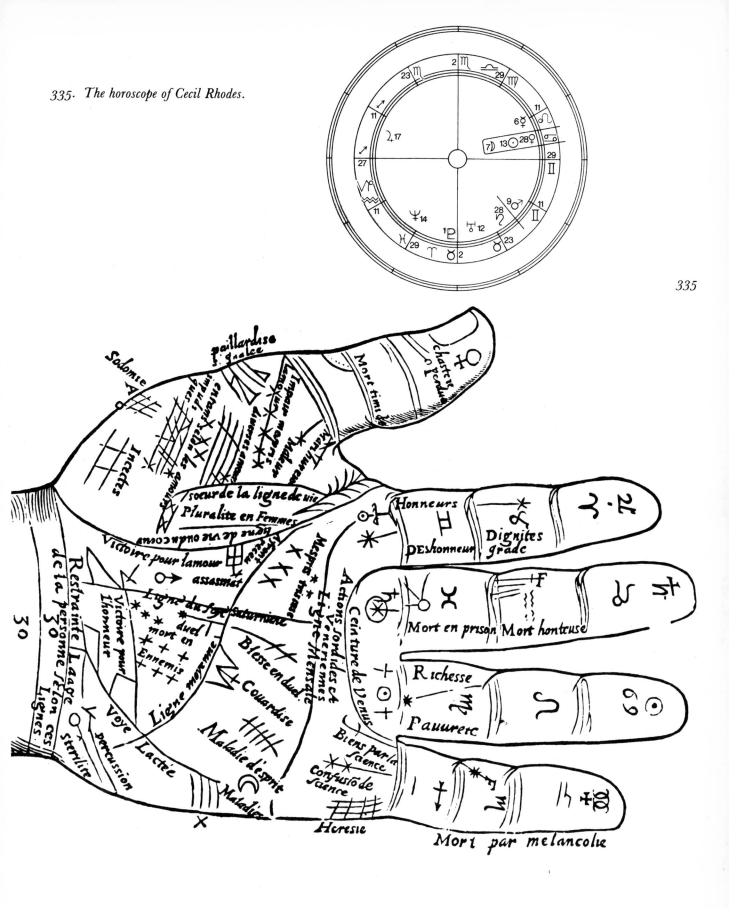

335

Conclusions

It is clear that many of the traditions concerned with astrology are being questioned, and a number will have to be rejected since, for all their validity in times past, they are no longer valid today. The important question is, what will be put in its place? Much within astrology will have to change if this science or art which deals with the basic algebra of life is to meet the challenge of the future, and indeed many changes are already taking place. Scientists are beginning to see that certain terrestial periodicities may be linked with certain celestial periodicities. One need only consider the work of Sanford on sunspots and Venusian conjunctions, of Maki Takata's work on the ovarian cycles in women and the flocculation index in blood serum linked with the Sun cycle, of Gauquelin's work on hereditary connexions between birth charts of children and parents, of Brown's work on lunar cycles: this sort of research is often quoted nowadays by astrologers who for some reason wish to show that astrology is 'scientific' – whatever that word may mean. Such changes may be taken as evidence of the fact that certain myths of nineteenth-century science are breaking down, and once more ancient knowledge is beginning to percolate – albeit in a new form – into Man's conscious world of intellectual experience.

More interesting than the gradual awakening of scientists – for indeed, one might ask why the attitudes and prejudices of modern scientists should necessarily be used as a touchstone for testing the validity of such an ancient science as astrology – is the rapid change which is taking place within astrology itself. Many of the older traditions have been completely rejected, and much of the ancient lore has been looked at in a new way, with the result that many teachings have proved to be more exciting than ever was dreamed of in the eighteenth or nineteenth century. For example, the glyph for Aries (figure 21), formerly regarded as a drawing of the horns of the ram, may be seen as representing the inner and downward movement of rebirth, and the outwards and upper movement of the transition we call death; physical life starts and ends with the head, which is ruled by Aries. In this way we can begin to sense something of the real depth of the ancient thinking which gave us that glyph. Again, the curious Taurus glyph (figure 21) represents a drawing of the bull's head, according to materialistic astrology. But we are suddenly presented with the fact that this is a drawing of the larynx with the eustachian canals moving upwards from the larynx region to the ears; and then, recalling the ancient connexion between Taurus and music, we begin to sense something of the mystery in these ancient glyphs. From such a sense of mystery is evolving an entirely new attitude to astrology, even within the world of astrology itself. There is already a search for a new form of astrology which will support the new spiritual understanding of man which is surely to grow in the next few centuries.

The search for a new astrology is leading into fascinating fields of human endeavour, and because of this it is true to say that nowadays, as at no other time in recorded history, there is almost no such thing as astrology, only numerous schools of astrology. Much work is being done by various associations and faculties in Germany, France, England and America; particularly notable are the Hamburg school, and the heliocentric systems of Sucher. Astrology is, as it were, exploding with a vibrant new force. And yet the danger is, as with all new movements however honest their original impetus, that in order to establish an identity and define a new path, it may be found necessary to reject totally the old methods. We must hope that this will not happen with astrology, for whilst it is true that much of the ancient tradition may appear to resemble a corpse, it is dead only for those who have not examined its beating heart.

If living astrology is in need of violent change, how much more so is palmistry! Much of the tradition has merely an antiquarian interest nowadays, though as the present text has attempted to show, elements of life – if only as a weak pulse beat – still show through in the most unexpected quarters. If palmistry is to continue as a study, then it will have to be rejuvenated from without – the world of palmistry has certainly lost contact with any modern reality, as the need to change basic terminologies has suggested. The most promising change which may revitalize this ancient art is likely to come from astrology, and in particular from an assessment of the valid relationships between the two. If it is possible to demonstrate, as was recently shown, that in the charts of 50 mongoloid children cast heliocentrically – see Sucher in the bibliography – Mercury was in a bad aspect to Venus, while the charts for 150 of their brothers and sisters show no such aspects, then we may deduce a connexion between the planets and mongolism. It must be remembered that one of the traits which identifies mongolism is a particular hand formation, so may we not therefore, even on an ordinary scientific and exoteric level, begin to suspect a direct contact between the planets and the hand? Or could it be, as the Ancients have ever proclaimed, that there is a unifying principle which connects everything, for all time?

Whatever the truth, we may be sure that our present direction of attempting to calibrate the universe with the intellect, as though this were some divine instrument of measurement, is leading into very sterile grounds. Fortunately the signs are that a spiritual awakening is near, and this will itself require a new way of looking at the world and at Man's place within the world. This new understanding of the world will of necessity have to consider Man as a meaningful spiritual unity in a system of spiritual forces; we shall have to reject the popular mode of thinking which tends to consider Man mainly as a physical unit caught up in a lifeless machine of huge balls spinning in meaningless orbits around a dying Sun. Astrology, even in its present stage of development, is a profound force which may help towards placing Man in that more spiritual position, whereby his very existence may take on momentous meaning.

A spiritual astrology is vital at this time for it may develop a spiritual defiance in the face of those two terrible forces which offer instant enlightenment and mere intellectual clarity, at the expense of eventual freedom.

Bibliography

There are few really good books on palmistry and astrology, which is very surprising when one considers the scope and implications of these subjects. The following list is intended to indicate essential reading for new students: most other books may be safely ignored by the beginner.

ASTROLOGY
CARTER C. E. O.
   Various titles, but in particular:
   Principles of Astrology
      The Theosophical Publishing House
   The Zodiac and the Soul
      The Theosophical Publishing House
COLLIN Rodney
   The Theory of Celestial Influences
      Routledge and Kegan Paul
DAVISON Ronald
   Astrology
      Arco
      (This is by far the best introduction to the study of astrology)
   The Technique of Prediction
      L. N. Fowler
DE VORE Nicholas
   Encyclopaedia of Astrology
      Philosophical Library
      (Certainly the best encyclopaedia in the English language)
EVANS Colin
   The New Waite's Compendium of Natal Astrology
      Routledge and Kegan Paul
      (This is a revised edition of a very useful compendium. The portraits of the twelve zodiacal personalities are rightly famous among astrologers. A few of the figures and symbols in the condensed ephemeris are inaccurate, especially in early editions; much of the remaining material is extremely valuable, but caution must be exercised when calculating horoscopes from these tables.)
GUAQUELIN Michel
   Astrology and Science
      Peter Davies
GETTINGS Fred
   The Book of the Zodiac
      Ward Lock Ltd.
HONE Margaret E.
   The Modern Textbook of Astrology
      L. N. Fowler
MAYO Jeff
   Various books, but especially recommended:
   The Planets and Human Behaviour
      L. N. Fowler
MORISH Furze
   Outline of Astro-Psychology
      Rider and Co.
PAGAN Isabelle M.
   From Pioneer to Poet
      (An old favourite with astrologers for the deftness with which the leading characteristics of the twelve zodiacal impulses are presented. It is a great pity that some of the horoscopes used to illustrate points are putative and inaccurate.)

ROBSON Vivian E.
  Fixed Stars and Constellations in Astrology
    The Aquarian Press
    (A useful extension of ordinary astrology
    into the fascinating star lore which was
    so important a part of astrology in past
    centuries. Students are advised to study
    fixed stars in regard to *karma*.)
RUDHYAR Dane
  Various books, but in particular as
  essential reading:
  The Astrology of Personality
    L. N. Fowler
  The Practice of Astrology
    Penguin Books
STEINER Rudolph
  In particular:
  Macrocosm and Microcosm
    Rudolph Steiner Press
SUCHER W.
  The Changing Countenance of Cosmology
    Meadow Vista, Rt. 1, Box 1282,
    California 95722
WEST J. A. and TOONDER J. G.
  The Case for Astrology
    Macdonald and Co.
WHITEMAN Edward E.
  The Influence of the Houses – Astro-kinetics
  The Influence of the Planets – Astro-kinetics
  Aspects and their Meanings – Astro-kinetics
    L. N. Fowler

PALMISTRY
BENHAM W. G.
  The Laws of Scientific Hand Reading
    Various publishers
GETTINGS Fred
  The Book of the Hand
    Paul Hamlyn
  Palmistry Made Easy
    Wiltshire Book Company
JAQUIN NOEL
  Various books, but in particular:
  The Signature of Time
    Faber and Faber
  The Hand Speaks
    Lyndoe and Fisher
SPIER J.
  The Hands of Children
    Routledge and Kegan Paul
WOLFF C.
  Various books, but especially:
  The Human Hand
    Methuen

  The only satisfactory modern publica-
  tion dealing with the relationship be-
  tween astrology and the hand is in
  French:
MUCHERY Georges
  *Traité Complet de Chiromancie Deductive et
  Experimentale*
    Editions du Chariot, Paris.

Glossary

The words in italics indicate cross-references within the glossary.

AIR One of the five *elements*. The term does not refer merely to the mixture of gases which we breathe: it refers to a condition of nature, in which materiality is expressed in a gaseous state. In palmistry it described a basic type of temperament and hand form, an example of which may be seen at figure 114.

AKASHYA The invisible fifth *element*, named thus by Pythagoras, but called by many names by different savants. It is the vivifying element, a kind of etheric light which binds together the four visible elements.

AQUARIUS The eleventh sign of the zodiac. It is an Air sign, traditionally ruled by *Saturn*, but in modern astrology ruled by *Uranus*. It is one of the four *Fixed* signs, of a mental disposition, and given to eccentricity. The *glyph* for this sign does not represent waves of water, any more than it represents waves of electricity, as some would maintain: the meaning is obscure, but originally the glyph consisted of three zigzag lines.

ARCH A finger pattern of papillary ridges which does not exhibit a *triadus*. Associated with the Earth element. Example at figure 210.

ASCENDANT The most important single point in the *horoscope*, marking the degree of a sign which is rising over the horizon at a given moment of time.

ASPECT An angular relationship between planets, or between planets and various nodal points, in a horoscope.

ASTROPALMISTRY An unfortunate and clumsy neologism which seeks to describe the study of the relationship between astrology and palmistry.

CANCER The fourth sign of the zodiac. It is a Water sign, ruled by the Moon. It is one of the four *Cardinal* signs, of an emotional disposition, and given to extremes of imagination. The *glyph* for this sign is supposed by some to be a drawing of the crab's pincer claws, but the early form of the glyph suggests that it depicts the influence of fixed stars, which raise up and push down according to their natures. The nature of Cancer is intimately connected with the *fixed stars* found in the area of the skies marked by this sign in the zodiacal belt.

CAPRICORN The tenth sign of the zodiac. It is an Earth sign, ruled by Saturn. It is one of the four Cardinal signs, of an austere though discriminative disposition, and given to a rigidity of outlook which seeks constantly to limit and control. The *glyph* for this sign draws the form of the goat-fish with which the sign was originally associated – the goat represents the aspirational half of the nature, the fish tail represents the force which drives the goat onwards, since the fear behind Capricorn is of losing hold on selfhood. The glyph admirably expresses the conflict of the sign – one half strictly linear, the other half curved.

CARDINALITY One of the three *modes*, explained on page 34. In astrology the modes are sometimes referred to as the Quadruplicities, since they each find expression through four signs. The four Cardinal signs are Aries, Cancer, Libra and Capricorn: we observe that each of these rules important parts of the body which are involved with movement, the essence of Cardinality. Aries rules the head, Cancer the upper part of the body, Libra the lower trunk, and Capricorn the entire skeletal frame.

CHIROGNOMY The study of the form of the hand, as opposed to *chiromancy,* which is more specifically concerned with studying the lines of the hand. In fact, serious palmistry does not draw such distinctions, for it regards form and linear structure as intimately connected.

CHIROMANCY Literally the word meant 'prediction of the future from the hand', but in past centuries its meaning has changed to accommodate the study of the line markings on the hand.

COMPLEX TYPE The term refers mainly to the kind of hand which to all intents and purposes appears to fall easily into one of the four main categories of classification, and yet by virtue of some striking formation (such as a *Simian* line) is lifted from that category, in which case the simple interpretation must be considerably amended.

CONJUNCTION An *aspect,* in which the planets are technically in the same degree of the same sign. A fairly wide *orb* of up to 8 degrees is allowed for this strong aspect.

CONSTELLATIONS The constellations are the series of star patterns in the skies, twelve of which bear the same names as the signs of the zodiac. These twelve constellations are not the same as the twelve signs, for they occupy different areas of the skies, and for thousands of years have not coincided in location with the twelve signs. There is an influential school of astrology which makes use of a zodiacal system closely related to the constellations along the *ecliptic.*

CUSP The term has a dual reference in astrology. Firstly it refers to the imaginary line which separates one sign from another, that is, the 30th degree of Aries from the 1st degree of Taurus. In popular astrology certain people are regarded as being 'cuspal' types, because they are not sure of which of two signs the Sun was in at the moment of birth. A glance at an *ephemeris* soon resolves this problem. There is no such thing as a 'cuspal' type in serious astrology. Secondly, it refers to the line which in certain systems (as in the system propounded in this book) marks the centrally most important and influential point in a given house: thus the *Ascendant* marks the cusp or centre-point of the first house, the *M.C.* the cusp of the tenth house, and so on. In other systems, such as the "equal house" system of measurement, the cusp marks the boundary between one house and the next: thus, the Ascendant would in theory, mark the beginning degree of the first house, and so on.

DESCENDANT The *cusp* of the seventh house, which links with Libra, and with the urge to escape the selfhood of the Ascendant, poised on the other side of the zodiac.

EARTH (element) One of the five *elements.* The term does not refer merely to the soils, rocks and minerals which compose

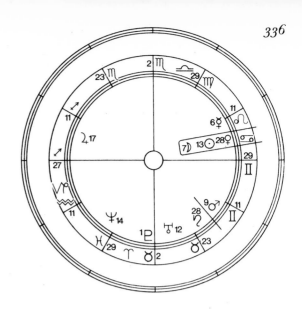

336. The horoscope of Rhodes. The greatness of the man stems from the influence of a fixed *star (see below). Sirius, which is conjunct his Sun, and which brings business success and advancement through military affairs. The fixed stars in Cancer largely account for the strength and genius of so many Cancerians. It is the effect of these which makes Cancer so difficult to understand as a zodiacal sign.*

the planet upon which we walk: it refers to a condition of nature, in which materiality is expressed as something solidified, non-fluid and heavy. In palmistry it describes a basic temperament, and also the hand form, an example which may be seen at figure

EARTH (planet) Most systems of astrology make measurements from a geocentric standpoint, regarding the Earth as the proper point from which to study celestial influences. In a horoscope chart, the Earth is symbolized sometimes as a central dot, sometimes as a circle within the concentric circles. The most common symbol is a circle enclosing a cross, representing a kind of miniature horoscope.

ECLIPTIC The imaginary line around the Earth, along which the Sun appears to travel. The other planets appear to follow courses fairly near to this imaginary line. The ecliptic belt is so named because it is along it that eclipses occur. The *zodiac* is the division of the ecliptic belt into twelve equal areas.

ELEMENT There are five elements, one of which is not discernible by ordinary means of perception. The remaining four between them represent the various conditions of nature in its material phase. The teachings which arise from the natures of the four elements pervade much of the occult tradition, and are of paramount importance in astrology, as well as in the system of palmistry outlined here. It is said that anyone who could rightly comprehend the nature of the five elements would have access to all knowledge. It is clear to anyone who studies the ancient

teachings that the four elements were never intended to refer to the conditions of Fire, Earth, Air and Water, as particularly manifest in material life.

EPHEMERIS (Plural, ephemerides.) A list of planetary positions on each day of a given year. The astrologer's ephemeris lists the positions from a geocentric point of view, and usually contains much additional material relevent to casting horoscopes.

FIRE One of the five *elements,* regarded by all occultists as the most powerful of the four material elements. The term does not refer merely to the incandescent gas of flame which we use on earth; it refers to a condition of nature, in which materiality is striving to attain a higher spiritual level of being. In palmistry it describes a basic type of temperament and hand form, an example of which may be seen at figure 102.

FIXED SIGNS see *Fixity*

FIXED STARS Something of a misnomer these days, since in terms of ordinary human time measurement all stars are fixed, and yet, from a more long-term system of time measurement, no star is fixed. The term arose originally to distinguish those stars which remained as it were, embedded against the sky, from those which wandered around – these being the *planets,* and our Sun and Moon. This accounts for the reason why astrologers refer to the *luminaries* as planets, which in terms of strict definition they are not. The interpretation of the fixed stars in astrology appears no longer to be given the attention it deserves: the force of certain horoscopes simply cannot be un-

188

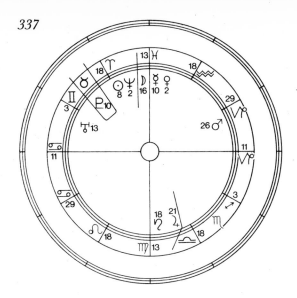

337. *The horoscope of Aristide Briand. The placing of Uranus in this chart illustrates the question of* houses *(see below). Uranus is in Gemini, and ten degrees from the twelfth house cusp. It is 28 degrees from the Cancerian Ascendant. Thus, the planet is in the twelfth house. In which house is Pluto?*

derstood if the influence of fixed stars in the formation of character, destiny and karma is not taken into account. Fixed stars have a reputation for producing extremes in personalities when these are conjunct with planets in the natal horoscopes; the traditional interpretations are doubtless a little unsubtle and in some cases even horrific, but there is an element of dramatic truth underlying the blood and thunder. See Robson in the bibliography.

FIXITY One of the three *modes,* explained on page 34. In astrology the modes are sometimes referred to as the Quadruplicities, since they each find expression through four signs. The four fixed signs are Taurus, Leo, Scorpio and Aquarius, and these have been symbolized in a rich variety of ways – in Christian symbolism they were represented by the four Evangelists.

GAZETTEER A geographic index. The astrologer requires a gazetteer which gives the latitude and longitude of all towns in the world, as an aid to casting horoscopes.

GEMINI The third sign of the zodiac. It is an Air sign, ruled by Mercury. It is one of the four *Mutable* signs, of a mental disposition, with a strong sense of duality, and usually finds expression through activity. The glyph for this sign represents the essential dualities of the world – above is the line which represents the spiritual heavens, below the line which represents the material world; separated by these two we find the dual polarities of left and right, good and bad, suggesting the choice which is perpetually open to Man with

every action.

GIRDLE OF VENUS A line, or series of lines, which arise between the fingers of Jupiter and Saturn, and run parallel to the line of Heart. See page 140.

GLYPH In astrology this word is used to denote certain symbols.

HOROSCOPE Although this word is now applied to the entire figure which is cast to symbolize the planetary relationships at a given time and place, it was originally applied to the 'hour of birth', which is to say the *Ascendant*.

HOUSES In very simple terms, the houses represent a static structure of twelve divisions, against which the position of the zodiac is measured in relation to the Earth. The first house marks the eastern horizon relative to a given point, the tenth house marks the highest point on the ecliptic relative to the Earth. There is much dispute among astrologers as to precisely which system of measurement should determine the parts of the zodiac on the intermediate cusps (not *angles*) at any place for a given time. Generally, a house spans the number of degrees which rise in a period of two hours at a given latitude. A good outline of the different 'house systems' is given by Waite (see bibliography), and an excellent analysis of the deeper significances of the twelve houses will be found in De Vore (see bibliography). The house question need not worry the beginner unduly, as it is fairly certain that he will (for good or evil) be compelled to use the Placidean system, as this is the one usually promulgated by publishers who produce ephemerides and

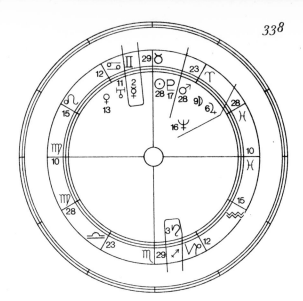

338. *The horoscope of Alexander II of Russia. This is to be compared with the horoscope of Feodorovna, opposite.*

tables of houses. The author himself prefers the tables of the Campanus system, originated in the thirteenth century by Giovanni Campanella.

ID A term used by certain psychologists to embrace the mass of undifferentiated energies which appear to lie behind conscious life. Astrology would suggest that these energies are less 'undifferentiated' than modern psychology would appear to grasp. It is certain that some energies appear to activate human beings without the conscious volition or even participation of those concerned, but there is much evidence that these energies are in fact highly disciplined, co-ordinated and meaningfully directed. If the theory of *karma* is accepted, then the nature of what is called the *Id* may be understood in quite a different way.

IMUM COELI Literally the 'lowest part of the heavens', but in fact the lowest part of the ecliptic, relative to a given place. The fourth house cusp.

JUPITER In astrology this is the beneficent planet which rules the expansive nature of the native, and the ease with which he fits into society in a manner useful to himself and others. See page 43. In palmistry Jupiter rules the index finger, the one which points at the world and differentiates. The glyph for Jupiter represents the half circle of potential spirit lifting the heavy cross of matter upwards, indicating the spiritualizing agency which works through Jupiterian impulses.

KARMA One of the most misunderstood of occult concepts. The nearest equivalent in European thought is contained in the idea of Fate, though the oriental term indicates that Fate is not a haphazard sequence of events or experiencings, but is dependent upon actions in previous lives or spiritual conditions. The idea is that a spirit undertakes to live in an earthly body for a given period of time, usually in order to learn something which cannot be learned in a disembodied state, and has to accept rewards and punishments for good and bad deeds committed in previous incarnations. In order that understanding may grow, any evil committed against another person will have to be experienced by the perpetrator. The working out of karma is not done consciously by ordinary people, and indeed the real reasons for the majority of people's actions and relationships may be understood only when the nature of their karma is grasped – which is tantamount to saying that it is virtually impossible to understand or judge another person when seen in the context of one material lifetime only.

LEO The fifth sign of the zodiac. It is a Fire sign, ruled by the Sun. It is one of the four important *Fixed* signs, of a warm and creative disposition. The glyph for this sign represents the heart (the small circle) projecting an energy which sweeps upwards and outwards, only to fall down if another creative impulse does not catch it, and project it further upwards. The glyph has nothing to do with the lion's mane, or with the tail of the lion, as some astrologers claim.

LIBRA The seventh sign of the zodiac. It is an Air sign, ruled by Venus. It is one of

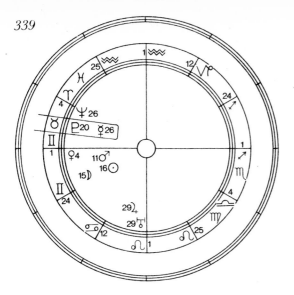

339 The running number *339* appears at top left of the chart.

339. *The horoscope of Alexander's wife shows a strong set of correspondences with his chart. Observe that her Mercury is conjunct his Sun, his Mercury conjunct her Venus, and her Neptune conjunct his Mars. People who are drawn together by* karma *(see below) always have such correspondences between their charts. The comparison of two horoscopes is called synastry.*

the four *Cardinal* signs, of a gentle disposition, insistent upon maintaining equilibrium. The glyph for this sign originated in the Egyptian hieroglyphic which shows the Sun setting over the Earth (see page 138): it is not a stylized drawing of scales.

LINE OF FATE The longitudinal line which, when present in the hand, separates the mounts of Moon, Mercury and Apollo from the rest of the hand. The line thus separates the more personal energies from those dedicated to influencing society and the external world. See page 145. This line does not show death by accident, as novices often believe, nor does its absence mean that the life of the subject is pointless. Such facile ideas are, unbelievably, still held by some people who call themselves astrologers.

LINE OF HEAD The lower transverse line of the hand. Its quality and termination relate to the mentality of the subject, according to the palmistic tradition, and this belief has largely been substantiated by modern research. See page 142.

LINE OF HEART The upper transverse line of the hand. Its quality, length and termination relate to the emotional life of the subject. See page 136.

LINE OF LIFE The line encircling the root of the thumb. Its quality relates to the vitality of the subject: significantly, this is the first line of the hand to develop in the embryo.

LINES It is generally believed that the lines of the hand are in fact 'crease lines', resulting from motor flexion. This is not true, for the lines develop quite early in the embryo, long before motor action of

so defined a nature is possible. The major lines of Head, Heart and Life rarely change from the formation established in the prenatal state, though the line of Fate, and various subsidiary lines, do change considerably.

LOOP A finger pattern of papillary ridges which incorporate a single *triadus.* Associated with the Air element. Example at figure 214. The two kinds are the radial loop in which the triadus is on the inner side of the finger towards Mercury, and the ulnar, in which the triadus is on the thumb side of the finger. The radial loop is fairly uncommon, save on the finger of Jupiter.

LUMINARIES The Sun and the Moon. A term sometimes used to avoid calling these bodies *planets,* and also to connote the power of these two in a horoscope.

MACROCOSM Literally the 'Great World' or universal womb in which Man, the *microcosm,* exists as a complete epitome of the larger pattern. It is held by occultists that the stellar world we see is a tiny fragment of a vast body, with which every human being is intimately connected. Astrology is the study of the interconnexion between the macrocosm and the microcosm.

MARS In astrology this is the active planet which rules the initiative nature of the subject; the degree to which the native is able to project himself as an individual unit into the larger group of society. The Mars impulse may be creative in outlook, but as it is selfish in orientation there is always the possibility that it may 'go too far' and become destructive, both to the

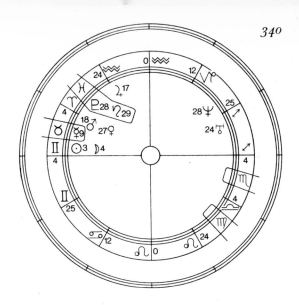

native and to the society in which he lives. See page 42. In palmistry Mars has traditionally been held to rule the *Plain of Mars*, a not very closely defined triangle in the centre of the palm, and it has always been associated with the thumb, sometimes specifically with the top phalange, at other times with both phalanges. The system of astropalmistry propounded nowadays claims that Mars rules over the phalanges of the thumb, and over the ring finger. The glyph for Mars is generally represented by the circle of spirit being carried up by an arrow – this modern interpretation of the glyph is interesting for it completely reverses the original significance it held. The arrow is in fact a vestigial remain of the cross, and the original glyph portrayed the cross of materiality weighing down the circle of spirit – a much more realistic representation of the actual nature of Mars.

MEDIUM COELI Literally, the middle of the sky, but in fact the highest point of the ecliptic, relative to a given place. The tenth house cusp. Sometimes called the Midheaven. See *zenith*.

MERCURY In astrology this is the planet which rules the communicative faculties in Man, as well as memory and manner of speech. Mercury is a great imitator, and is not ashamed to appropriate other people's mannerisms and ideas for his own purposes. Such tendencies may be studied in a chart from the placing and aspects to Mercury. See page 40. In palmistry Mercury has traditionally been held to rule over the little finger, and has been connected specifically with money. The modern idea is that the finger of Mercury relates to sexuality and, through its repression, with money or material compensation. In the system of astropalmistry presented here, Mercury is held also to rule (through its connexion with Gemini) over the line of Life. The glyph for Mercury represents the summation of the Earth/Spirit struggle giving rise to productivity, for the cross of earth is being lifted by the circle of spirit, and these between them support a half circle which acts as a receptacle for spiritual energies. This glyph was not derived from the caduceus, the wand carried by Mercury, which has quite a different significance.

MICROCOSM Literally the 'Small World', or Man, who is held to be a tiny image of the whole cosmos, an image of God, a complete or potential model of the great *Macrocosm*. This idea is contained in those ancient diagrams which show the rulerships of the signs and planets over parts of the body. The real significance of these diagrams is almost lost, but originally they did not simply attempt to portray the fact that the head is ruled by Aries, or that the feet are ruled by Pisces. The diagrams hinted at the esoteric connexion between the individual man and the cosmos, thus setting out the basic tenet of astrology, which is the study of the inter-connexion between macrocosm and microcosm.

MODES The astrological concept of *Cardinality*, *Fixity*, and *Mutability*. See page 34.

MOON In astrology this is the planet which rules the personality of the native, those behavioural traits which reflect the

341. Every student of palmistry must develop the habit of making prints with a view to studying the hand. Equipment required include a roller, and ordinary lino-printing ink. The best kind of ink is the black water-based kind, as the oil-based is difficult to wash off. Both roller and ink may be purchased in most art shops. A supply of fine paper is required for printing, whilst a soft rubber pad facilitates a delicate impression (see below).

341

society and educational system of the world around, in much the same way as the visible Moon may be regarded as a mere reflection of the Sun. Astrology does not visualize the human being as a 'tabula rasa', a kind of great big zero which merely reflects society, but it does claim that the individual may be understood only in terms of the society in which he or she lives. It is the function of the Moon in astrology to portray the nature of this relationship, or reflection. See page 39. In palmistry the Moon has always been held to rule over the lower hypothenar eminence, and to this area has been accorded the fount of the imaginative faculties in man. The area is certainly one of great sensitivity, with potential for destruction and construction, depending upon the quality of lines and papillary patterns found upon it. See page 120. The glyph for the Moon is an attempt to show it as a fragment of the Sun. It is not uncommon for astrologers and artists to depict the Moon in an unrealistic relationship to the Sun – that is, pointing away from the Sun, rather than towards it, as must happen in the phenomenal world. This is itself an attempt to show the esoteric concept that the conscious mind of Man (the Sun) is not in harmony with the subconscious mind of Man (the Moon). Man is living in a state of guilt – an idea which is, of course, expressed in many religious teachings.

MOUNTS In traditional palmistry there were six mounts – the mounts of Venus and Moon, as described in the present book, and four mounts of Jupiter, Saturn,

342. *The hand is rolled as evenly as possible, after a thin coat of ink has been rolled on to a sheet of paper or glass. A separate rolling is required for each impression. Care must be taken to prevent the ink clogging the papillary canals, otherwise the print will smudge.*

342

Apollo and Mercury, localized under the relevant fingers. The qualities of these mounts were supposed to indicate the qualities of the planets in their operation upon the individual, though there was much confusion about how this was manifested.

MUTABILITY One of the three *modes*, explained on page 34. In astrology the modes are sometimes referred to as the Quadruplicities, since they each find expression through four signs. The four Mutable signs are Gemini, Virgo, Sagittarius and Pisces.

MYSTIC CROSS This is a linear cross which is present in some hands, localized under the finger of Jupiter. It is supposed to indicate great spirituality, and is sometimes called the Cross of Solomon or the Cross of Jupiter.

NADIR In ordinary usage this term applies to the point of the heavens directly opposite to the *zenith,* and is the point in the sky directly underneath the observer. However, in astrology the term is applied to the lowest point in the ecliptic band relative to a chosen point – it is thus the lowest point which the Sun reaches in its apparent path around the Earth. In this sense the term is synonymous with the fourth house cusp.

NATAL CHART A horoscope for a moment of birth. It is sometimes necessary to distinguish a horoscope for a moment of birth from horoscopes cast for other moments. Some astrologers cast horoscopes for prenatal moments, certain of which are called Epoch charts, other astrologers cast horoscopes for the moment of death, from which they assess certain life characteristics of the personality. It is possible to cast horoscopes for happenings other than birth or death: an astrologer may cast a horoscope to determine the propitious moment for launching a ship or beginning a business activity. In days past it would have been regarded as folly to begin a new venture without looking into its astrological considerations, especially in such matters as marriage.

NATIVE The human subject of a horoscope, a term derived from 'natus', birth.

NEBULA A cloud-like cluster of stars, in which the individual lights from the stars merge to give the impression of a single, indistinct mass. There are numerous such nebulae in the heavens, and the presence of one on the Ascendant is traditionally supposed to bring blindness. See *fixed stars.*

NEPTUNE In astrology this is one of the so-called 'new' planets. The planet rules sensitivity, especially that of an artistic or mediumistic kind. In its rulership over liquids and drugs, it is having a great influence at the present time over people who for one reason or another wish to undergo gratuitous body-free experiences. See page 46. In palmistry this planet does not find a specific rulership, save through the modern connexion which has been established between Neptune and Pisces. If any part of the hand is particularly emphasised when Neptune is strong in a chart it is not, in fact, the finger of Jupiter which is connected with Pisces, so much as the mount of Moon. This is not unreasonable when one considers that Neptune is

343. *The inked hand is pressed down fairly gently. The aim at this point is not to make a precise impression. The hand must be relaxed, and the print is generally best made with the subject seated with his elbow level with the printing surface.*

344. *The hand is lifted, with the paper adhering to the surface. The paper is then gently rubbed down on to the palm. If care is taken, this is by far the most*

linked with feelings, emotions, imagination, intuitive faculties, and psychism. One cannot help but subscribe to the general astrological idea that Neptune is connected with faculties as yet undeveloped in man, though it must be understood that those faculties which may be developed under its aegis must be developed consciously, and through a sense of responsibility.

NODAL In a general sense the term applies to any point within a chart which is emphasised for one reason or another. A degree may be nodal because it is occupied by a planet, or by one of the house cusps, for example. In a more specific sense the nodes are the points at which the orbits of planets intersect the ecliptic. Particularly important in astrology are the nodes called the Dragon's Head and the Dragon's Tail, which are in fact the Ascending and Descending nodes of the Moon.

OPPOSITION An *aspect* in which two planets are in degrees diametrically opposed in the zodiac. The force of the opposition is generally disruptive, though the nature depends upon the planets involved. See page 48.

ORB This is the space, measured in degrees, in which an *aspect* may be regarded as remaining in force. The wider the orb from an exact aspect, the weaker the force of that aspect to be experienced in the chart. There is no strict agreement among astrologers as to precisely what orbs should be allowed for different planets and different aspects, though those set out on page 48 may be taken as working very well

on a practical level.

PAPILLARY RIDGES The surface of every hand is covered with a series of closely packed papillae or 'nipples', arranged in distinctive curvilinear patterns. The literary indications are that palmists in past centuries did not consider these patterns to be very important, but in recent years their significance, especially the individual patterns on the finger ends and on the mounts, has received a great deal of attention. See *Arch*, *Loop* and *Whorl*.

PHALANGE In anatomy the term applies to the individual bones of the fingers and toes, a term derived from the word phalanx, which is used to denote a body of people massed together for some purpose. The word is particularly appropriate therefore in palmistry, where the first phalange refers to the topmost of the three divisions of the fingers – that part of the finger which is most completely involved with both self-expression and with manipulating the world.

PISCES The twelfth sign of the zodiac. It is a Water sign, traditionally ruled by Jupiter, but in modern astrology ruled by *Neptune*. It is one of the four *Mutable* signs, of an emotional and retiring disposition, though romantically inclined. The glyph for this sign is supposed to show two fishes, bound together by a silver cord and pulling against each other, suggesting the indecision to which Pisceans are subject.

PLAIN OF MARS See entry under *Mars*.

PLANETS The word is derived from the Greek, meaning 'wandering star' used

satisfactory method of taking a print, for in this way the most delicate lines may be recorded. Direct printing by pressure often leaves 'islands' – see figure 347.

345. *The print is peeled away, and examined before it is completely removed. If an area is unsatisfactory, then the paper may be laid down again and rubbed, as in 343.*

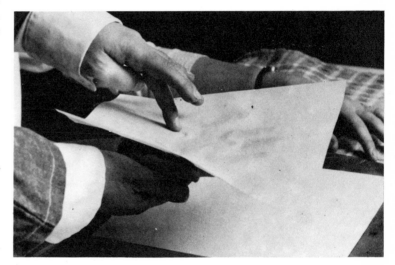

to distinguish these bodies from the *fixed stars*. The astrological concept of planets appears to bear little relationship to the astronomical concept. For the astrologer, planets are living entities. There is no agreement as to precisely how the planets affect human beings, but it is evident from a purely pragmatic point of view that they do, and that the influences may be studied with the tools offered by the various astrological systems.

PLUTO The most recently discovered of the important new planets, first observed by astronomers in 1930, though used as a hypothetical planet much earlier by certain astrologers. The influence of Pluto is disruptive, though it induces a penetrative outlook on life. When it is strongly placed in a chart, it is of paramount importance that its force be integrated into the life pattern, otherwise an anti-social and criminal tendency may result. It is closely linked with sexual energies, though many astrologers suggest that, like *Neptune*, it is linked with faculties in Man as yet undeveloped. The glyph for Pluto is of modern origin, and consequently contains none of the esoteric quality of the earlier glyphs.

PRINTS Prints are essential as a palmist's permanent record of the papillary and linear formations of hands. They are most conveniently made by rolling the hand with an ordinary lino-roller, lightly inked with a black water-based lino ink. The palm of the hand is pressed down lightly on to a wad of paper, and then it is lifted up, with the paper still adhering to it. The paper is then pressed lightly down

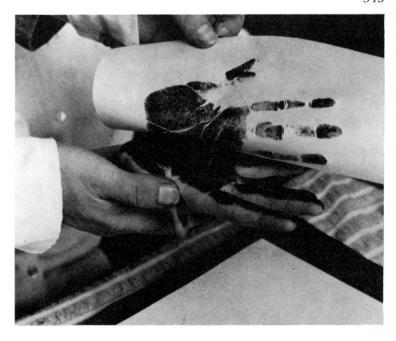

onto the palm, in order to record patterns on the various hollows and indentations of the hand. Extremely hard and extremely soft hands are very difficult to print in a satisfactory manner. A serious student will combine handprints with photography, though the first applies mainly to the *chiromantical* aspect of palmistry, while the latter applies mainly to the *chirological*.

PROGRESSION Serious astrologers regard a *natal chart* not as a fixed statement of personality, but as a variable theme which will develop in a temporal sequence. Progression is the term applied to the various complicated calculations used to determine how and when various psychological traits, events and accidents will emerge in the life of the native from the initial themal statement which the natal horoscope represents. There are very many different methods of calculating progressions; the most popular takes the day after birth as representing the quality of the first year after birth, and so on. A progression for the thirty-fifth year of life would be a horoscope cast for a time thirty-five days after birth. Progression reveals the pattern and rhythm of spiritual, psychological and material changes in the life of the native. A fairly advanced knowledge of astrology is required to interpret progressed charts accurately.

RADIAL LOOP See entry under *Loop*.

RULER In astrological terminology this word has a very loose application. Strictly speaking the 'ruler of a chart' is the planet which rules the Ascending sign, but some astrologers refer to the ruler as the most strongly placed planet in the chart. See page 58, and also *rulerships*, below.

RULERSHIPS This astrological concept is based on congeniality – on the idea that certain planets and signs are congenial with each other, and that these are in turn congenial with material manifestations in the world. For example, the Sun is said to rule Leo, because both are warm, creative and filled with light. Then again, Leo is said to rule Italy, and Rome, because (some would say) these places 'feel' Leo. Others would say that Italy is under the charge of spiritual hierarchies who are themselves under the force of Leo. Individuals are generally ruled by the sign Ascending at their birth, or by signs strongly emphasised in the natal chart, and this determines basic character. There are, however, periods when the native will come under other rulerships. For example, Leo types often work very hard and seriously, in spite (as it would seem) of their general flamboyant and sometimes irresponsible nature; this is because their Ascendant Leo will eventually progress into the domain of Virgo, and stay there for approximately thirty years. After that time, it will progress into the ease of Libra. Such considerations of rulerships applies to all types, of course. Again, it is observed pragmatically that as a person grows older the rule of the Ascendant, though never entirely lost, weakens in favour of the Sun sign.

SAGITTARIUS The ninth sign of the zodiac. It is a Fire sign, ruled by the expansive Jupiter. It is one of the four

346. A triadus *(see below, on page 202). The number of* triadi *determine the nature of the papillary pattern on the phalange. Two* triadi *give a Whorl, one* triadus *gives a Loop, and the absence of* triadi *implies that the pattern is an Arch.*

Mutable signs, of an inspirational disposition, and given to great dignity of expression, and love of enjoyment in life. The glyph for this sign, appropriately enough for a type so aspirational, represents the arrow of desire lifting the cross of materiality upwards.

SATURN In astrology this is the planet of limitation, which rules the underlying fears of the native, and indicates the frustrations and limitations which he will experience in life and within the spirit. See page 44. In palmistry Saturn rules the middle finger. The modern glyph is a deviant reversal of that used for Jupiter: it originally showed the cross of materiality weighing down the half circle of potential spirit.

SATELLITIUM A term used to denote a group of three or more planets in a single sign. As one might imagine from such a heavy conjunction, a satellitium is always emphatic in a chart and sometimes a satellitium may outbalance the force of an unteneted Ascendant, with the result that the 'type' of the native may not depend upon the Ascendant. It is not uncommon for Sun, Mercury and Venus to form satellitiums, as the latter two are in orbits nearer to the Sun than is the orbit of the Earth. Another synonymous term is *Stellium.*

SCORPIO The eighth sign of the zodiac. It is a Water sign, traditionally ruled by Mars, but in modern astrology ruled by *Pluto.* It is one of the four important *Fixed signs,* of a passionate and deeply emotional nature. In some early astrological traditions, as in Christian iconography, Scorpio

347. *The unsatisfactory white 'island' on the line of Heart is a result of attempting to print down by direct pressure. Had the print been made following the technique laid down in figures 342 to 344, then no such island would have resulted.*

347

was depicted as an Eagle, and not as a scorpion. The glyph for this sign is linked with the sexuality associated with the type, and its derivation is explained in figure 159.

SEMI-SQUARE An *aspect* in which the planets or nodal points concerned are separated by 45 degrees, or half of the 90 degrees of a *square*. It is a 'difficult' aspect, productive of discord. An *orb* of only a few degrees is usually allowed for this aspect..

SEXTILE An *aspect* in which the planets or nodal points concerned are separated by 60 degrees. It is an 'easy' aspect, productive of harmony of working for the planets involved, though not as beneficial as the *trine*.

SIDEREAL TIME A method of reckoning time from the stars, in which the beginning of the year is considered as starting at the precise moment of time when a specific fixed star passes directly over a given point in relation to the Earth. Sidereal time is not exactly the same as solar time, by which ordinary clock time is measured. The differences between these time systems need not concern the astrologer, save that he should observe that sidereal time, as given in the ephemerides, must be converted to ordinary clock time in order to determine the Ascendant and M.C. for any given place and time.

SIGN One of the twelve divisions of the *Zodiac*, each of 30 degrees.

SIMIAN Literally, 'monkey-like', and used mainly to describe certain atavistic signs in the hand. In palmistry, the term refers specifically to the Simian line, which in its pure form combines the lines of Head and Heart into a single line running transversally across the palm, as in figure 228. See page 149.

SQUARE An *aspect* in which the planets or nodal points concerned are separated by 90 degrees. It is a 'difficult' aspect, productive of discord, and always requiring attention from the native. It is sometimes regarded as a 'cross to be borne', and is openly linked with the more difficult side of karma.

STELLIUM American usage for *Satellitium*.

SUBSIDIARY LINES In palmistry, used to denote long lines which are not obviously identifiable as being part of the major lines. They must be regarded as carrying energies from one part of the hand to another, and interpreted in terms of the harmonies or conflicts which would arise from the meeting of the energies represented by the different zones.

SUN In astrology the beneficent, life-giving 'planet' which rules the conscious principle, the consciously held sense of selfhood in the native. A strongly placed Sun confers great dignity and creativity. See page 38. In palmistry the Sun traditionally rules the ring finger. The glyph for the Sun represents the entire solar system with the central Sun contained at the centre, and yet at the same time it represents any seed contained within the nutrient.

TAURUS The second sign of the zodiac. It is an Earth sign, ruled by Venus. It is one of the four important *Fixed* signs, of a practical, energetic and sensuous nature. The glyph for this sign represents the larynx, with the eustachian tubes which run up to the ears. The glyph is not a drawing of the bull's head.

TRIAD The triad of astrology and the triad of palmistry are intimately connected. The first is derived from the fact that the Ascendant, ruled by Mars, is positioned between the Jupiter of Pisces, and the Venus of Taurus (figure 346). The second is derived from precisely the same relationship within the hand: the Mars of the thumb phallange is embedded in the Venus of the thenar eminence, and the space between the thumb and finger of Jupiter must be traversed for the thumb to become effective – that is to grip something. Mars is, so to speak, continually pulled down by the materiality of Venus, and lifted up by the spiritually expansive Jupiter.

TRIADUS A term used by dermatologists and palmists to designate the triangular link established when one papillary pattern meets another one. Ultimately it is the number of triadi which determine the nature of a finger pattern, when there is doubt from mere appearances. The *arch* does not have a triadus, the *loop* has only one, and the *whorl* pattern stands freely upon two (figures 210 to 214).

TRINE An *aspect* in which the planets or nodal points concerned are separated by 120 degrees. It is a beneficial aspect, productive of ease and harmony. It is linked with the 'Golden Triangle' formed periodically between Jupiter and Saturn (see page 180). A fairly wide *orb* is allowed for this powerful aspect.

ULNAR LOOP See entry under *loop*.

URANUS In astrology this is the planet of disruption and originality, and when emphasised in a chart it is usually productive of genius. See page 46. This is one of the so-called 'new' planets, and many astrologers maintain that while genius may be responsive to its power, the mass of humanity has not yet developed to a point at which its forces may be assimilated. Its forces may, on the other hand, be experienced in mass movements, in which things happen without reference to dialectic. Within this context we may see how genius could be defined as a particular sensitivity to the anima mundi and what it wants to be expressed.

VENUS In astrology this is the planet of harmony, love and the arts. See page 41. In palmistry Venus has rule over the thenar eminence, or the base phalange of the thumb, and is co-ruler with the Sun over the area of Libra (figure 226), which is dominated by the Girdle of Venus and the line of Apollo. The glyph for Venus shows the circle of spirit lifting the cross of matter skywards.

VIRGO The sixth sign of the zodiac. It is an Earth sign, in the tradition ruled by Mercury, though some astrologers suggest the rulership of a hypothetical planet called Vulcan. It is one of the *Mutable* signs, of a critical disposition, and given to assimilation. The glyph for this sign points to the essential objectivity and intellectual calibre of its nature, as the explanation on page 100 indicates.

WATER One of the five elements. The term does not refer merely to the liquid we use, and of which the material body is so largely composed; it refers to a condition of nature, in which materiality is expressed in a fluid state. In palmistry it describes a basic type of temperament and hand form; an example is shown at figure 120.

WHORL A finger pattern of papillary ridges which exhibits two *triadi*. The pattern is associated with individualism, and with the Fire element.

ZENITH In ordinary usage this term applies to the point of the heavens directly overhead at any point on Earth. However, in astrology the term is frequently applied to the highest point in the ecliptic band, relative to the observer; it is thus the highest point which the Sun reaches in its apparent path around the Earth. In this sense, the term is synonymous with the tenth house cusp, the midheaven, for the Sun is indeed at the midheaven halfway through the day.

ZODIAC Apparently the word originally meant a circle of animal pictures. It is an imaginary belt in the heavens, 18 degrees wide, its centre on the ecliptic. The planets all run in orbits within this imaginary belt, and their positions may be recorded by reference to it.

Credits

I would like to thank Helen Piers for some of the photographs, John Hardy and Beverley Cook for most of the horoscope diagrams, Charles Rice for the drawings of the modern zodiac images, and all those people who have allowed me to use pictures of their hands and horoscopes in this book.